Artificial Intelligence - Latest Advances, New Paradigms and Novel Applications

Edited by Eneko Osaba, Esther Villar, Jesús L. Lobo and Ibai Laña

Published in London, United Kingdom

IntechOpen

Supporting open minds since 2005

Artificial Intelligence - Latest Advances, New Paradigms and Novel Applications
http://dx.doi.org/10.5772/intechopen.87770
Edited by Eneko Osaba, Esther Villar, Jesús L. Lobo and Ibai Laña

Part of IntechOpen Book Series: Artificial Intelligence, Volume 5
Book Series Editor: Marco Antonio Aceves-Fernandez

Contributors
Valentina Talimonchik, Wided Ali, Fatima Bouakkaz, Kumar S. Ray, Juan Jose Saucedo-Dorantes, David Alejandro Elvira-Ortiz, Arturo Yosimar Jaen-Cuellar, Manuel Toledano-Ayala, Aran Hansuebsai, Kosuke Takano, Somkiet Leanghirun, Thunchanok Tangpong, Gideon Samid, Clemence Alla Takam, Aurelle Tchagna Kouanou, Odette Samba, Thomas Mih, Daniel Tchiotsop, Mrinmoy Roy, Eneko Osaba, Ibai Laña, Jesús L. Lobo, Esther Villar

First published in London, United Kingdom, 2021 by IntechOpen
IntechOpen is the global imprint of INTECHOPEN LIMITED, registered in England and Wales, registration number: 11086078, 5 Princes Gate Court, London, SW7 2QJ, United Kingdom
Printed in Croatia

British Library Cataloguing-in-Publication Data
A catalogue record for this book is available from the British Library

Additional hard and PDF copies can be obtained from orders@intechopen.com

Artificial Intelligence - Latest Advances, New Paradigms and Novel Applications
Edited by Eneko Osaba, Esther Villar, Jesús L. Lobo and Ibai Laña
p. cm.
Print ISBN 978-1-83962-387-5
Online ISBN 978-1-83962-388-2
eBook (PDF) ISBN 978-1-83962-389-9
ISSN 2633-1403

For EU product safety concerns:
IN TECH d.o.o., Prolaz Marije Krucifikse Kozulić 3, 51000 Rijeka, Croatia, info@intechopen.com or visit our website at intechopen.com.

IntechOpen Book Series
Artificial Intelligence
Volume 5

Dr. Eneko Osaba works at TECNALIA as a senior researcher. He obtained his Ph.D. in Artificial Intelligence in 2015. He has participated in more than twenty-five local and European research projects, and in the publication of more than 130 papers. He has performed several stays at universities in the United Kingdom, Italy, and Malta. Dr. Osaba has served as a program committee member in more than forty international conferences and participated in organizing activities in more than ten international conferences. He is a member of the editorial board of the *International Journal of Artificial Intelligence*, *Data in Brief*, and *Journal of Advanced Transportation*. He is also a guest editor for the *Journal of Computational Science, Neurocomputing, Swarm, and Evolutionary Computation* and *IEEE ITS Magazine.*

Dr. Esther Villar obtained a Ph.D. in Information and Communication Technologies from the University of Alcalá, Spain, in 2015. She obtained a degree in Computer Science from the University of Deusto, Spain, in 2010, and an MSc in Computer Languages and Systems from the National University of Distance Education, Spain, in 2012. Her areas of interest and knowledge include natural language processing (NLP), detection of impersonation in social networks, semantic web, and machine learning. Dr. Esther Villar made several contributions at conferences and publishing in various journals in those fields. Currently, she is working within the OPTIMA (Optimization Modeling & Analytics) business of TECNALIA's ICT Division as a data scientist in projects related to the prediction and optimization of management and industrial processes (resource planning, energy efficiency, etc).

Dr. Jesus L. Lobo (Ph.D. in Information and Communications Technologies in Mobile Networks since 2018) is currently working at TECNALIA as a data scientist and machine learning/artificial intelligence researcher. His research topics include stream learning (online learning and concept drift), lifelong machine learning, ensemble building, and spiking neural networks. He is a member of the GEI-Big Data, an international excellence group at TECNALIA, and a member of the JRLab. He writes and reviews manuscripts for scientific journals and conferences, and he has worked as a data science trainer. He has dealt with real problems such as robotics planning, electricity fraud detection, and EEG signals to identify fatigue of pilots in aircrafts. He designs predictive/descriptive models working with the latest machine learning and optimization techniques.

Dr. Ibai Laña works at TECNALIA as a data analyst. He received his Ph.D. in Artificial Intelligence from the University of the Basque Country (UPV/EHU), Spain, in 2018. He is currently a senior researcher at TECNALIA. His research interests fall within the intersection of intelligent transportation systems, machine learning, traffic data analysis, and data science. He has dealt with urban traffic forecasting problems, applying machine learning models and evolutionary algorithms. He has experience in origin-destination matrix estimation or point of interest and trajectory detection. Working with large volumes of data has given him a good command of big data processing tools and NoSQL databases. He has also been a visiting scholar at the Knowledge Engineering and Discovery Research Institute, Auckland University of Technology.

Editors of Volume 5:
Eneko Osaba, Esther Villar, Jesús L. Lobo and Ibai Laña
TECNALIA, Basque Research and Technology Alliance (BRTA)
Derio, Bizkaia, Spain

Book Series Editor: Marco A. Aceves-Fernandez
Universidad Autónoma de Querétaro
Faculty of Engineering, Querétaro, México

Scope of the Series

Artificial Intelligence (AI) is a rapidly developing multidisciplinary research area that aims to solve increasingly complex problems. In today´s highly integrated world, AI promises to become a robust and powerful mean for obtaining solutions to previously unsolvable problems. This book series is intended for researchers and students alike, as well as all those interested in this fascinating field and its applications, in particular in areas related to the topics on which it is focused.

Contents

Preface

Artificial Intelligence (AI) is widely known as a knowledge field that aims to make computers, robots, or products that mimic the way humans think. In the current scientific community, AI is an intensively studied area composed of multiple branches. Historically, machine learning and optimization are two of the most studied fronts thanks to the development of novel and challenging research topics such as transfer optimization, swarm robotics, and drift detection and adaptation to evolving conditions in real-time. In addition, the emergence of new paradigms such as deep learning and explainable AI has kept this field as one of the principal cornerstones of computer science. This book collects radically new theoretical insights, reporting recent developments and evincing innovative applications regarding AI methods in all fields of knowledge. It also presents works focused on new paradigms and novel branches of AI science. This volume is a great resource for researchers, lecturers, and practitioners interested in AI and its potential applications.

Eneko Osaba, Esther Villar, Jesús L. Lobo and Ibai Laña
TECNALIA,
Basque Research and Technology Alliance (BRTA),
Derio, Bizkaia, Spain

Chapter 1

Introductory Chapter: Artificial Intelligence - Latest Advances, New Paradigms and Novel Applications

Esther Villar, Eneko Osaba, Jesus L. Lobo and Ibai Laña

1. Introduction

In the current technological society, data are considered the new oil of the digital economy. For this reason, Artificial Intelligence (AI), a knowledge field that emerges and flourishes on data, can be arguably deemed as the principal driving force of the current social and economical revolution. AI makes possible to extract knowledge from data, in order to infer, decide and proactively act in diverse critical areas for the human being, such as transportation, energy, industry, health, security or the financial sector.

Today, AI services and products can be found in many daily applications, such as those mobile tools that enrich user experience with our mobile devices or in the online shopping sector, where AI intervenes in the whole process from the targeted advertising to the recommendation systems. Furthermore, the application of AI algorithms in the industry has been a recurrent research topic for some years, and represents one of the catalyst technologies of the entire digital transformation movement that the industry is experiencing [1]. In this context, we can find heterogeneous systems such as predictive analytics methods, decision support techniques or artificial vision systems. Many additional applications are being developed and deployed by different companies for helping in diverse contexts such as the assistance with diagnosis and planning decisions, automated inspections, robotic applications or advanced manufacturing [2].

In any case, we are still at the very dawn of a technological revolution. It is widely considered that in an increasingly interconnected and automated world, those companies who master AI technologies will exercise control over the market.

2. Main areas of artificial intelligence

Artificial Intelligence is a wide field of knowledge dedicated to the design, modeling and implementation of intelligent systems so that they automatically give a response to complex problems arisen in the real-world. In this regard, several subfields can be found in this broader paradigm, being Machine Learning (ML) and Optimization the ones that stand out.

ML comprises those algorithms targeted to extract knowledge from data, relying on fundamental concepts in computer science, statistics or probability. Apart from

IntechOpen

that, ML goes one step further, being capable of unveiling additional features from the data, such as causality or advanced cognitive reasonings. Thus, ML techniques are meant to properly represent raw data featuring past experience and rendering it into a model able to gain insights and make either decisions or predictions. ML is closely related to data mining, although the latter fundamentally concentrates on the exploratory analysis whilst the former draws upon other artificial intelligence disciplines such as computational statistics or pattern recognition.

ML algorithms comprises both descriptive and predictive techniques. On the one hand, descriptive refers to those solvers aiming at describing the data, summarizing or categorizing it. On the other hand, predictive analysis is focused on finding trend, behaviors or conclusions which could be valuable for anticipating future outcomes. With respect to the learning style applied to the model generation, ML algorithms are typically categorized as supervised, unsupervised, semi-supervised and reinforcement learning:

- Supervised Learning [3]: in this category, labeled input data feeds a learning algorithm in the training phase. The model or inferred function will be generated under the premise of minimizing an error function or, on the contrary, of maximizing the precision. These systems are intended to correctly map unseen examples. Mostly addressed problems in this case are classification and regression.

- Unsupervised Learning [4]: no label for any input vector is provided. The objective in this case is to find the structure behind the patterns, with no supervisory or reward signal. These models analyze and deduce peculiarities or common traits in the instances so as to discover similarities and associations among the samples. Example problems are clustering and latent variable models.

- Semi-Supervised Learning [5]: labeled and unlabeled instances feed the algorithm, hence falling between the previously mentioned categories. The acquisition of labeled data is fairly expensive and often requires human skills while unlabeled data can be of great practical value in order to surpass the performance of any other previous learning approaches. The goal of this kind of systems can be oriented towards a transductive learning (deriving the labels of the unlabeled data by searching for analogies) or inductive learning (inferring the mapping from initially labeled vectors to their corresponding categories).

- Reinforcement Learning [6]: in this last category, the system interacts with its environment by producing actions and receiving either a positive or a negative stimulus from the events in response. These stimuli prompt the translation of that feedback into a learning process aiming at minimizing the punishment or maximizing the gained reward. This sort of learning is typical of robotics and its realistic environments which require algorithms for identifying relevant peripheral events in the stream of sensory inputs.

Apart form these classical categories, the natural flow of this field along with the technological advances happened in last years have led to the proposal of more sophisticated paradigms. This sophistication can come from the way the knowledge is acquired, like in the case of transfer and online learning; the way knowledge is shared (Federated Learning) or the inner complexity of models that allows for the representation of complex knowledge (Deep Learning). Furthermore, the growing complexity of the systems developed in these areas has created a demand for understanding the behavior of the applications created. All this with the purpose of reaching comprehensible and reliable systems for users foreign to the AI technologies, and also for automating tasks for researchers and practitioners (with paradigms such as AutoML [7]). As a result of this need, the field known as Explainable AI has recently emerged [8], which objective is to facilitate the interpretation and visualization of complex ML models (mainly Deep Learning models).

In another vein, optimization is the other widely studied topic within the wide field of AI. Hundreds of studies are published every year fully focused on giving an answer to many diverse real-world problems of this kind. In a nutshell, an optimization problem can be defined as the intelligent search of the best solution from the whole group of feasible ones. In this regard, a feasible solution is this alternative that can be placed within the boundaries demarcated by the established constraints. Analogously, the specific word *best* refers in this context to the most desired solution related to any objective function (or fitness function) which is expected to be maximized or minimized. In other words, an optimization procedure consists of finding the optimal solution to a problem taking into account i) the previously mentioned objective function, which provides a quantitative measure of the performance ii) the decision variables that compose the optimization problem and the parameters on which the solving algorithm is based on, and iii) the constraints to be compulsorily met which delimits the allowable search space.

The nature and characteristics of the above described objective function, variables or restriction give rise to a broad variety of optimization problems, such as numerical optimization, linear, continuous or combinatorial optimization. We can also distinguish about single-optimization, which objective is to optimize one sole objective; or multiobjective optimization [9], which entails the finding of a group of solutions which provide the optimal balance among different objectives. We would like to highlight dynamic optimization [10], in which constraints and/or fitness function of the problem can vary dynamically along time; stochastic optimization [11], defined as the process of optimizing a problem in which one or more of its values are subject to randomness; or Transfer Optimization [12], devoted to the exploitation of the knowledge acquired throughout the optimization of one problem to solve another related or unrelated problem. Additional categories are multimodal optimization or robust optimization among many others.

The interest of solving optimization problems can be justified in two different ways. On the one hand, optimization problems are usually modeled for giving an efficient solution to a real-world problem, entailing their resolution a both social and business interest. To be more precise, this means that different real situations can be modeled as optimization problems to be treated and solved with greater efficiency [13]. On the other hand, many optimization problems are highly complex to solve. For this reason, finding efficient solutions constitutes an attractive challenge for researchers. Being more specific, a large number of these problems are classified as NP-Hard. According to the theory of computational complexity, a problem is considered NP-Hard when there is no technique capable of finding an optimal solution for all its instances in polynomial time.

3. Motivation behind the book edition

Regarding the scientific production, AI symbolizes one of the most high-growing area in the current research community, with more than 350 000 papers published since the nineties. Just a quick glance to renowned Scopus® database confirms this statement, and unveils a clear upward trend. More concretely, AI related scientific production evolves at a significant rate from nearly 3 500 papers in 1990, 14 100 in 2010 and more than 35 000 in 2020. For this reason, and considering the interest that this area is generating in the current community, the edited book that this chapter is introducing revolves around recent prominent theories and developments of AI methods, as well as their application to different fields covered by the engineering. Thus, this material supposes a great opportunity for practitioners, lectures and researchers interested in AI topic as a whole.

Author details

Esther Villar, Eneko Osaba*, Jesus L. Lobo and Ibai Laña
TECNALIA, Basque Research and Technology Alliance (BRTA), Derio, Bizkaia, Spain

*Address all correspondence to: eneko.osaba@tecnalia.com

References

[1] Matt, C., Hess, T., Benlian, A.: Digital transformation strategies. Business & Information Systems Engineering **57**(5) (2015) 339–343

[2] Lee, J., Davari, H., Singh, J., Pandhare, V.: Industrial artificial intelligence for industry 4.0-based manufacturing systems. Manufacturing letters **18** (2018) 20–23

[3] Caruana, R., Niculescu-Mizil, A.: Anempirical comparison of supervised learning algorithms. In: Proceedings of the 23rd international conference on Machine learning. (2006) 161–168

[4] Barlow, H.B.: Unsupervised learning. Neural computation **1**(3) (1989) 295–311

[5] Zhu, X., Goldberg, A.B.: Introduction to semi-supervised learning. Synthesis lectures on artificial intelligence and machine learning **3**(1) (2009) 1–130

[6] Sutton, R.S., Barto, A.G.: Reinforcement learning: An introduction. MIT press (2018)

[7] He, X., Zhao, K., Chu, X.: Automl: A survey of the state-of-the-art. Knowledge-Based Systems **212** (2021) 106622

[8] Samek, W., Montavon, G., Vedaldi, A., Hansen, L.K., Müller, K.R.: Explainable AI: interpreting, explaining and visualizing deep learning. Volume 11700. Springer Nature (2019)

[9] Abraham, A., Jain, L.: Evolutionary multiobjective optimization. In: Evolutionary Multiobjective Optimization. Springer (2005) 1–6

[10] Nguyen, T.T., Yang, S., Branke, J.: Evolutionary dynamic optimization: A survey of the state of the art. Swarm and Evolutionary Computation **6** (2012) 1–24

[11] Schneider, J., Kirkpatrick, S.: Stochastic optimization. Springer Science & Business Media (2007)

[12] Osaba, E., Del Ser, J., Martinez, A. D., Lobo, J.L., Herrera, F.: At-mfcga: An adaptive transfer-guided multifactorial cellular genetic algorithm for evolutionary multitasking. Information Sciences (2021)

[13] Osaba, E., Villar-Rodriguez, E., Del Ser, J., Nebro, A.J., Molina, D., LaTorre, A., Suganthan, P.N., Coello, C.A.C., Herrera, F.: A tutorial on the design, experimentation and application of metaheuristic algorithms to real-world optimization problems. Swarm and Evolutionary Computation (2021) 100888

Chapter 2

Big Data Framework Using Spark Architecture for Dose Optimization Based on Deep Learning in Medical Imaging

Clémence Alla Takam, Aurelle Tchagna Kouanou, Odette Samba, Thomas Mih Attia and Daniel Tchiotsop

Abstract

Deep learning and machine learning provide more consistent tools and powerful functions for recognition, classification, reconstruction, noise reduction, quantification and segmentation in biomedical image analysis. Some breakthroughs. Recently, some applications of deep learning and machine learning for low-dose optimization in computed tomography have been developed. Due to reconstruction and processing technology, it has become crucial to develop architectures and/or methods based on deep learning algorithms to minimize radiation during computed tomography scan inspections. This chapter is an extension work done by Alla et al. in 2020 and explain that work very well. This chapter introduces the deep learning for computed tomography scan low-dose optimization, shows examples described in the literature, briefly discusses new methods for computed tomography scan image processing, and provides conclusions. We propose a pipeline for low-dose computed tomography scan image reconstruction based on the literature. Our proposed pipeline relies on deep learning and big data technology using Spark Framework. We will discuss with the pipeline proposed in the literature to finally derive the efficiency and importance of our pipeline. A big data architecture using computed tomography images for low-dose optimization is proposed. The proposed architecture relies on deep learning and allows us to develop effective and appropriate methods to process dose optimization with computed tomography scan images. The real realization of the image denoising pipeline shows us that we can reduce the radiation dose and use the pipeline we recommend to improve the quality of the captured image.

Keywords: Deep Learning, Computer Tomography Scan Image, Big Data technologies, Low Dose Optimization, Spark Framework

1. Introduction

Machine Learning (ML) technics are widely used in medical imaging in the form of many successful optimization, clustering, prediction and classifier algorithms. ML is a branch of artificial intelligence (AI) and has been used in a heterogeneity of applications. It is used to analyze complex data sets and find similarity, correlation and patterns between such data without explicit programming [1]. ML technology is an important part of medical imaging research. Recently, a highly flexible ML method called deep learning (DL) has emerged as a disruptive technology to improve the performance of existing ML methods and solve previously difficult problems [2]. DL comes from the ML and computer vision communities. The key to the success of the DL-based method lies in its independence from the explicit imaging model, backup of big data in a specific field, and optimization of image quality by learning features in an end-to-end manner [3]. Recently, it has been applied to natural language processing, facial recognition, speech recognition, image classification, automatic diagnosis and other problems, and has achieved good results [4, 5]. Nowadays, DL allows many applications in CT and helps to improve interpretation speed, diagnostic accuracy and clinical efficiency. In addition, for research purposes and clinical purposes, CT is widely used for detection, diagnosis and image-guided treatment [6, 7]. CT is a well-known imaging technique that can observe the inside of objects non-invasively [8]. The main problem of CT scans is the optimization and minimization of radiation dose during the examination, especially in pediatric skull scans. The development and optimization of dosimetry protocols in pediatric skull scans is a huge social interest, as well as the medical community worldwide. Indeed, because the radiosensitivity is much higher than that of adults, patient-specific dosimetry has aroused great interest in pediatric skull applications. This is because children have a higher risk of cancer compared with adults receiving the same dose [9]. In view of the possible risk of X-ray radiation to pediatric patients, low-dose CT has attracted considerable interest in the field of biomedical imaging [10]. However, the main problem with low-dose CT is image noise and the quality of the results obtained. To overcome this shortcoming, DL with a convolutional neural network (CNN) algorithm is used. In fact, one of the goals of various DL and ML algorithms is to improve the consistency, quality and/or applicability of diagnostic data interpretation. DL can improve the image quality during low-dose CT skull scans.

This chapter is an extended work done by Alla et al. in 2020 (https://doi.org/10.1016/j.imu.2020.100335), and explains the work well. In this chapter, we mainly focus on the dose optimization in pediatric skull scans using CNN for DL and the image processing performed in [4]. We completed the expansion of the work in [4], giving more explanations and more papers. The workflow performs the following steps: image denoising, image segmentation, CNN, image retrieval, image diagnosis and storage. We described the importance of using big data technology (Spark framework) to build our proposed architecture through the MapReduce method. We will discuss with the pipeline and architecture discussed in the literature. The implementation of FCNN has been implemented. The rest of the work is arranged as follows: Section 2 introduces the latest status of published works in this field. In Section 3, theoretically, these works are fully utilized in our paper, and the architecture we propose is proposed. Section 4 introduces the implementation of our architecture and the different results obtained. Section 5 examines and discusses the results. Section 6 provides conclusions and future work.

2. State of the art

ML and DL are becoming established disciplines in a wide range of AI fields in terms of analyzing and using data-concentrated patterns [11, 12]. The DL model of CNN refers to a class of computers that can learn the hierarchical structure of elements by constructing high-level attributes from low-level attributes, thereby automatically executing the process of element builders [13, 14]. In CT scan images, DL is usually used for the purpose of minimizing radiation exposure, noise images and CT image reconstruction. CT accurately uses gamma rays, X-rays, ultrasound or other types of beams in conjunction with sensitive detectors to sequentially scan various parts of the human body [15]. However, obtaining excellent image quality from CT scans requires very high radiation doses to the patient during the examination.

In addition, because the radiosensitivity is much higher than that of adults, patient-specific dosimetry has aroused great interest in pediatric skull applications [16]. Therefore, in these cases, low-dose CT is essential. In the past few years, low-dose CT biomedical imaging technology has become the focus of attention to alleviate people's concerns about exposure to X-ray radiation and the widely used CT scan [16]. According to [17], the author reviewed the dosimetry applications in pediatric diagnostic methods (including CT and nuclear medicine applications) in 2018.

Based on these challenges, a lot of work was done during the CT examination to reduce the radiation dose and maintain the quality of the captured images. In [18–20], the author proposed a news method to optimize the dose during CT scans. However, sometimes the reduction of radiation leads to a reduction in image quality. DL can overcome this problem through reconstruction technology and prevent useful information from being deleted into the original CT image. Many types of research and publications have been conducted in the literature. In order to reduce radiation dose, some work is based on traditional methods (protocol optimization), while others are based on DL and ML methods. In Ref. [21], the author proposes a method for optimizing radiation dose based on the study of the scheme used. Dalmazo et al. in [22] investigated the radiation dose of the CT program through the phantom and ionization chamber, and conducted the research in the university hospital. Their research is based only on equipment surveys. In 2012, Dougeni et al. reviewed the patient dose and optimization procedures in CT scans of adults and children [23]. They discussed and compared various literary works in CT dose optimization, but did not propose their method. Recently, in 2019, Smith-Bindman et al. conducted a study in 151 institutions in seven countries and proposed a good practical plan from more than 2 million adult CT examinations to optimize the dose of radiation during CT scans or other radiological examinations [24]. In 2020, Abdukkadir et al. conducted a study to optimize current local practices by investigating the radiation dose distribution of pediatric head and abdomen CT examinations and existing routine scanning procedures at the Kelanta Radiology Department in Malaysia [25]. In addition, Cui et al. in [26], proposed a work to optimize the dose and image quality of various exposure conditions and phantom diameters in pediatric abdominal CT scans. In [27], the authors evaluated the image quality of dose-optimized (DO)C spine CT in patients who can pull down their shoulders in an emergency to reduce exposure and improve image quality. Chen et al., based on a survey in 2017, observed how to improve image quality after CT scan [28]. Nowadays, many works based on DL or ML are studying how to reduce the radiation dose during CT scan inspection and maintain good resolution and the quality of captured images.

Regarding ML and DL in dose optimization, Kang et al. in 2017, developed an algorithm using CNN, which was applied to the window wavelet transform coefficients of low-dose CT images. Their CNN is built with a residual learning architecture, which can speed up network training and improve performance. The execution results of their proposed algorithm show that the complex noise patterns are effectively eliminated in the CT images obtained from the reduced X-ray dose, and the wavelet domain CNN is effective in reducing the noise of low-dose CT [29]. Jung et al. performed a survey in 2017 on the latest applications of DL in CT and magnetic resonance imaging (MRI) biomedical image analysis in a range of tasks and target organs, with a focus on improving the accuracy and productivity of current diagnostic analysis [30]. They introduced some promising applications that have greatly changed the current flow of biomedical imaging [30]. However, they did not provide any workflow for the described method. Xuy et al. in [31] performed literature on

DL method to solve the problem of PET image reconstruction quality. In their work, an excellent clinical diagnosis can be obtained when the radiation dose during the capture of biomedical images using PET Scan is low [31]. They are based on encoder-decoder residual deep networks with chain skip connections. Liu et al. evaluated how to use DL-based low-dose coronary CT angiography (CCTA) optimization algorithm for image noise reduction and image quality (IQ) improvement [32].

Wurfl et al. proposed a new DL framework for 3-D CT reconstruction in [33]. They developed a new type of cone beam back-projection layer, which can effectively calculate the forward pass, and their framework can jointly optimize the volume and the correction steps in the projection domain. Although the performance is encouraging, their methods are limited to post-processing methods. Shan et al. launched a transmission path-based convolutional codec (CPCE) network in 2018, which performs low-dose CT noise reduction based on transfer learning in 2D and 3D configurations within the framework of Generative Adversarial Networks (GAN) [34]. Tian et al., based on CNN, we combined the two networks to increase the width of the network, thereby obtaining more functions. This allows them to design a novel network called Batch Renormalized Noise Reduction Network (BRDNet) to eliminate a lot of noise on the image [35]. However, the author did not use CT images. Lee et al. developed a method using DL and its CNN which can analyze CT image tasks, such as object detection and semantic segmentation, or analyze other biomedical imaging modes, such as MRI and positron emission tomography (PET) scans [36]. However, their method is not based on low-dose CT. Recently, in 2019, Gu et al. combined random forest with dictionary learning to reduce CT scan radiation while ensuring the new low-dose CT super-resolution reconstruction and CT image quality [22]. In the same year, Meineke et al. proved that ML can comprehensively detect chest CT examinations with the potential of dose optimization [37]. They used 139 CT chest examinations to train and test different neural network layers and components, improved and optimized the construction model, and predicted the volumetric CT dose index (CTDIvol) based on the scanned patient indicators [37]. However, in the previous three works, the author did not provide a framework based on big data technology and DL to optimize the dose in children's cranial CT scans.

According to these cited works, and as far as we know, no author does not provide a specific pipeline and big data architecture to use DL, Spark framework and MapReduce processing model to manage low-dose and efficient cranial CT scan images. This shortcoming is the main interest of this article. In fact, we have performed a pipeline that implements a full CNN (FCNN) for processing CT scan images and proposed a method to divide biomedical images into image blocks before applying FCNN. Therefore, we can use the Spark framework and MapReduce programming, and shorten the processing time to our proposed architecture. Our proposed architecture allows adjustment of the low dose in the low dose skull CT image for correct diagnosis.

3. Methods

Biomedical image processing is not new. Many software and programming methods always divide the image into many blocks for processing. In fact, dividing the image into small pieces, processing and merging them is a routine engineering work that will be used in any medical imaging pipeline. However, the new concept introduced in this article is to perform parallel processing, and for biomedical images, parallel processing is not actually completed. Traditionally we divide the image into many chucks. Instead of processing each block one by one, we use the Spark framework, but process many blocks or all blocks of the image at the same time. This section discusses our recommended workflow.

As the use of CT in modern medicine continues to increase, people are beginning to pay attention to increasing the radiation dose from biomedical imaging to the community and the associated increase in the estimated risk of radiation-induced cancer [38]. The optimization of the scanning method is important, so the necessary clinical information can be collected or captured while minimizing the radiation dose [39]. The proposed general workflow for biomedical image denoising is presented in **Figure 1**.

In **Figure 1**, the first step includes data collection from various hospitals, medical centers, and laboratories. The data include the images of various medical applications. In this chapter, we used CT image to perform our work. The second step consist to choose the denoising techniques to use. We list various techniques and we used DL into this chapter. Feature extraction and selection are actually a critical step for image denoising using DL. Feature extraction methodologies evaluate the preprocessed images in order to extract the most prominent features which represent different sets of features based on the pixel intensity relationship statistics.

We proposed also in this part the best pipeline for CNN-based low-dose CT image diagnosis. Our proposed pipeline relies on four main parts: captured images, multiprocessing images, denoising and diagnosis, sharing or storage. **Figure 2** shows us all the parts of our proposed pipeline [4].

3.1 Image denoising theory in CT Scan: overview

Image denoising has always been a basic problem in the field of image processing [40]. For researchers, removing noise on the original captured image is still a challenging problem in digital image processing. Solving image details and eliminating random noise as much as possible is the goal of image denoising methods. Many noise reduction techniques rely on mathematical methods. The problem of image denoising cans mathematically modelled by Eq. (1) [41]:

$$y = x + b \tag{1}$$

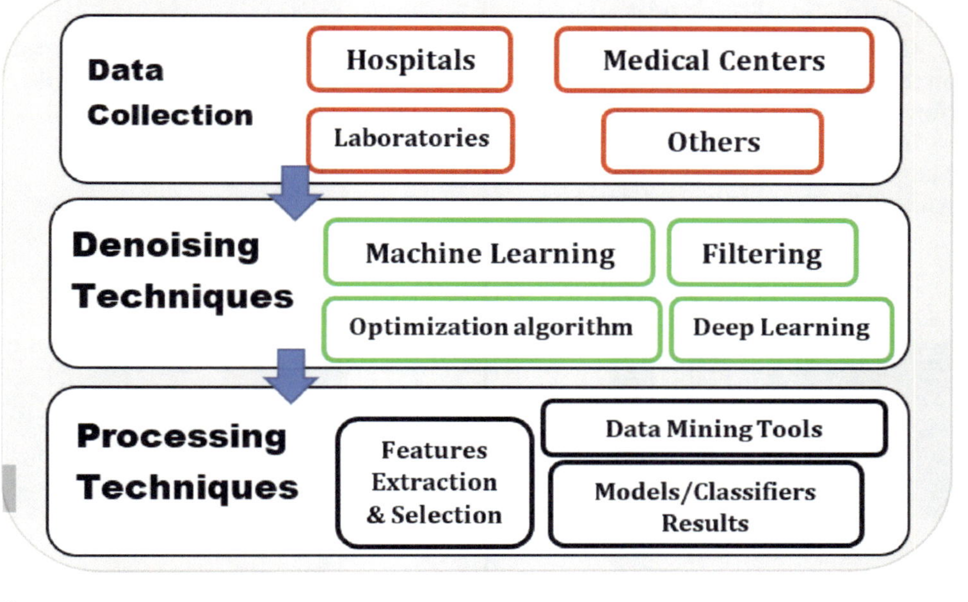

Figure 1.
Proposed General workflow for biomedical image denoising.

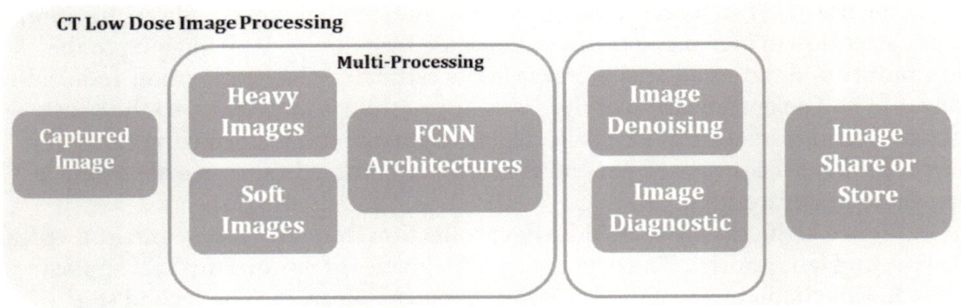

Figure 2.
Pipeline for low-dose CT image reconstruction. Using the Spark framework will only design multi-processing steps.

In Eq. (1), y represented the image noising, x the clean image, and b the noise. The noising is modelled by using an additive white Gaussian noise (AWGN) with standard deviation. The authors from [40–43], shown that the technics of denoising image rely on the transform domain and spatial domain. In this part, we based of work done in [44] and present the FCNN architecture used to applied in our work. Through mathematical explanation, the parameter update process in the CNN architecture is introduced in detail. In this section, we deal with the CNN model for image denoising.

The mathematical model of CNN that allows us to predict a clean version from noisy images based on the CNN architecture and training process will develop. Image noise reduction and noise removal with structure preservation function is one of the important tasks integrated in medical diagnostic imaging systems (such as X-ray, computer tomography (CT)). When the area considered by the patient is exposed under X-ray/CT, X-ray and CT images are formed and the resulting attenuation is captured. The **Figure 3** presents the CNN architecture for image denoising from [42, 43].

The CNN model usually has three layers: Input layer, hidden layer and output layer. **Figure 4** shows a set of layers used to reduce image noise in the CNN architecture. All descriptions of this architecture are presented in [4].

CNN method is based on the following idea: the model operates normally based on the local understanding of the image. By reusing the same parameters multiple times, it uses fewer parameters than a fully connected network.

In the "multi-processing" step in **Figure 2**, we propose our method based on a large number of research results provided by the CT low-dose optimization study using Deep CNN [12]. FCNN is composed of multiple layers of neuron-like

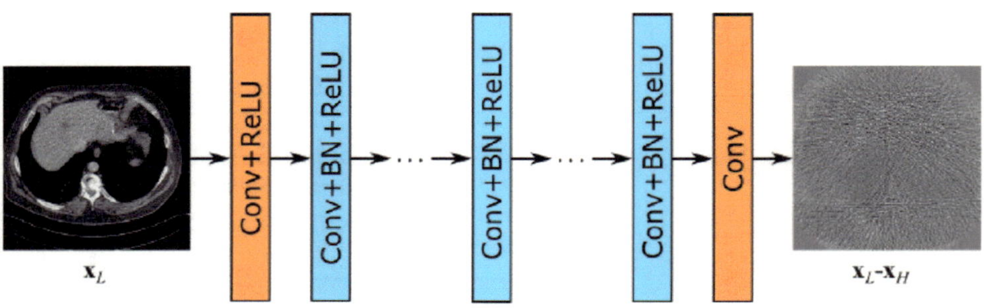

Figure 3.
The structure of the CNN denoiser [42].

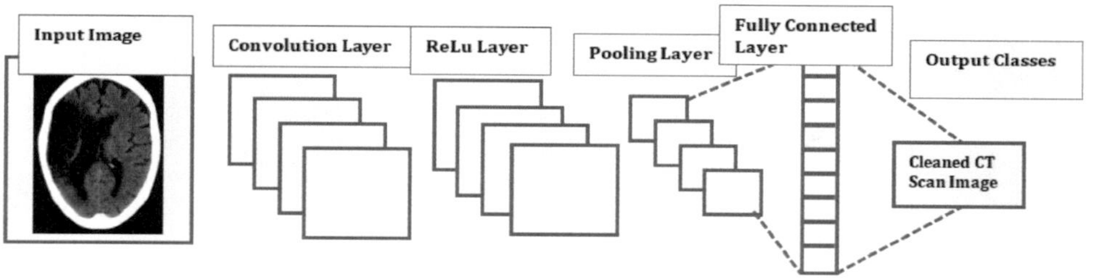

Figure 4.
Layers name for CT image denoising.

computational connections, and has minimal step-by-step processing, thus achieving significant improvements [12]. In FCNN, each layer is completely connected to the upper layer, so there is no need to preserve spatial relationships. However, the training of FCNN is computationally demanding and requires a large number of data sets that may not be easily available. In order to solve the usually long training time problem, a large community of machine learning engineers and programmers is committed to research and development of more general and faster software platforms for DL use cases. There are many examples, such as Keras, Pytorch, Torch, etc., which provide an exciting experience, a practical interface, and a fast and efficient memory implementation to train and test many deep learning architectures [12, 45]. Nowadays, almost every framework includes convolution, deconvolution, max pooling, full connection, exit technology and batch normalization, and almost all popular optimization methods are implemented. Due to the lack of a powerful computer, we propose a DNN-based architecture in this chapter, which uses Spark to accelerate and improve CT low-dose image reconstruction. In this chapter, we set up a cluster with one master node and two slave nodes to reduce computation time. After the FCNN-based CT low-dose image reconstruction step, we can turn to the image diagnosis step in **Figure 2**, where the expert will view the new image and make a suitable diagnosis. In addition, low doses can be used to carry on the health of the patient. According to our pipeline technic, experts can always make correct diagnosis on captured images.

3.2 Suggested FCNN method for CT scan image denoising

The development and training of FCNN is still the subject of research. In the process, we use DL for low-dose CT image reconstruction. In the next session, we will use the best big data framework (Spark) with MapReduce to design the best architecture to build effective and appropriate technics for processing low-dose CT scan images. In this part, we will introduce the Spark architecture to handle the most important steps of the pipeline described in **Figure 1**. The main goal of this architecture is to see how to process CT images for reconstruction. Apache Spark is based on MapReduce for parallel programming and extends the data sharing abstraction called *Resilient Distributed Data Set (RDD)* [4, 5]. Spark's DL has two main advantages: large-scale prediction and hyperparameter adjustment [5]. In addition, Spark Framework provides easy-to-use APIs to enable DL in a few lines of code in its Spark MLib library. **Figure 5** shows us the Apache Spark architecture with different layers, and **Figure 6** shows us the Spark architecture with FCNN for low-dose CT image optimization. In **Figure 6**, we can see how to use MapReduce programming and FCNN with back propagation and forward propagation to train the input image. We need to divide the image into a set of image blocks (with heavier images). Digital CT scan images are usually too large, thus increasing the

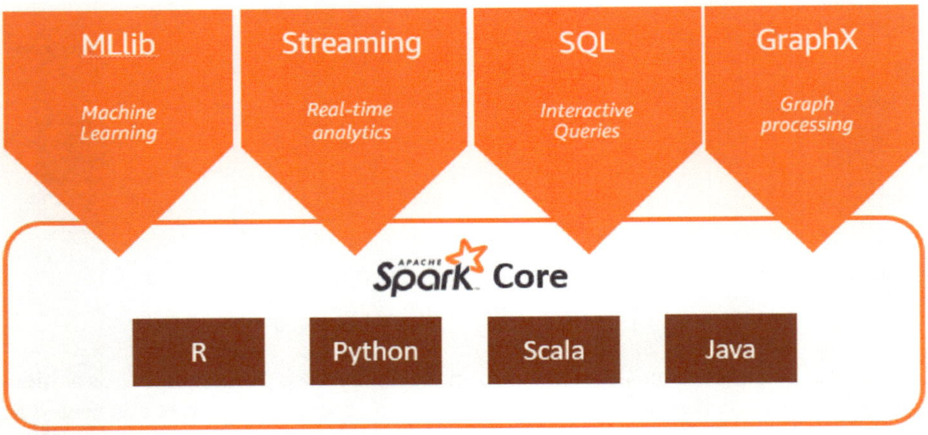

Figure 5.
Apache spark features.

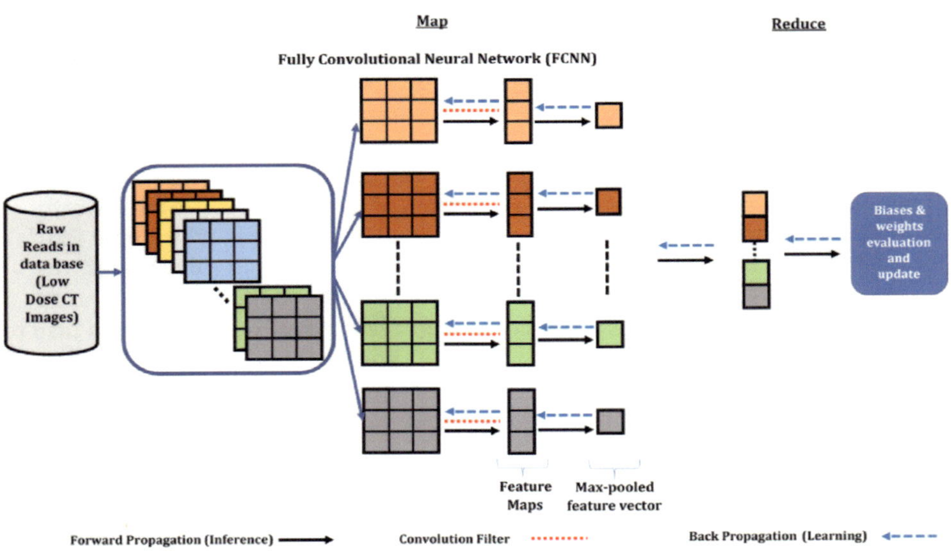

Figure 6.
FCNN-based spark map reduce pipeline for low-dose CT image reconstruction.

complexity of processing. To overcome this complexity, we divide the image into many image blocks and process each part of the image independently. By using a programming parallel method like MapReduce, we can execute the processing of these blocks at the same time, thus saving processing time compared to traditional methods. **Figure 6** outlines how FCNN reconstructs CT low-dose images into Spark. In fact, the Spark architecture allows us to develop effective and appropriate techniques to utilize a large number of images. **Figure 6** outlines image processing in Spark. Training our FCNN model on the Spark framework involves two main steps (MapReduce programming), these steps will happen repeatedly and repeated until the total initialization error is small enough: Map and Reduce Step [4].

The scenario or concept of **Figure 6** allows us to process many CT images at the same time and optimize the processing time. Using the Spark framework and using the DL architecture, the process of dose optimization in pediatric skull scans is complete, easy and fast.

4. Results

In this section, we are based on the architecture proposed in **Figure 6** and implement our CT image noise reduction algorithm. Our goal is to use FCNN to learn Eq. (1) by minimizing function of equations presented in [4]. We treat the image from Kaggle [46] as a clean/real image: *yi*. The data set contains information on 37 women and 45 men, so a total of 82 patients obtained 4615 CT images. However, due to insufficient computer capabilities, we reduced the number of images. **Figure 7** shows us some noisy and clean images from the dataset. For each pixel, we will generate a noisy version by adding Gaussian white noise: $x_i = y_i + b_i$ (see Eq. (1)), where b where is a CT image, where each pixel is an independent implementation of zero-mean Gaussian distribution, Has a standard deviation $\sigma = 30$.

Indeed, when we reduce the dose during the CT scan, the captured image is noisy. Here, we treat the noise as a Gaussian distribution. Since the sizes of CT images are different, we will consider random crops with a size of 180 × 180. As mentioned in [47], it is very important to initialize the weights in the process of training the model. The training loss and training PSNR according to number of epochs are also presented in this section. The PSNR is defined in [7, 48] by (2)

$$PSNR = 10\log_{10}\left(\frac{255^2}{MSE}\right) \quad (2)$$

$$\text{Where } MSE = \frac{1}{M \times N}\sum_{i=0}^{M-1}\sum_{j=0}^{N-1}\left(x(i,j) - y(i,j)\right)^2 \quad (3)$$

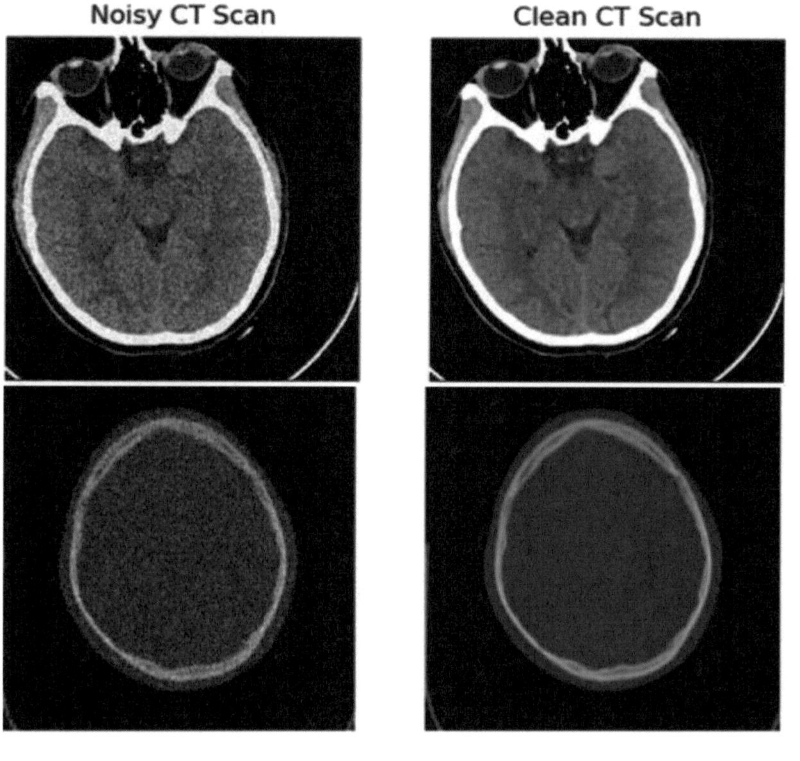

Figure 7.
Clean and noisy CT images.

PSNR gives an objective measure of distortion; a higher PSNR (greater than 30 dB) equals good image quality [7, 48]. **Figure 8a** and **b** respectively show the training loss and training PSNR according to several periods. We notice that in **Figure 8**, the training loss is close to 0.001, which proves the effectiveness of our training model, and the training PSNR is close to 33 dB (**Figure 8b**). Therefore, our DL method can efficiently denoise CT scan images. This effect can be seen

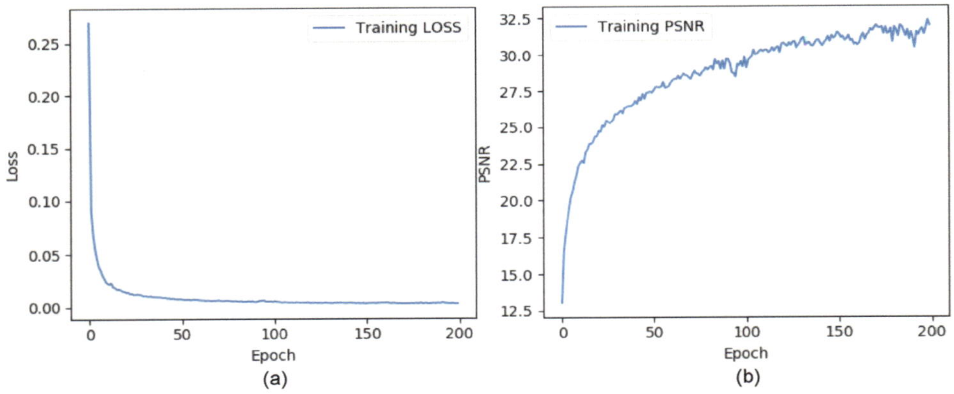

Figure 8.
(a & b) Results of training model. (a) Training Loss (b) Training PSNR.

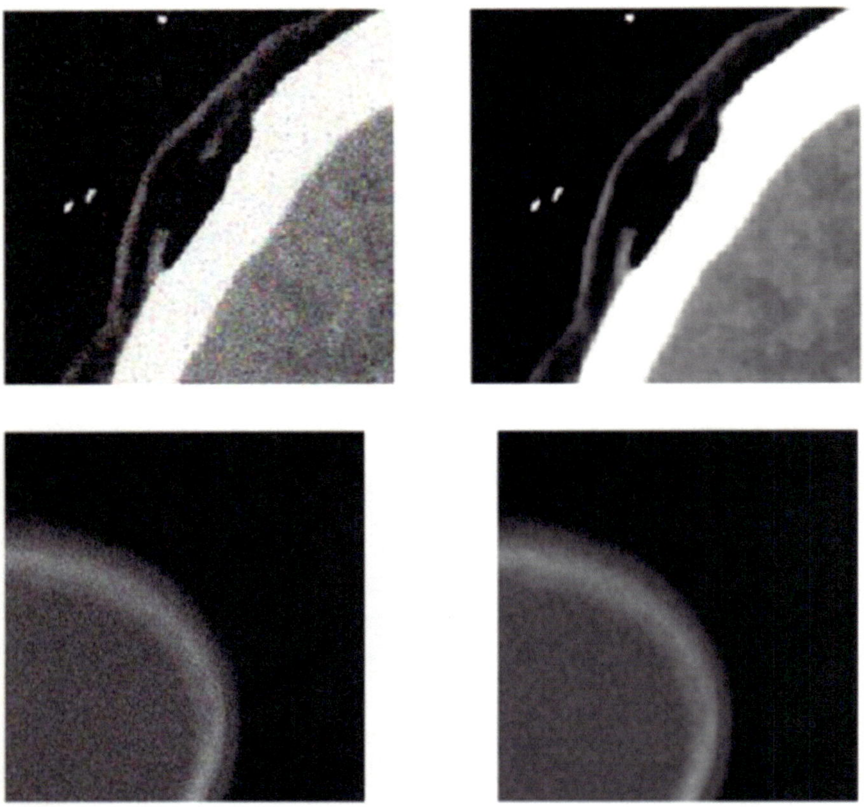

Figure 9.
Image noisy and obtained image denoising from our model.

Number of epochs	Training Loss	PSNR (dB)	Training Time (s)
20	0.021	22.6	423
50	0.014	26.7	850
100	0.011	29.8	1621
200	0.003	32.6	3112

Table 1.
Summary of our Training simulation Model.

in **Figure 9**, where we show a noisy and denoised image. To implement this work, we use a computer with Ubuntu OS, Spark and work locally in one cluster that we built with one node. **Table 1** present a summary of our different results.

5. Discussion

Nowadays, new workflows, pipelines, and architectures are always suggested in other areas to improve the field of biomedical imaging. This work proposes a workflow for CT low-dose image reconstruction relying on FCNN and Spark. The uniqueness of our workflow is that it gives the best techniques, methods and algorithms that can be used in every design phase. By using the features of MapReduce, we can perform parallel processing on the proposed architecture. Based on the observations in the previous section, our proposed pipeline and architecture have a new concept for low-dose optimization in pediatric skull scans. They can be customized and adapted to many other biomedical applications. In order to effectively understand our proposed architecture, we compared this architecture with another architecture suggested in the literature. In [8], the author proposed an architecture based on FCNN for CT low-dose optimization. However, his proposed architecture is not based on the Spark, so it cannot process many bio medical images at the same time. As shown in [8], we propose two main training steps: forward propagation, in which low-quality images are passed through the network, and the output is obtained by calculating a set of convolutions. Backpropagation, where the derivative of the loss function with respect to each network parameter is calculated, and the calculated gradient is used to update these values to reduce the loss. Similarly, in [49], the author designed a DL architecture for CT reconstruction based on the plug-and-play framework, and obtained good results. Nevertheless, the authors did not use DL for low-dose reconstruction. They are only used for image noise reduction. As mentioned in Section 2, they did not rely on the literature of the Spark framework for CT low-dose reconstruction using DL.

6. Conclusion

Deep learning has shown encouraging results in clinical studies because they can perform major reconstructions during a reduced-dose CT scan while maintaining a useful diagnosis. In this article, we outline some important research in the field of low-dose CT optimization, and study the problem of low-dose CT reconstruction from the perspective of DL. We propose a pipeline for low-dose image reconstruction using FCNN to Spark framework. To design our pipeline, we conducted a literature review to determine the most suitable method for CT low-dose image optimization. Therefore, we are able to provide a way to finally obtain the best architecture for each stage of the pipeline. To outline our proposed method, we built a Spark architecture that uses FCNN for low-dose CT reconstruction. The results got prove the efficiency and effectiveness of our proposed method. The training data greatly affects the noise reduction performance of the model, which is a common problem in discriminative learning methods. In the future, we will build our own data set to improve the process of CT scan image noise reduction. We will also try to used quantum computing with deep learning for a large dataset in order to improve quantitatively the work done in this chapter.

Author details

Clémence Alla Takam[1], Aurelle Tchagna Kouanou[2,3]*, Odette Samba[1,4], Thomas Mih Attia[2] and Daniel Tchiotsop[5]

1 Unité de Recherche de Matière Condensée d'Electronique et de Traitement du Signal (URMACETS), Faculty of Science, University of Dschang, Dschang, Cameroon

2 Department of Computer Engineering, College of Technology, University of Buea, Cameroon

3 Department of Training, Research, Development and Innovation, InchTech's Solutions, Yaounde, Cameroon

4 Service de Radiothérapie, Hôpital Général de Yaoundé-Cameroun, Cameroon

5 Unité de Recherche d'Automatique et d'Informatique Appliquée (URAIA), IUT-FV de Bandjoun, Université de Dschang-Cameroun, Bandjoun, Cameroon

*Address all correspondence to: tkaurelle@gmail.com

References

[1] Lakhani P, Prater AB, Hutson RK et al., Machine Learning in Radiology: Applications Beyond Image Interpretation, J Am Coll Radiol 2018;15: 350-359. https://doi.org/10.1016/j.jacr.2017.09.044

[2] Kim J, Hong J, Park H, Prospects of deep learning for medical imaging, Precision and Future Medicine 2018; 2(2):37-52. https://doi.org/10.23838/pfm.2018.00030

[3] You C, Li G, Zhang Y et al., CT Super-resolution GAN Constrained by the Identical, Residual, and Cycle Learning Ensemble (GAN-CIRCLE), IEEE 2018, asarXiv:1808.04256v3.

[4] Alla Takam C, Samba O, Tchagna Kouanou A, Tchiotsop D (2020) Spark Architecture for deep learning-based dose optimization in medical imaging, Elsevier Informatics in Medicine Unlocked 29 1-13. https://doi.org/10.1016/j.imu.2020.100335

[5] Tchagna Kouanou A, Tchiotsop D, Kengne R, Djoufack Tansaa Z, Ngo Moelas AA, Tchinda R, An optimal big data workflow for biomedical image analysis, Elsevier Informatics in Medicine Unlocked 11 (2018) 68-74. https://doi.org/10.1016/j.imu.2018.05.001

[6] Sandfort V, Choi Y, Symons R, Chen MY, Bluemke DA, An Optimized Test Bolus Contrast Injection Protocol for Consistent Coronary Artery Luminal Enhancement for Coronary CT Angiography, Academy Radiology 27 (2019) 371-380. https://doi.org/10.1016/j.acra.2019.05.003

[7] Tchagna Kouanou A, Tchiotsop D, Tchinda R, et al., A Machine Learning Algorithm for Biomedical Images Compression Using Orthogonal Transforms, International Journal of Image, Graphics and Signal Processing (IJIGSP), 10, (2018), 38-53.DOI: 10.5815/ijigsp.2018.11.05

[8] Bazrafkan S, Nieuwenhove VV, Soons J, Beenhouwer JD, Sijbers J, Deep Learning Based Computed Tomography Whys and Wherefores, 2019, arXiv: 1904.03908v1.

[9] Papadimitroulas P, Kostou T, Chatzipapas K et al., A review on personalized pediatric dosimetry applications using advanced computational tools, IEEE Transactions on Radiation and Plasma Medical Sciences 2018. DOI 10.1109/TRPMS.2018.2876562.

[10] Chen H, Zhang Y, Kalra MK et al., Low-Dose CT with a Residual Encoder-Decoder Convolutional Neural Network (RED-CNN), IEEE Transactions on Medical Imaging, DOI 10.1109/TMI.2017.2715284

[11] Pehrson LM, Nielsen MB and Lauridsen CA, Automatic Pulmonary Nodule Detection Applying Deep Learning or Machine Learning Algorithms to the LIDC-IDRI Database: A Systematic Review, MDPI diagnostics 2019, 9, 29; doi:10.3390/diagnostics 9010029

[12] Lou B, Doken S, Zhuang T, An image-based deep learning framework for individualising radiotherapy dose: a retrospective analysis of outcome prediction, Elsevier Lancet Digital Health 2019, 1: e136-47.

[13] Landers A, Neph R, Scalzo F, Ruan D, Sheng K, Performance Comparison of Knowledge-Based Dose Prediction Techniques Based on Limited Patient Data, Technology in Cancer Research & Treatment, 2018, 17, 1-10. DOI: 10.1177/1533033818811150

[14] Kim T, Heo J, Jang DK et al., Machine learning for detecting moyamoya disease in plain skull radiography using a convolutional neural network, Elsevier EBioMedicine,

2018. https://doi.org/10.1016/j.ebiom.2018.12.043

[15] Gu P, Jiang C, Ji M et al., Low-Dose Computed Tomography Image Super-Resolution Reconstruction via Random Forests, Sensors 2019, 19, 207; doi: 10.3390/s19010207.

[16] Papadimitroulas P, Kostou T, Chatzipapas K et al., A review on personalized pediatric dosimetry applications using advanced computational tools, IEEE Transactions on Radiation and Plasma Medical Sciences 2018. DOI 10.1109/TRPMS.2018.2876562.

[17] Rensselaer Polytechnic Institute, Machine learning approach for low-dose CT imaging yields superior results: Findings make a strong case for harnessing the power of artificial intelligence in CT, ScienceDaily. ScienceDaily, 10 June 2019. www.sciencedaily.com/releases/2019/06/190610111505.htm (Assessed on 11 Aug 2019)

[18] Serna A, Ramos D, Garcia-Angosto E, Optimization of CT protocols using cause-and-effect analysis of outliers, Physica Medica 55 (2018) 1-7. https://doi.org/10.1016/j.ejmp.2018.10.010

[19] Hedgire S, Ghoshhajra, Kalra M et al., Dose optimization in cardiac CT, Physica Medica (2017). http://dx.doi.org/10.1016/j.ejmp.2017.04.021

[20] Mhaylov IB, Moros EG, Integral dose based inverse optimization objective function promises lower toxicity in head-and-neck, Physica Medica 54 (2018) 77-83. https://doi.org/10.1016/j.ejmp.2018.06.635

[21] Miglioretti DL, Johnson E, Williams A, The Use of Computed Tomography in Pediatrics and the Associated Radiation Exposure and Estimated Cancer Risk, JAMA Pediatr. 2013;167(8):700-707. doi:10.1001/jamapediatrics.2013.311

[22] Dalmazo J, Júnior JE, Brocchi MAC, Costa PR, Azevedo-Marques PM, Radiation dose optimization in routine computed tomography: a study of feasibility in a University Hospital, Radiol Bras. 2010; 43(4):241-248.

[23] Dougeni E, Faulkner K, Panayiotakis G, A review of patient dose and optimisation methods in adult and paediatric CT scanning, Elsevier European Journal of Radiology 81 (2012) e665– e683. doi: 10.1016/j.ejrad.2011.05.025

[24] Smith-Bindman R, Wang Y, Chu P *et al.*, International variation in radiation dose for computed tomography examinations: prospective cohort study, BMJ 2019; 364:k4931 http://dx.doi.org/10.1136/bmj.k4931

[25] Abdulkadir MK, Yusra Mat Rahim NA, Mazlan NS, Daud NM, Shuaib IL, Osman ND, Dose optimisation in paediatric CT examination: Assessment on current scanning protocols associated with radiation dose, *Radiation Physics and Chemistry* (2020), doi: https://doi.org/10.1016/j.radphyschem.2020.108740

[26] Choi HR, Kim RE, Heo CW, Kim CW, Yoo MS, Lee Y, Optimization of dose and image quality using self-produced phantom with various diameters in pediatric abdominal CT scan, Optik 168 (2018) 54-60. https://doi.org/10.1016/j.ijleo.2018.04.066

[27] Tozakidou M, Yang SR, Kovacs BK et al., Dose-optimized computed tomography of the cervical spine in patients with shoulder pull-down: Is image quality comparable with a standard dose protocol in an emergency setting? European Journal of Radiology 120 (2019) 108655. https://doi.org/10.1016/j.ejrad.2019.108655

[28] Chen GP, Noid G, Tai A et al., Improving CT quality with optimized image parameters for radiation treatment

planning and delivery guidance, Physics and Imaging in Radiation Oncology 4 (2017) 6-11. https://doi.org/10.1016/j.phro.2017.10.003

[29] Kang E, Min J, Ye JC, A deep convolutional neural network using directional wavelets for low-dose X-ray CT reconstruction, Med. Phys. 44 (10), (2017) e330-e337.

[30] Jung KH, Park H and Hwang W, Deep Learning for Medical Image Analysis: Applications to Computed Tomography and Magnetic Resonance Imaging, Hanyang Med Rev 2017;37:61-70 https://doi.org/10.7599/hmr.2017.37.2.61

[31] Xuy J, Gongy E, Pauly J and Zaharchuk G, 200x Low-dose PET Reconstruction using Deep Learning, 2017, arXiv:1712.04119v1

[32] Liu P, Wang M, Wang Y et al., Impact of Deep Learning-based Optimization Algorithm on Image Quality of Low-dose Coronary CT Angiography with Noise Reduction: A Prospective Study, Acad Radiol (2019) 1-8. https://doi.org/10.1016/j.acra.2019.11.010

[33] Wurfl T, Hoffmann M, Christlein V *et al.*, Deep Learning Computed Tomography: Learning Projection-Domain Weights from Image Domain in Limited Angle Problems, IEEE Transactions on Medical Imaging, 2018. http://dx.doi.org/10.1109/TMI.2018.2833499

[34] Shan H, Zhang Y, Yang Q *et al.*, 3D Convolutional Encoder-Decoder Network for Low-Dose CT via Transfer Learning from a 2D Trained Network, IEEE TRANSACTIONS ON MEDICAL IMAGING (2018). DOI 10.1109/TMI.2018.2832217

[35] Tian C, Xu Y, Zuo W, Image denoising using deep CNN with batch renormalization, Neural Networks 121 (2020) 461-473. https://doi.org/10.1016/j.neunet.2019.08.022

[36] Lee H, Kim M and Do S, Practical Window Setting Optimization for Medical Image Deep Learning, Machine Learning for Health (ML4H) Workshop at NeurIPS 2018. arXiv:1812.00572v1

[37] Meineke A, Rubbert C, Sawicki LM, Thomas C et al., Potential of a machine-learning model for dose optimization in CT quality assurance, Springer European Radiology 2019, 9p. https://doi.org/10.1007/s00330-019-6013-6

[38] Singh S, Kalra MK, Moore MA, Dose Reduction and Compliance with Pediatric CT Protocols Adapted to Patient Size, Clinical Indication, and Number of Prior Studies, Radiology 252 (1), 2009, 200-208. https://doi.org/10.1148/radiol.2521081554

[39] Ferrero A, Takahashi N, Vrtiska TJ et al., Understanding, justifying, and optimizing radiation exposure for CT imaging in nephrourology, Nat Rev Urol. 2019; 16(4): 231-244. doi:10.1038/s41585-019-0148-8

[40] Motwani MC, Gadiya MC, Motwani RC, Survey of Image Denoising Techniques, https://www.cse.unr.edu/~fredh/papers/conf/034-asoidt/paper.pdf

[41] Fan L, Zhang F, Fan H, Zhang C, Brief review of image denoising techniques, Springer Visual Computing for Industry, Biomedicine, and Art (2019) 2:7. https://doi.org/10.1186/s42492-019-0016-7

[42] Thanh DNH, Prasath Prasath VBF and Hieu LM, A Review on CT and X-Ray Images Denoising Methods, Informatica 43 (2019) 151-159. https://doi.org/10.31449/inf.v43i2.2179

[43] Wu D, Kim, El Fakhri G, Li Q, A Cascaded CNN for X-ray Low-dose CT Image Denoising. 2017. arXiv: 1705.04267v2

[44] Zhang Y, Lin H, Li Y, Ma H, A Patch Based Denoising Method Using Deep

Convolutional Neural Network for Seismic Image, IEEE Access 7 (2019), 156883-156894. Doi: *10.1109/ACCESS.2019.2949774*

[45] Deisenroth MP, Faisal AA, Ong CS, Mathematics for Machine Learning, Cambridge University Press, 2020, 417p.

[46] Ioffe S and Szegedy C, Batch normalization: Accelerating deep network training by reducing internal covariate shift, in *Proc. Int. Conf. Mach. Learn*, 2015, 448-456.

[47] CT Scan Image dataset. https://www.kaggle.com/vbookshelf/computed-tomography-ct-images/ (accessed on 19/02/2020)

[48] Tchagna Kouanou A, Tchiotsop D, Fozin Fonzin T, Bayangmbe Mounmo, Tchinda R, Real-Time Image Compression System Using an Embedded Board, Science Journal of Circuits, Systems and Signal Processing, 7(4) (2019), 81-86. doi: 10.11648/j.cssp.20180704.11

[49] Ye DY, Srivastava S, Thibault JB, Hsieh J, Sauer K, Bouman C, Deep Residual Learning for Model-Based Iterative CT Reconstruction Using Plug-And-Play Framework, https://engineering.purdue.edu › pdf › ICASSP-2018

Chapter 3

Novelty Detection Methodology Based on Self-Organizing Maps for Power Quality Monitoring

Juan Jose Saucedo-Dorantes, David Alejandro Elvira-Ortiz, Arturo Yosimar Jaen-Cuéllar and Manuel Toledano-Ayala

Abstract

The inclusion of intelligent systems in the modern industry is demanding the development of the automatic monitoring and continuous analysis of the data related to entire processes, this is a challenge of the industry 4.0 for the energy management. In this regard, this chapter proposes a novelty detection methodology based on Self-Organizing Maps (SOM) for Power Quality Monitoring. The contribution and originality of this proposed method consider the characterization of synthetic electric power signals by estimating a meaningful set of statistical time-domain based features. Subsequently, the modeling of the data distribution through a collaborative SOM's neuron grid models facilitates the detection of novel events related to the occurrence of power disturbances. The performance of the proposed method is validated by analyzing and assessing four different conditions such as normal, sag, swell, and fluctuations. The obtained results make the proposed method suitable for being implemented in embedded systems for online monitoring.

Keywords: condition monitoring, power quality, novelty detection, self-organizing feature maps, feature extraction

1. Introduction

The development and application of intelligent systems in the modern industry lead to the implementation of improved devices capable of acquiring, processing, storing, and sending any kind of information from any process to perform its continuous assessment. These novelty systems and devices lead to the industry 4.0 and aim to increase the value of the work developed to handle the complexity of all the available data from industrial processes. Indeed, this information is not only directly related to the sensors that are installed in the equipment involved in processes, but the information could also be the electrical consumption that the equipment, the supply to the machinery. Due to an adequate electrical supply has a lot of inference in all the processes in the industrial, commercial, and residential equipment [1].

Therefore, the monitoring of Power Quality (PQ) has been increased and reached its importance to ensure the appropriate functioning of the electrical equipment in the industrial processes, avoiding unexpected interruptions which may cause and lead to the loss in the production or utilities. Moreover, the importance of developing new strategies and methodologies for monitoring PQ has gained more interest in the scientific field in recent years [2]. The increase in the electrical power system and the loads connected to supply sources highlight the importance of the availability of monitoring systems to detect and face the occurrence of anomalies presented in the system [3]. Despite in the literature has been identified that problems related to PQ are caused by the supply system or non-linear behaviors of the loads, the opportunity of detecting the occurrence of electrical power disturbances represent a critical challenge to the monitoring systems [4].

In this regard, condition monitoring strategies focused on the assessment of PQ are mainly related to data-driven approaches. In these cases, the acquisition and processing of electrical power signals are performed in order to estimate a useful and meaningful set of features. These, in turn, allow a high-performance characterization of different kinds of electrical power disturbances that may be presented in electrical power systems. In this sense, most of the classical approaches focused on the identification of electrical power disturbances are related to the use of signal processing that transforms the original space of electric power signals through processing techniques such as Fourier Transform, Hilbert Transform, Wavelet Transform, among others [5–7].

Additionally, these proposed approaches focused on obtaining a useful set of features, then use common machine learning-based classification structures to carry out the pattern recognition and classification of assessed power disturbances. Indeed, the most used classifier structures are represented by Support Vector Machines (SVM), Artificial Neural Networks (ANN), infrared Fuzzy Classifiers, among others [8, 9]. On the other side, self-organizing maps (SOM) is a well-studied technique that is based on a grid of neurons and by a procedure performed under unsupervised learning, the topology of an input data space is represented by a discrete distribution [10]. In this regard, the application of SOM as a part of a monitoring strategy focused on PQ, may lead to extend its application to solve different tasks such as feature reduction, multiple class classification, remaining life prediction, and even novelty detection [11, 12].

Thereby, the main contribution of this chapter lies in the proposal of novelty detection methodology based on Self-Organizing Maps (SOM) for the monitoring of Power Quality (PQ). The proposed methodology faces the occurrence of power disturbances from the viewpoint of detecting novel events that do not belong to pre-established normal conditions. Thus, the originality of this proposal includes the characterization of different electric power signals by means of calculation a meaningful set of statistical time domain-based features and, then, its posterior data distribution modeling through individual SOM neuron grid models to perform the diagnosis and novelty evaluation. The effectiveness of the proposed methodology is evaluated by analyzing synthetic electric power signals that consider the normal condition, sag, swell, and fluctuations. The obtained results make the proposed method a suitable option for being implemented in embedded systems for online monitoring purposes.

2. Theoretical basis

2.1 Electric power disturbances

The ideal electric power signals have specific parameters such as fundamental frequency and a specific range of amplitudes that are also known as nominal values. Thus, any deviation from these values is determined as an electric power disturbance and its occurrence may be detected through PQ monitoring [13]. According to the IEEE Std 1159 [14], a sag is defined as a decrease of the rms value of the voltage for durations that comprises 0.5 cycle to 1 minute with typical decreases of 0.1 per unit (pu) to 0.9 pu. On the other side, a swell is defined as an increase of the rms value and it may occur for values up to 1.1 pu with a duration of 0.5 cycles to 1 min. Otherwise, fluctuations are defined as a series of voltage changes that may appear randomly in the envelope of the signal with typical values between 0.95 pu to 1.05 pu. In the category of waveform distortions are included the harmonics, which are sinusoidal voltages or currents with frequencies that are integer multiples of the fundamental frequency. In addition, other kinds of disturbances are known as transient, which depicts a phenomenon that presents variations between two consecutive steady states, that is, during a short interval of time and can be a unidirectional impulse or an oscillatory wave [15].

2.2 Self-organizing maps

Machine learning represents a suitable tool that may be considered in condition assessment methodologies applied to the monitoring of PQ to detect the occurrence of electric power disturbances. In this regard, the SOM is an unsupervised technique based on a neural network that has been used with multiple purposed, such as clustering, classification, prediction of novelty detection. The main objective of SOM is based on the non-linear projection of an original and high-dimensional input data space into a low-dimensional space represented by a pre-defined number of neurons. Through this mapping, the data distribution of the input space, which commonly is represented by a defined number of features, resembles the mapped neurons since the topology of the data is preserved. In this regard, the consideration of SOM for PQ monitoring may lead to detecting the occurrence of power disturbance from a novelty detection viewpoint. Until now, other reported methodologies used for PQ analysis require to be continuously supervised and they use a predefined topology of the data, meanwhile, the SOM automatically adjusts to different data topologies. These are important advantages since they allow to be trained only once, while other techniques are retrained every time the conditions change. This is possible of being implemented whether the available data distribution related to the normal condition is initially modeled and then, eventual novelty patterns are detected due to the topological characteristics of the initial data distribution are highly associated with the normal condition. Indeed, SOM performance is qualitatively measured in terms of the average quantization error, $\bar{E}q$, that also provides information to the degree of novelty detection (Nd) described by Eq. (1) [12]:

$$N_d = \begin{cases} E_q \leq \bar{E}_{q-training}, & 0 \\ d_{\max} > E_q > \bar{E}_{q-training}, & 1 - \dfrac{E_q - \bar{E}_{q-training}}{d_{\max-training} - \bar{E}_{q-training}} \\ E_q > d_{\max-training}, & 1 \end{cases} \tag{1}$$

3. PQ-based novelty detection method

The proposed novelty detection methodology for PQ is composed by five different steps as **Figure 1** depicts. Thus, in the first step, a complete database composed

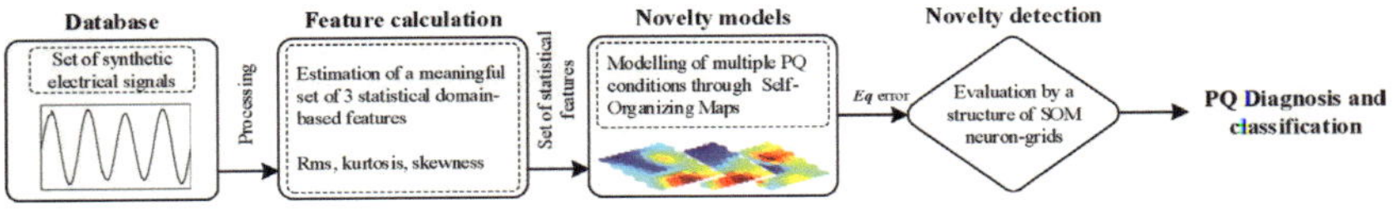

Figure 1.
Proposed novelty detection strategy based on SOM for monitoring and detecting different PQ events.

Root mean square	$RMS = \sqrt{\frac{1}{n} \cdot \sum_{k=1}^{n} (x_k)^2}$	(1)
Kurtosis	$Ku = \frac{\sum_{k=1}^{n} \left[(x_k - \bar{x})^4 \right]}{\sigma^4}$	(2)
Skewness	$S_k = \frac{\sum_{k=1}^{n} \left[(x_k - \bar{x})^3 \right]}{\sigma^3}$	(3)

Table 1.
Statistical time domain-based set of features.

by several synthetic signals is generated. The database is generated in Matlab following the corresponding definitions established by the IEEE Std 1159 [13]. In this regard, the synthetic signals are related to different power signals including normal conditions and different disturbances such as sag, swell, and fluctuations.

Subsequently, in the second step, a meaningful set of 3 statistical time domain-based features is estimated from all the synthetic signals, this set of features is composed by the rms value, kurtosis, and skewness [16]. Indeed, the calculation of a numerical set of statistical-time domain features allows obtaining a significant characterization due to its capability for characterizing trends and eventual changes over these trends in the analyzed signals [12, 15]. The mathematical equations of the considered statistical time domain features are listed in **Table 1**.

Then, in the third step, the modeling of all considered power signals is carried out through different SOM neuron grid structures. Thereby, in this modeling stage, the data distribution of each one of the events is modeled and represented by a unique and specific SOM neuron grid model, i.e. the normal condition is represented by SOM_1, and the power disturbances such as sag, swell, and fluctuations are represented by SOM_2, SOM_3, and SOM_4, respectively.

Afterward, the continuous assessment of electric power signals and the detection of events is performed by a novelty detection stage, such detection is carried out by analyzing the resulting $\bar{Eq}$ value of each one of the considered SOM's neuron grids. Specifically, the $\bar{Eq}$ values are successively analyzed by each SOM neuron grid. That is, a measurement is assessed, first, through the SOM_1 in order to analyze its normal condition. Subsequently, a novel event is detected if an abrupt change in the $\bar{Eq}$ value is obtained. In this regard, the electric power signal under inspection is subsequently analyzed by a second, third and fourth SOM's neuron grids aiming to find the SOM model that best represents such power signal in Eq terms. Indeed, the increase of the $\bar{Eq}$ value lies to achieve a novelty detection. Such increase is due to the topological characteristic of the database considered during the modeling of each SOM neuron grid and its difference with the topological characteristics of the measurement under inspection.

Finally, the diagnosis and classification of different power disturbances follows. Synthetic signals with multiple power disturbances are analyzed in this step, in order to validate the effectiveness of the proposed fault detection and identification methodology.

It worth mentioning that the PQ monitoring problem is addressed by the novelty detection technique since changes in the Eq values would be analyzed to conclude if effectively a power disturbance occurs, or if simply the electrical equipment reaches a new condition that falls between an operating range that stills remains normal. In counterpart, techniques focused on outlier/anomaly detection could lead to misclassifications.

4. Results

The proposed novelty detection methodology has been implemented in Matlab, a software platform used to develop multiple engineering applications such as condition monitoring of industrial systems.

4.1 Synthetic signal database

As it has been aforementioned, a database composed of different synthetic signals is generated by taking into account the corresponding definitions established by the standards. In this sense, it should be highlighted that any power disturbance must fulfill specific characteristics for being considered as a specific disturbance, otherwise, there will be no appropriate category to which it could belong. Thus, all synthetic signals are generated by considering a sampling frequency of 8 kHz and 50 Hz as fundamental frequency; additionally, different levels of noise are also considered with the aim of increasing the variability of the database.

Consequently, a database with four different patterns is generated, such patterns are related to different electric power conditions representing the normal condition and, three disturbances such as sag, swell, and fluctuations. Hence, for each one of the considered electric power conditions, twenty synthetic signals are produced with a signal duration of 5 seconds.

4.2 Signal processing and data modeling

Subsequently, as it has been described, all synthetic signals are processed by estimating a set of statistical time-domain based features. The proposed feature estimation is considered attempting to highlight the most meaningful characteristics that may describe the incidence of unexpected electric power disturbances.

In this regard, due to there exist specific disturbances that may appear instantly, the statistical set of features is individually estimated for each one of the cycles that compose a complete electric power signal; indeed, a zero-crossing detector is considered to identify the beginning and end of each cycle. Thus, for each one of the considered conditions, twenty synthetic signals with 250 cycles are subjected to this feature estimation, as a result, a feature matrix with 5000 files (samples) and 3 columns (features) is obtained for each specific condition.

Then, the data distribution of each one of the electric power signals, represented by its corresponding feature matrix, is modeled and represented by a unique and specific SOM neuron grid model. Thereby, the considered SOM's neuron grids consist basically of a predefined number of neurons (10 x10) which is known as the Matching Unit (MU). Subsequently, during a training process, each SOM neuron grid is randomly initialized and consecutively is adapted to the data distribution under evaluation aiming to retain as much as possible its topological properties.

Furthermore, the performance achieved for each SOM neuron grid model may be quantitatively defined in terms of its quantization error. Specifically, the average quantization error, $\bar{E}q$, represents the mean distance from each measurement to the nearest neuron that is activated (Best Matching Unit-BMU). Thus, after modeling the data distribution of the electric power signal in normal conditions, the first SOM_1 neuron model achieves a mean quantization error equal to 0.0016.

4.3 Novelty detection and PQ diagnosis

In order to demonstrate the effectiveness of this first SOM_1 neuron grid for modeling the normal condition and to evaluate its achieved performance, three different electric power signals, with an electric disturbance, are assessed through the SOM_1 model. Thus, in **Figure 2** is shown the mean quantization, $\bar{E}q$, obtained by the first SOM_1 model during the evaluation of the first electric power signal that includes a power disturbance. From **Figure 2**, it should be clarified that each sample of the horizontal axis represents each analyzed cycle from the electric power signal under evaluation. In this regard, it is possible to observe that an abrupt increase of the $\bar{E}q$ is achieved between samples 89 and 93, this increase depicts the sudden occurrence of an abnormal condition, indeed, such occurrence is also known as novel detection.

Due to a novelty detection is performed by the SOM_1, the electric power signal under evaluation has to be analyzed in order to confirm the occurrence of disturbances. Hence, in **Figure 3a** is shown the complete electric power signal and, through visual inspection, it is possible to identify an abnormality on the signal (amplitude reduction), where, such abnormality describes a sag. A detailed visualization of the affected part of the power signal is shown in **Figure 3b**, thus, from **Figure 3b**, and by following the definitions established by the IEEE Std 1159, it may be determined that three cycles of the power signal are affected by the occurrence of sag.

Afterward, a second and a third electric power signal that also includes power disturbance are also assessed under the SOM_1 model. In this sense, the $\bar{E}q$ value achieved during the evaluation of the second signal is graphically represented and shown in **Figure 4**. For this electric power signal, the novelty detection is placed between samples 175 and 178, on the other hand, when this electric power signal is visually inspected an instantaneous amplitude increase is detected. In **Figure 5a** is shown the complete electric power signal evaluated and, in **Figure 5b** is shown a detailed visualization of the affected part of the second power signal, that, according to the established definitions represents the occurrence of swell and affects the power signal during two cycles.

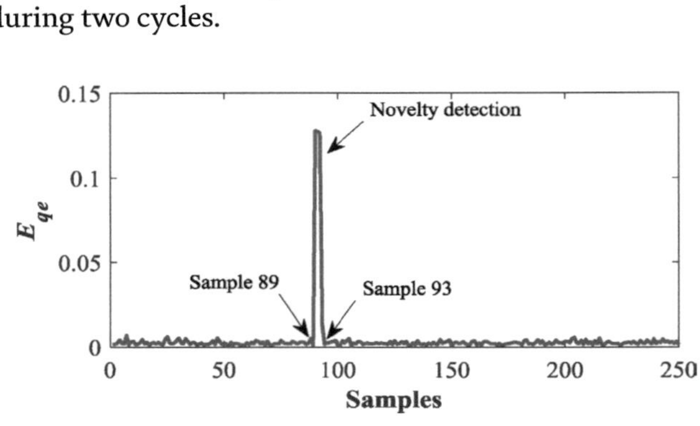

Figure 2.
Graphical representation of the resulting mean quantization error ($\bar{E}q$) that is obtained during the evaluation of an electric power signal that includes an unknown power disturbance (sag), in the first SOM_1 model.

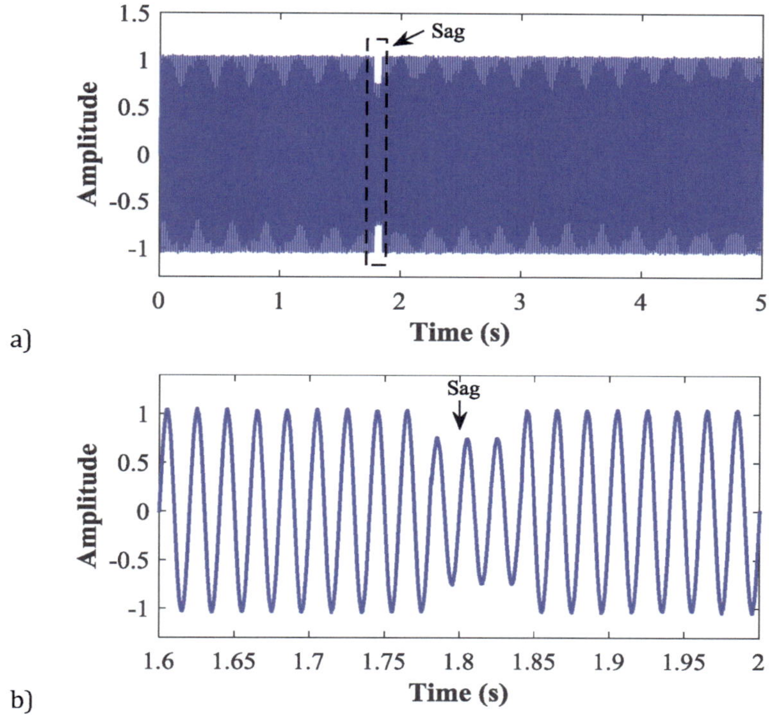

Figure 3.
Electric power signal with a power disturbance, SAG, evaluated under the first SOM_1 model. (a) Complete signal with 5 seconds of duration and, (b) zoom of the detailed signal that shows the signal affectation.

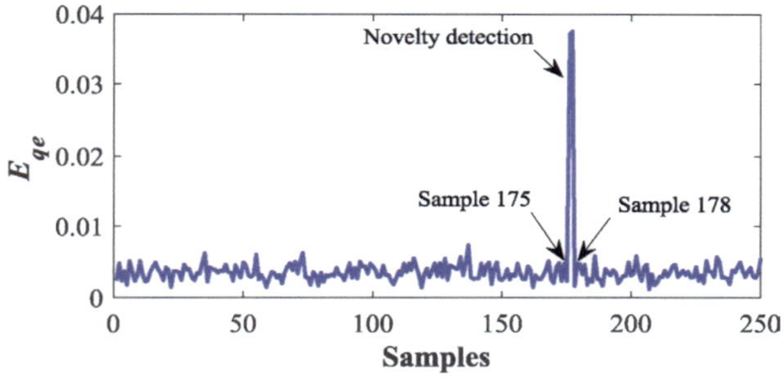

Figure 4.
Obtained mean quantization error during the evaluation of an electric power signal that includes an unknown power disturbance (swell), in the first SOM_1 model.

Later, the third electric power signal is finally evaluated through the first SOM_1 model, the $\bar{E}q$ value obtained during its evaluation is graphically represented in **Figure 6**, where, the novelty detection is performed between samples 21 and 32. Thus, when this electric power signal is visually inspected, it is noted that several amplitude variations appear over the power signal, as in **Figure 7a** is shown. In **Figure 7b** is shown a detailed visualization of the affected part of the third power signal, that, in terms of the established definitions, such amplitude variations represent the occurrence of fluctuations. Thereby, through the evaluation of these three electric power signals, which include power disturbances such as sag, swell, and fluctuations, is validated the effectiveness of considering a specific SOM neuron grid to model and represent the data distribution of electric power signals in normal conditions.

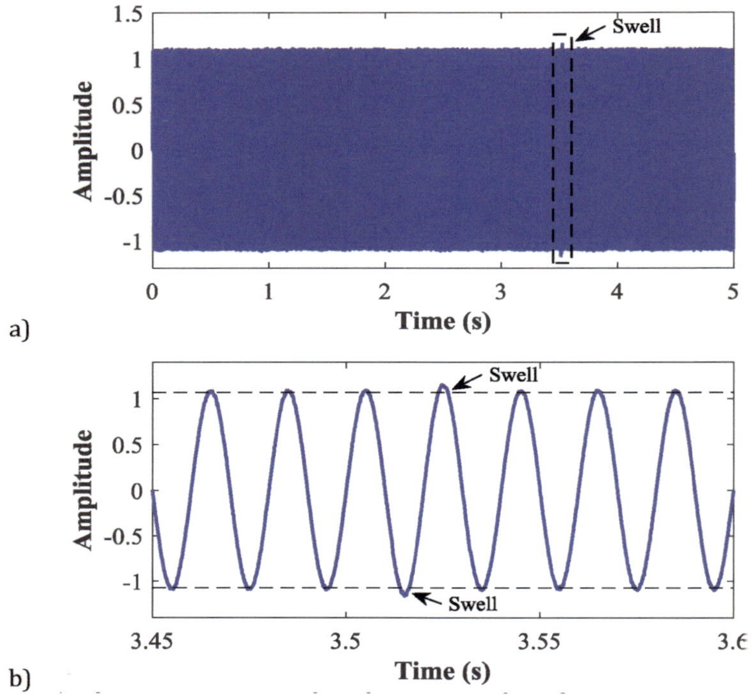

Figure 5.
Electric power signal with a power disturbance, SWELL, evaluated under the first SOM_1 model. (a) Complete signal with 5 seconds of duration and, (b) zoom of the detailed signal that shows the signal affectation per two cycles.

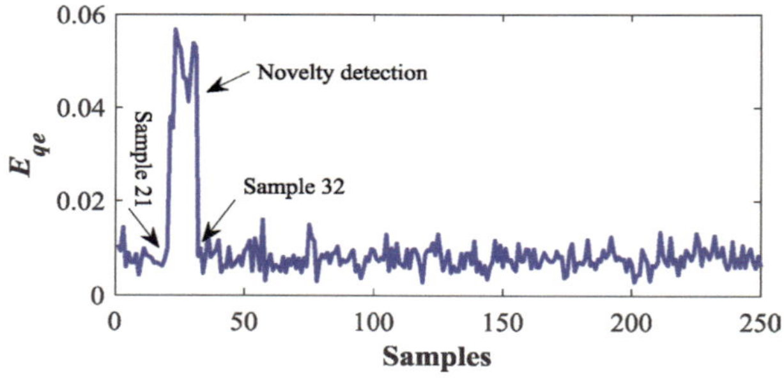

Figure 6.
Achieved mean quantization error obtained during the assessment of an electric power signal that includes an unknown power disturbance (fluctuations), in the first SOM_1 model.

Regarding the proposed methodology, the modeling of the data distributions related to synthetic electric power signals with different disturbances such as sag, swell and fluctuations, is also performed by three individual SOM neuron models, SOM_2, SOM_3 and SOM_4 respectively. Thereby, SOM_2 represents the sag power disturbance, SOM_3 represents the swell power disturbance and, SOM_4 represents the fluctuation power disturbance. The mean quantization error, $\bar{E}q$, achieved during the training of each SOM neuron model is 0.003, 0.0023 and 0.0016, for each one of the considered disturbances, sag, swell and fluctuations, respectively.

Accordingly, in order to evaluate the performance achieved by each modeled SOM neuron model, an electric power signal that includes all considered conditions, normal, sag, swell and fluctuations, is evaluated through the four SOM

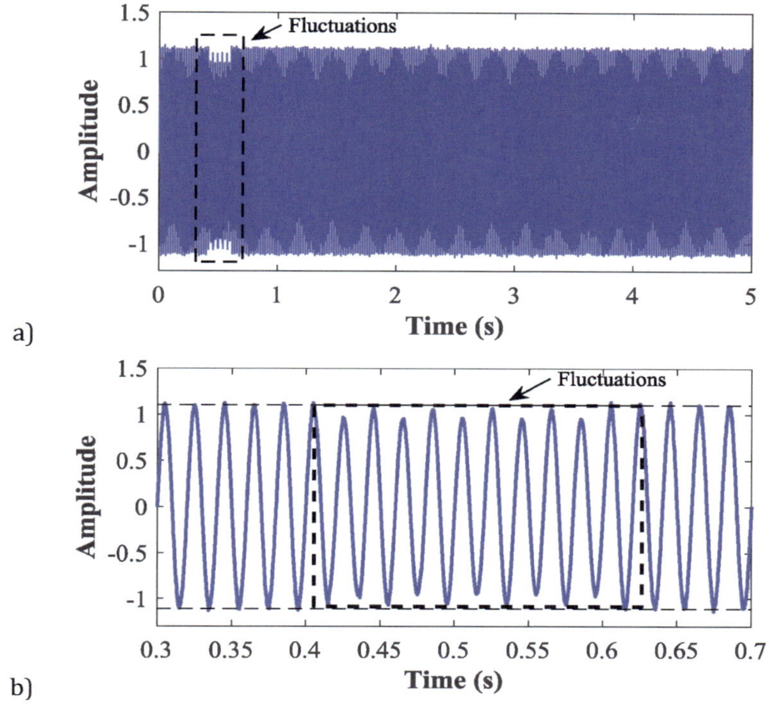

Figure 7.
Electric power signal with a power disturbance, fluctuations, evaluated under the first SOM_1 model. (a) Complete signal with 5 seconds of duration and (b) zoom of the detailed signal that shows the signal affectation.

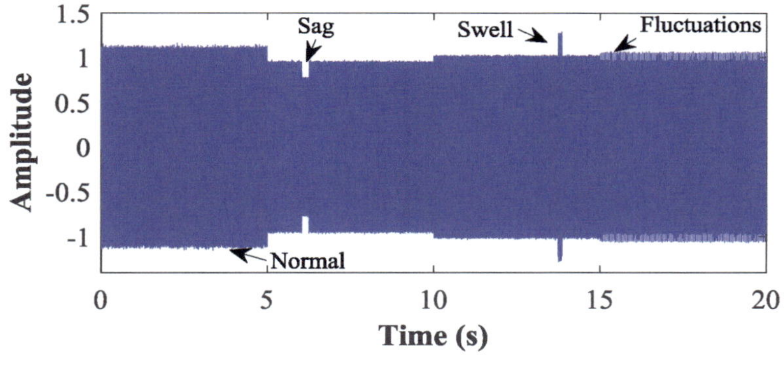

Figure 8.
Electric power signal with three power disturbances, sag, swell and fluctuations, used by the subsequent evaluation through SOM_1, SOM_2, SOM_3 and SOM_4.

neuron models, SOM_1, SOM_2, SOM_3 and SOM_4. Thus, as it has been mentioned, the electric power signal is first evaluated through the SOM1 neuron model and, in case of novelty detection, such electric power signal is subsequently analyzed by SOM_2, SOM_3 and SOM_4 neuron grids aiming to find the SOM model that best represents such power signal in terms of its $\bar{Eq}$ value. In **Figure 8** is shown the electric power signal used to evaluate the SOM neuron grid structure, this electric power signal is composed by concatenating an electric power signal in a normal condition of 5 seconds of duration with the electric power signals shown in **Figure 3a**, **Figure 5a** and **Figure 7a**.

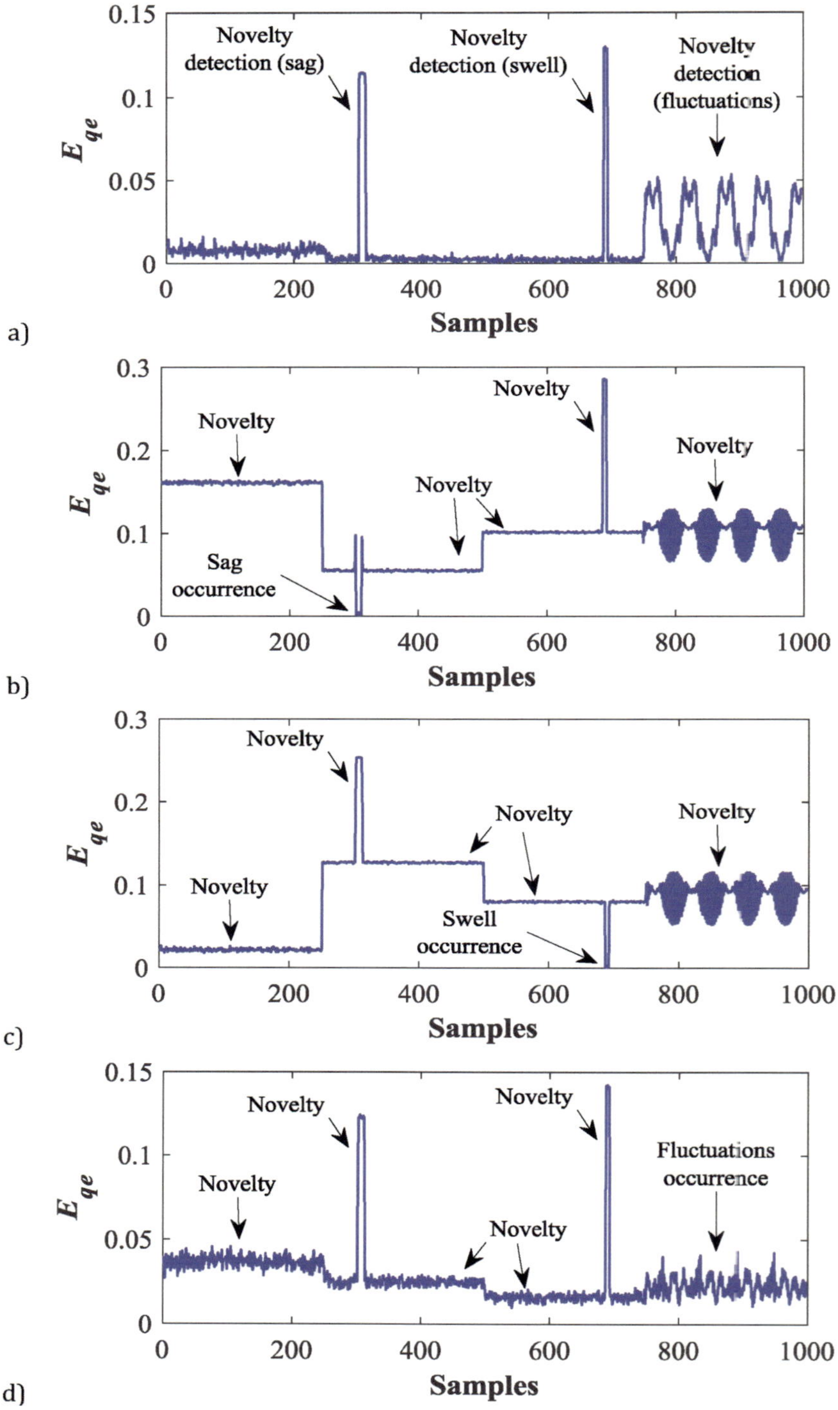

Figure 9.
Mean quantization error achieved by each SOM neuron model during the evaluation of an electric power signal that includes power disturbance such as sag, swell, and fluctuations. (a) SOM_1, (b) SOM_2, (c) SOM_3 and (d) SOM_4.

The $\bar{E}q$ values achieved by each SOM neuron model are individually shown from **Figure 9a-d**, for SOM_1, SOM_2, SOM_3 and SOM_4, respectively. Therefore, by analyzing the $\bar{E}q$ value of **Figure 9a**, from SOM_1, it is possible to notice the occurrence of different events detected as novelties. In this regard, when the first novelty detection occurs, the $\bar{E}q$ values of the following SOM's neuron models have to be analyzed. That is, while a novelty detection is performed by the SOM_1 neuron grid, for these specified number of samples, in the second SOM neuron grid, SOM_2, is achieved the lowest $\bar{E}q$ value; whereas, the rest of SOM's neuron models present an abrupt increase of the $\bar{E}q$ value. Consequently, the first novelty detection of SOM_1 belongs to the appearance of sag.

Subsequently, when the second novelty detection appears over the $\bar{E}q$ value of SOM_1 (**Figure 9a**), in the SOM_3 is achieved the lowest $\bar{E}q$ value; while the rest of SOM's neuron models the abrupt increasing and change of the $\bar{E}q$ value is described; thus, the occurrence of swell produces the second novelty detection. Finally, the third novelty detection that occurs in the $\bar{E}q$ value of SOM_1 trend to produce abrupt and variable changes of the $\bar{E}q$ value, indeed, this variable behavior also appears over the $\bar{E}q$ values of SOM_2 and SOM_3 neuron grids, and, the unique SOM neuron model that do not present these abrupt and variable changes in the $\bar{E}q$ value is the SOM_4 neuron grid. Hence, the third novelty detected by the SOM_4 neuron grid depicts the occurrence of fluctuations.

Therefore, the obtained results prove the effectiveness of the proposed methodology to perform the PQ monitoring and for detecting the occurrence of electric power disturbances. In fact, the proposed diagnosis methodology also has the advantage of considering additional disturbances for being modeled through additional SOM's neuron grids models. Definitely, this proposed structure is suitable to be implemented in embedded systems such as field-programmable gate arrays (FPGA) for online monitoring purposes.

Moreover, aiming to summarize the obtained results in **Table 2** are shown the resulting classification ratios that were achieved during the training and validation of each SOM neuron grid model; thus, three test cases are evaluated. As in **Table 2** is observed, the test case 1 consists on evaluating the available data related to the Normal and Sag conditions through the first SOM_1 model and, in the case of the Normal (evaluated as the known condition) condition is achieved 100% of the global classification ratio; whereas, in the case of Sag (evaluated as the unknown condition) or novelty detection 100% of the global classification is also obtained. Subsequently, for the second test set, the conditions considered as known are the Normal and Sag conditions and, the occurrence of Swell is evaluated as the known condition; in the third test case, the known conditions are Normal, Sag and Swell; while the Fluctuation represents the unknown condition. Therefore, it should be highlighted that all the samples that were evaluated have been correctly identified and diagnosed to its corresponding class (assigned condition) with a membership probability higher than 97% for all cases.

Regarding other novelty detection methods, one-class support vector machine (OC-SVM) remains as the most classical approach that has been implemented under condition monitoring strategies to perform novelty detections. In this sense, the consideration of OC-SVM with classical feature reduction techniques, such as PCA (Principal Component Analysis) and LDA (Linear Discriminant Analysis),

Test case	*Known class* (%)	*Unknown class* (%)
1	Normal (100%)	Sag (100%)
2	Normal (100%), Sag (100%)	Swell (>98%)
3	Normal (100%), Sag (100%), Swell (100%)	Fluctuation (>97%)

Table 2.
Resulting diagnosis and novelty detection ratios for each SOM neuron grid model.

are used to evaluate the available data to detect novelties during the PQ monitoring. Thus, by evaluating the available data by means of such approach a global classification ratio about 62% is approximately obtained for each evaluated condition. Therefore, it must be mentioned that the consideration SOM neuron grids as a part of a novelty detection structure leads to obtain advantageous results over classical approaches such as OC-SVM.

4.4 Experimental validation by analyzing a photovoltaic generation system

Additionally, the proposed method is evaluated under a real scenario in order to highlight the effectiveness and performance during the novelty detection of PQ disturbances. In this regard, experimentation is performed in a 30-MW wind farm located in northwest Spain. A proprietary data acquisition system (DAS) is used for collecting and storage the electrical signals. This DAS is based on field programmable gate array (FPGA) technology and it is able to acquire data from 7 channels simultaneously. Three of these channels are devoted to collect the voltage signals, whereas the four remaining channels are intended to receive current signals. The FPGA-based DAS operates at a sampling rate of 8000 samples per seconds and has a 16-bit analog to digital converter that ensures the proper representation of the acquired data. Finally, the DAS incorporates a 128 GB SD memory that allows performing the uninterrupted data storage for periods up to 11 days. When the memory is full, it can be easily replaced to continue with the acquisition process. The DAS is located at the substation of the windfarm, which means that the production of the complete farm can be monitored. The measurements are taken from a measuring transformer, so the DAS must measure voltages up to 110 Vrms. The commercial current clamps SCT-013-010 from YHDC are used to perform the current measurements in this location.

Therefore, the proposed novelty detection method for detecting the occurrence of PQ disturbances is applied to real data acquired from a real scenario as follows:

1. One of the voltage signals that was acquired during the monitoring of the transformed is processed as is described in Section 3, this processing is performed in order to compute the proposed set of 3 statistical features.

2. Subsequently, the set of statistical features that represent the voltage signal is evaluated though all the SOM neuron grids models that were obtained during the training procedure, in which, the synthetic signals were considered. Specifically, such set of statistical features is evaluated through the neuron grid model: SOM_1, SOM_2, SOM_3 and SOM_4, which represent the normal condition, the occurrence of sag, swell, and fluctuations, respectively.

3. The mean quantization error, $\bar{Eq}$, is analyzed aiming to determine the novelty detection and aiming to determine whether the occurrence of a PQ disturbance is detected by one of the SOM models.

In this regard, after evaluating the set of the statistical features through each one of the SOM neuron grid models, SOM_1, SOM_2, SOM_3, and SOM_4, the $\bar{Eq}$ value is obtained. Thereby, the $\bar{Eq}$ value achieved by each SOM model is represented and show from **Figure 10a-d**, respectively. From these obtained results it should be highlighted that the graphical representation of the $\bar{Eq}$ value of **Figure 10a, c** and **d**, presents an abrupt increase. This increase is produced due to the neuron grid models SOM_1, SOM_3 and SOM_4 detect a novelty; on the other hand, the $\bar{Eq}$ value achieved by the SOM_2 neuron grid does not show the increase since it could be considered that the novelty detection belongs to the occurrence of sag.

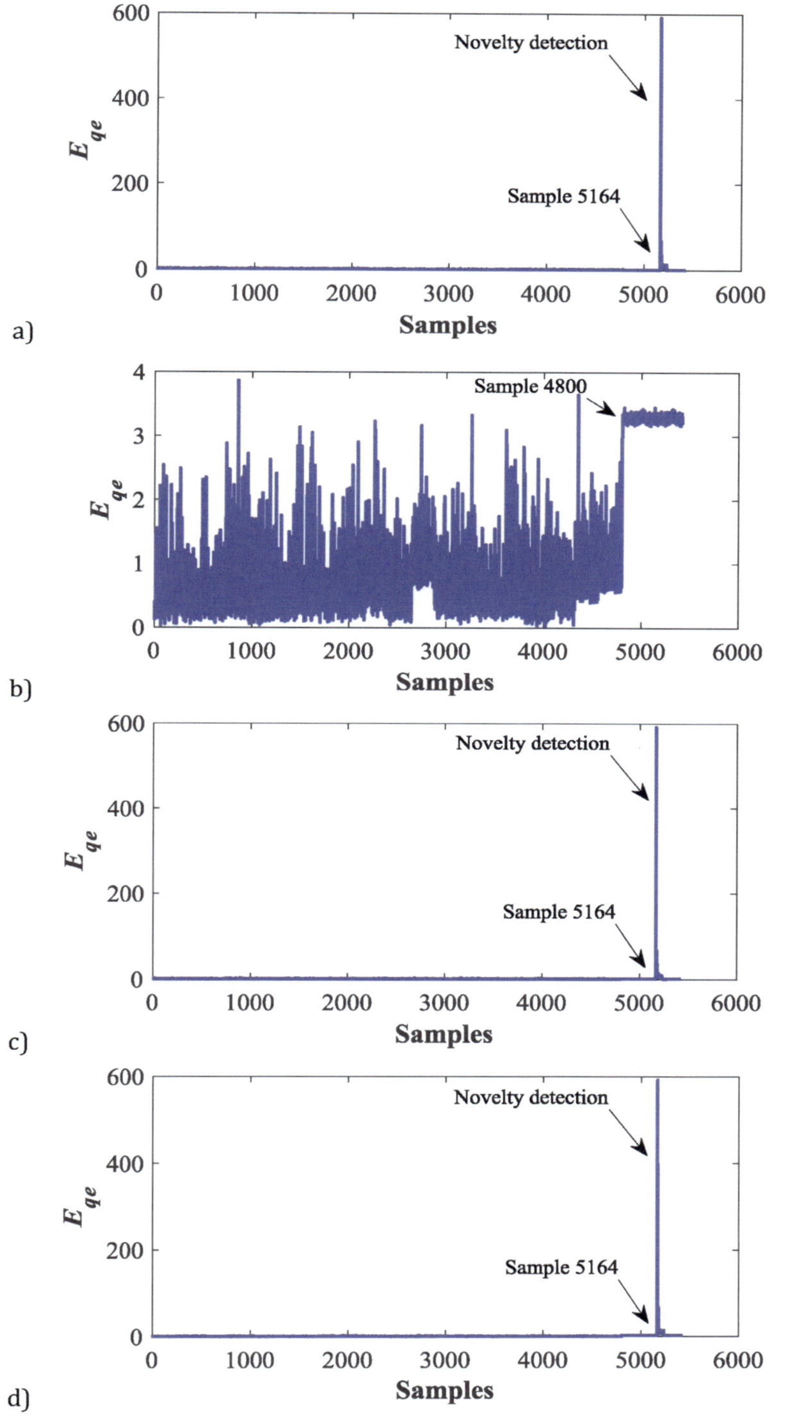

Figure 10.
Achieved mean quantization error by each SOM neuron model by evaluating the electric power signal of a transformer in: (a) SOM_1, (b) SOM_2, (c) SOM_3 and (d) SOM_4.

Afterward, in order to validate the occurrence of the sag, the voltage signal is analyzed by visual inspection to find and detect such PQ disturbance; in this sense, in **Figure 11a** is shown the voltage signal and it may be observed that

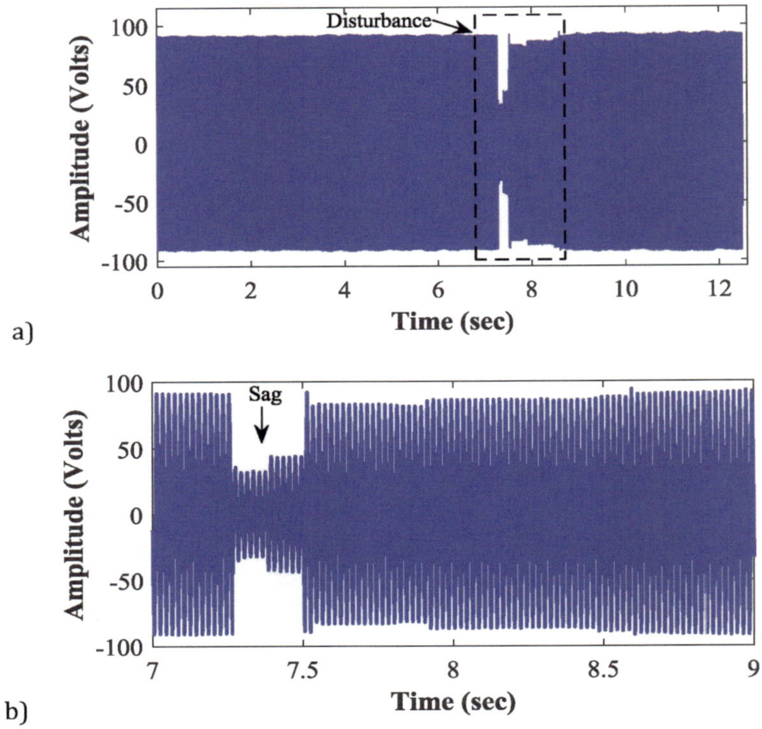

Figure 11.
Voltage signal acquired during the monitoring of the electric transformer in which a novelty detection is detected. (a) Complete voltage signal, (b) zoom over the specific area in which the disturbance is detected and identified as sag.

around the eight-second a disturbance is presented. Also, in **Figure 11b** is shown a zoom of such specific area in which the disturbance is presented and, it can be appreciated that the disturbance has the specific characteristics that belong to the occurrence of sag. In this sense, it should be highlighted that the effectiveness of the proposed novelty detection methodology has been proved by analyzing real data acquired from a real scenario that includes the monitoring of a transformer.

5. Conclusions

This chapter proposes a novelty detection methodology based on Self-Organizing Maps to perform the monitoring of Power Quality. The obtained result proves the effectiveness of the proposed method for detecting the occurrence of unexpected and undesirable electric power disturbances such as sag, swell, and fluctuations.

Thus, two main important key points must be highlighted from this proposal. First, the characterization of the electric power signals through statistical time-domain based features leads to achieving a high-performance representation of the data distribution. Second, the modeling of the available data by means of SOM's neuron grids allows preserving the topology of the data, which is a key feature that leading the detection of novelty events. Additionally, the consideration of a collaborative SOM neuron structure based on the analysis of the mean quantization error effectively detects all novel electric power disturbances considered.

Finally, the proposed method is evaluated under a synthetic database of electric power signals that considers the occurrence of four conditions, normal, sag, swell, and fluctuations. In fact, the proposed PQ monitoring structure may be extended to other power disturbances. The obtained results depict that this proposal is a suitable option to be implemented in embedded systems, such as field-programmable gate arrays (FPGA), as a tool for online monitoring with application in industrial processes.

Acknowledgements

This research work has been partially supported by the FONDEC-UAQ-2019 under the registered project FIN202011.

Conflict of interest

The authors declare no conflict of interest.

Author details

Juan Jose Saucedo-Dorantes*, David Alejandro Elvira-Ortiz, Arturo Yosimar Jaen-Cuéllar and Manuel Toledano-Ayala
Engineering Faculty, Autonomous University of Queretaro, San Juan del Rio, Mexico

*Address all correspondence to: jsaucedo@hspdigital.org

References

[1] D. A. Elvira-Ortiz, R. A. Osornio-Rios, D. Morinigo-Sotelo, H. Rostro-Gonzalez, and R. J. Romero-Troncoso, "Power quality monitoring system under different environmental and electric conditions," Proc. Int. Conf. Harmon. Qual. Power, ICHQP, vol. 2018-May, pp. 1-6, 2018.

[2] M. A. Rodriguez-Guerrero, A. Y. Jaen-Cuellar, R. D. Carranza-Lopez-Padilla, R. A. Osornio-Rios, G. Herrera-Ruiz and R. d. J. Romero-Troncoso, "Hybrid Approach Based on GA and PSO for Parameter Estimation of a Full Power Quality Disturbance Parameterized Model," in IEEE Transactions on Industrial Informatics, vol. 14, no. 3, pp. 1016-1028, March 2018, doi: 10.1109/TII.2017.2743762.

[3] L. Morales-Velazquez, R. de J. Romero-Troncoso, G. Herrera-Ruiz, D. Morinigo-Sotelo, and R. A. Osornio-Rios, "Smart sensor network for power quality monitoring in electrical installations," Meas. J. Int. Meas. Confed., vol. 103, pp. 133-142, 2017.

[4] S. M. Blair, C. D. Booth, G. Williamson, A. Poralis, and V. Turnham, "Automatically Detecting and Correcting Errors in Power Quality Monitoring Data," IEEE Trans. Power Deliv., 2017.

[5] S. Jamali, A. R. Farsa, and N. Ghaffarzadeh, "Identification of optimal features for fast and accurate classification of power quality disturbances," Meas. J. Int. Meas. Confed., vol. 116, no. August 2017, pp. 565-574, 2018.

[6] J. Li, Z. Teng, Q. Tang, and J. Song, "Detection and Classification of Power Quality Disturbances Using Double Resolution S-Transform and DAG-SVMs," IEEE Trans. Instrum. Meas., vol. 65, no. 10, pp. 2302-2312, 2016.

[7] W. Qiu, Q. Tang, J. Liu, Z. Teng, and W. Yao, "Power Quality Disturbances Recognition Using Modified S Transform and Parallel Stack Sparse Auto-encoder," Electr. Power Syst. Res., vol. 174, no. February, p. 105876, 2019.

[8] S. Karasu and Z. Saraç, "Investigation of power quality disturbances by using 2D discrete orthonormal S-transform, machine learning and multi-objective evolutionary algorithms," Swarm Evol. Comput., vol. 44, no. November 2018, pp. 1060-1072, 2019.

[9] S. Wang and H. Chen, "A novel deep learning method for the classification of power quality disturbances using deep convolutional neural network," Appl. Energy, vol. 235, no. November 2018, pp. 1126-1140, 2019.

[10] A. E. Lazzaretti1, V. H. Ferreira and H. V. Neto, "New trends in power quality event analysis: novelty detection and unsupervised classification," Journal of Control, Automation and Electrical Systems, vol. 27, pp. 718-727, 2016.

[11] Z. Li, H. Fang, M. Huang, Y. Wei and L. Zhang, " Data-driven bearing fault identification using improved hidden Markov model and self-organizing map," Computers & Industrial Engineering, vol 116, pp. 37-46, 2018.

[12] J, J. Saucedo-Dorantes, M. Delgado-Prieto, R. A. Osornio-Rios and R. J. Romero-Troncoso, "Industrial data-driven monitoring based on incremental learning applied to the detection of novel faults," IEEE Transactions on Industrial Informatics, Feb 2020, DOI: 10.1109/TII.2020.2973731.

[13] M. H. J. Bollen and I. Y. H. Gu, Signal Processing of Power Quality Disturbances. 2005.

[14] IEEE, IEEE Std 1159 - IEEE Recommended Practice for Monitoring

Electric Power Quality., vol. 2009, no. June. 2009.

[15] O. Florencias-Oliveros, J. J. González-de-la-Rosa, A. Agüera-Pérez and J. C. Palomares-Salas, " Power quality event dynamics characterization via 2D trajectories using deviations of higher-order statistics," Measurement, vol. 125 pp. 350-359, 2018.

[16] J. J. Saucedo-Dorantes, M. Delgado-Prieto, R. A. Osornio-Rios and R. de Jesus Romero-Troncoso, "Multifault Diagnosis Method Applied to an Electric Machine Based on High-Dimensional Feature Reduction," in IEEE Transactions on Industry Applications, vol. 53, no. 3, pp. 3086-3097, May-June 2017, doi: 10.1109/TIA.2016.2637307

Chapter 4

AI-Powered Workforce Management and Its Future in India

Mrinmoy Roy

Abstract

Day in and day out, the Workforce Department faces new problems and operational demands. It is very important for the department to respond quickly and understand the best possible action to be taken in each single case. It is unknown in a compromised setting of near-constant shifts in forecast and scheduling, increased customer demands, and changing recruitment and retention of employees. Workforce management around the world has begun to use artificial intelligence (AI)-based workforce management (WFM) software to solve the above problems and reach goals. These tools transform workforce management by helping to anticipate and plan short- and long-term planning. These tools improve Workforce Management by helping to predict short- and long-term scheduling and recruiting requirements, communicate with staff, and at the right time bring customers in contact with the right agent. This chapter addresses AI workforce management intervention and WFM instruments with industry-specific case studies and its experience with the product Workforce Dimensions. Present status and future expectations are also critically reviewed. Techniques of AI and machine learning (ML) are transforming industries, as are goods from thermostats to cars. The global enterprise value generated from AI continues to grow, according to Gartner, and is projected to reach up to $ 3.9 trillion by 2022. But what do these approaches mean for workforce management in the field? The current chapter examines the growing use of artificial intelligence (AI) in various HRM functions, as well as the ongoing debate about the expected decline in the usability of human resources in organizations. In the presence of AI in the workplace, HR practitioners are constantly afraid of being replaced by computers/robots/smart business machines. The study aims to recognize AI's important contribution to enhancing organizational decision-making processes, as well as to enhance awareness of AI's acceptability and inclusion in the HRM department. Despite the fact that the combination of AI and HRM is attracting a large number of researchers, many aspects of the field remain unexplored. The current research proposes a collaborative approach by stressing the complementary role of HRM in the successful use of AI, and it contributes to the existing literature. Since AI and HR are so intertwined, organizations should concentrate on incorporating AI as a supporting tool for HR rather than attempting to take over HR's function. Business systems and smart business machines should be designed in such a way that they cannot produce results without the help of HR.

Keywords: AI Powered Workforce Management, WFM, Artificial Intelligence

1. Introduction

Artificial intelligence (AI), also known as machine intelligence in computer science, is intelligence exhibited by computers as opposed to natural intelligence shown by humans and other species. AI research is characterized in computer science as the study of "intelligent agents," or devices that perceive their environment and take actions to increase their chances of achieving their objectives. "A system's ability to accurately interpret external data, learn from those data, and use those learnings to accomplish clear goals and tasks through flexible adaptation," say Kaplan and Haenlein. When a computer mimics "cognitive" tasks that humans associate with other human brains, such as "learning" and "problem solving," the word "artificial intelligence" is used [1].

The reach of AI is debatable: as machines become more efficient, tasks previously considered to require "intelligence" are increasingly excluded from the concept, a phenomenon known as the AI effect, leading to Tesler's Theorem's quip, "AI is whatever hasn't been done yet." Optical character recognition, for example, is often left out of discussions of "artificial intelligence," despite the fact that it has become a commonplace technology. Successfully understanding human voice, playing at the highest level in strategic game systems (such as chess and Go), autonomously driving vehicles, and intelligent routing in content distribution networks and military simulations are all examples of digital computer capabilities that are commonly known as AI.

Artificial intelligence is categorized into three forms by Kaplan and Haenlein: analytical, human-inspired, and humanized artificial intelligence. Analytical AI only has features that are associated with cognitive intelligence, such as the ability to produce cognitive representations of the environment and the ability to learn from previous experiences to guide future decisions. Human-inspired AI combines cognitive and emotional intelligence, recognizing, in addition to cognitive components, human emotions and taking them into account while making decisions. Humanized AI demonstrates all forms of competencies (cognitive, emotional, and social intelligence), as well as the ability to be self-aware and self-conscious in interactions with others.

Although AI and automation may be replacing workers, it's easy to overlook the fact that these same innovations play a critical role in recruiting, hiring, and retaining employees." "Finding the right talent is more difficult than ever in this period of constant change and digital skills shortages. Businesses can quickly and efficiently find a wide range of top candidates using AI and automation, and at a speed that keeps up with the frantic pace of modern business."

Screening chatbots and automated social media scraping tools are two examples of simple artificial intelligence applications that can assist recruiters with the sourcing and screening processes. These tools are intended to provide just a sliver of information about an applicant's chances of succeeding at the business. According to the Society for Human Resource Management, Mya, an AI hiring assistant created by FirstJob, communicates with applicants to verify they meet job criteria, answer questions, and keep them updated on their application's status. This bot provides help 24 hours a day, seven days a week via chat, text message, Skype, or e-mail, and will contact a person if it is unable to complete a mission. Another form of artificial intelligence recruitment tool is social media scraping software. These bots will gather a lot of information from an applicant's social media accounts and use it to predict those activities, such as potential interaction levels.

Tests, gamification, and simulations that gather data directly from the candidate are examples of intermediate artificial intelligence systems used in the hiring process. Unilever is one organization that has introduced a competitive artificial intelligence screening method developed in partnership with Pymetrics. Applicants would spend approximately twenty minutes playing neuroscience-based Pymetrics games as part of the hiring plan. These scientific games covertly test a candidate's memory, risk tolerance, ability to read contextual cues, and ability to concentrate. These intermediate AI applications typically offer hiring managers a clear indication of whether an applicant is a good match for the role, but they do not rely on precise job metrics.

Advanced artificial intelligence solutions, on the other hand, employ custom algorithms designed specifically to relate specific job performance metrics to potential candidates who best exhibit these characteristics. HireVue is a firm dedicated to the development of innovative AI human resource solutions. Their most effective program currently entails a video interview with questions "specifically crafted to evoke answers indicative of work satisfaction and find the right behaviors." Every applicant's responses, body language, speech, emotional state, and keywords are analyzed by the HireVue artificial intelligence program. Affectiva has also developed emotion detection software that can be used to assess a candidate's authenticity and emotional intelligence. These AI software systems are so advanced that they can "detect the flash of disdain that passes over an applicant's face as he mentions his ex-boss," according to WirePiazza [2].

2. Human resource functions and artificial intelligence

2.1 Personalized employee experiences

IBM officials addressed how AI can be successfully woven into an employee's onboarding program in their report. New workers who want to meet people and learn more about the company can be unsure where to go. They might inquire of their desk neighbor. But what if she's allocated to a different division? "What if Joe had been greeted with new recruit details customized to his first task on his mobile device?" In a paper on transforming HR with AI, IBM officials wrote. IBM is developing a system that can respond to a new employee's most urgent or job-critical concerns in order to help them get up to speed quickly. For example, an AI might recommend training or provide the names, places, and contact details for people he should meet on his first day or so. AI engines can also remind the same employee that a new recruit website provides a wealth of useful information.

2.2 Decision-making with cognitive support

IBM officials, who are promoting their own AI capabilities through IBM Watson, also demonstrated how cognitive engines could assist employees in making key day-to-day decisions in the workplace. Normally, HR team members will be in charge of the following tasks:

- Holiday requests - Workers who request vacation days are told that they are unlikely to be accepted because many people have already scheduled time off during that period.

- Assessing your mood - A worker answers a phone call from a customer. Following the call, the employee is told that he is stressed and that he should take a break before his meeting.

- Team planning - When a company wishes to take a more comprehensive approach to employee training, team members are offered a list of training choices to choose from.

- Recruiting practices - A hiring manager is told that the company's recruitment policy is unsuccessful because it interviews far too few applicants. Cognitive solutions can help businesses tap into various data sources and uncover new insights, among other things, to help them create applicant profiles. Automatically and leverages historical data patterns, seasonality and cyclicality to make forecasting more accurate.

2.3 Automation of 'repetitive, low-value add tasks'

AI gives HR the chance to automate "repetitive, low-value add tasks" and concentrate on more strategic work. HR teams will concentrate on "value-add work including mentoring and continuous feedback" by saving time on the steps of onboarding a new employee (allocating space, provisioning a laptop, etc.).

HR teams will be "free to do some of the innovative and strategic work that has a bigger effect on the performance of their companies" as AI tools automate basic HR activities like benefits management and triaging common questions and requests.

Companies have been gathering data on their consumers for years in order to obtain information and predict future actions. HR departments have a long way to go in terms of using these people analytics. AI would be able to play a bigger role in HR if it can find out what data to monitor, evaluate, handle, and secure. "In the never-ending battle for talent, businesses will seek out novel approaches to attracting top talent. Companies can be differentiated from one another by innovations that boost the candidate experience and fulfil the candidate's digital expectations."

2.4 Removing biases

According to the Human Resources Professional Association's study, even when managers try to be inclusive, they can subconsciously favor applicants that are similar to them, a phenomenon known as "unconscious bias." Another bias, language bias, has been discovered by the Implicit Association Test (IAT), a psychological instrument that shows that people's subconscious word associations suggest bias. "These prejudices are ingrained in job descriptions and resume selections. "Now, thanks to AI, algorithms can be programmed to assist employers in recognizing and eliminating prejudice trends in the language they use to enhance their recruiting communications and accept diverse applicants," according to HRPA researchers. AI may also present managers with applicants who were previously filtered out due to the human propensity to prefer candidates with similar characteristics or skills. HRPA researchers' algorithms are free of these tendencies, enabling managers to focus on data-driven evaluations rather than gut feelings.

2.5 Detecting workers on their way out

Veriato's AI systems are built to detect employees who are on their way out. It keeps track of employee computer activity — emails, keystrokes, web surfing, and so on — for a month and then uses an AI system to analyze the data to create a baseline of normal activity patterns in the company. "It flags outliers and reports them to the employer based on that knowledge," HRPA researchers wrote, "and also identifies shifts in the overall tone of employees' communications to predict when employees may be thinking about leaving."

2.6 Litigation strategy

Employment-related cases are typically fact-based, so collecting documentation and other facts is crucial. However, according to Littler's study, only 5% of respondents use advanced analytics to direct their litigation strategy. According to Crews, employers can be unaware of the advantages of using analytics in this scenario. "It's groundbreaking to be able to use data early in a case to eke out insights before taking a deposition or testing the credibility of witnesses." Having the opportunity to locate key records allows an employer to see what employees were doing at a given time and can aid in the construction of a tale, he explained.

Consider the case of a refrigerator repair technician who travels to people's homes and files a wage and hour class action alleging that he or she was not paid for all hours worked. The employees' version of their days will be exposed in the lawsuit and subsequent depositions, but analytics may be used to validate or refute their narrative. Crews said, "The more knowledge you have, the better the decision-making process you will participate in." GPS data from work vehicles, routing orders, messages about the technicians' assignments, invoices, and cellphone and login information could all be collected by the employer. These numbers can help to build an image.

The data could show that the technicians did not work off the clock and were properly paid for all hours worked, in which case the employer has some good proof on its hand. However, if the data shows that the workers' arguments are legitimate, it is best to check the data and know about it up front rather than going through time-consuming and expensive litigation, according to Crews.

2.7 Pay equity

Pay equity can also be assessed using data analytics. At the state and local levels, legislation in this region is increasingly evolving. At least 12 states, for example, have enacted legislation banning employers from questioning work applicants about their past pay. The aim of such legislation is to bring an end to long-standing wage inequalities based on gender, race, and ethnicity.

Crews recommended that employers keep an eye on employee salaries for disparities based on protected groups, adding that certain jurisdictions with pay equity regulations offer a safe haven for employers who perform investigations and strive to close gaps.

He went on to say that there are resources available that make it simple to create a user-friendly experience as well as evaluate, understand, and communicate data. "You don't have to rely on a math-filled Excel spreadsheet any longer." Having a clear view of what is going on in the company is beneficial, according to Crews. "HR practitioners will have the dialogue with the compensation committee, executives, and other decision-makers when advanced technology is combined with strong storytelling and visualization."

2.8 Chatbots

Using apps like chatbots, workers can get crucial policy and procedure information from anywhere and at any time. Chatbots are text-based chatbots that can answer basic employee questions. According to a 2017 ServiceNow survey of 350 HR leaders, two-thirds of respondents believe workers are more comfortable using chatbots than other means of communication for transactional inquiries about paid-time-off policies, open enrollment, and leaves of absence. ServiceNow, based in Santa Clara, California, is a cloud computing company. Employers who use chatbots must ensure that they are in compliance with federal and state data protection, disabilities, and other jobs laws.

2.9 Legal pitfalls

When using AI to direct human resource planning, HR practitioners must keep an eye out for prejudice in the systems. They must be on the lookout for differential effects, which occurs when an apparently equal or neutral norm is unequal in reality. A recruitment tool, for example, can weed out applicants who live more than 10 miles from the job site. What if the surrounding communities are mostly made up of wealthy white families? This hiring criterion will have a racially and ethnically unequal effect [3].

2.10 Recruiting

We make a lot of choices based on intuition. According to one report, most hiring managers make a decision about an applicant within the first 60 seconds of meeting them, mostly based on the candidate's appearance, handshake, wardrobe, or voice. Is it really possible to predict which attributes, experiences, schooling, and personality traits would lead to success in a specific role? We do not have any. Despite spending billions of dollars on assessments, evaluations, simulations, and games to recruit applicants, many managers and HR professionals tell me that they still get 30–40% of their candidates wrong.

AI-based algorithms can sift through resumes, identify successful internal applicants, profile top performers, and even decode video interviews to give us clues on who will succeed. One company uses Pymetrics' AI-based gamified evaluation to screen applicants for marketing and sales positions, and their performance rate has increased by over 30% thus removing both of the existing process's "interview bias" and "educational pedigree bias." The use of artificial intelligence in recruiting would be enormous. Although we are all concerned with work skills (software skills, sales skills, math skills, and so on), most research indicates that technological skills account for only a small portion of a person's performance. According to a recent report on High-Impact Talent Acquisition, level 4 maturity firms, which have the highest financial return from recruiting, devote nearly 40% of their hiring requirements to emotional and psychological qualities such as ambition, learning agility, enthusiasm, and sense of intent. Will AI be able to find this out as well? It's possible. LinkedIn, Pymetrics, Entelo, HiredScore, IBM, Textio, Talview, Unitive, PredictiveHire, and others are among the vendors in this market.)

2.11 Employee growth and learning

We have no idea how to perfectly "train" people. Most learning professionals estimate that at least half of the global L&D market is wasted (forgotten, incorrectly implemented, or simply wasting people's time). However, we have no idea which half this is!

Do you know what you "need to learn" to boost your job performance? What if we had algorithms that tracked and analyzed the talents, attitudes, and actions of the top performers in our teams and then simply instructed us how to be more like them? These "Netflix-like" algorithms are now finding their way into the world of learning platforms, making learning as useful and enjoyable as watching cable television. The market is still young, but the potential is immense. According to study, the average employee has less than 25 minutes a week to train and learn; if that time is made more important, everyone will benefit.

Improve your results through getting trained and automatizing the work process via Degreed, EdCast, Filtered, Volley, Axonify, BetterUp, Clustree, Workday etc.

2.12 Leadership and management

We work like Zen masters in terms of management and leadership. We read books, attend seminars, emulate the bosses we respect, and extol the accomplishments of today's popular leaders. Do we have a firm grip on the science of leadership? I assume it is a passing fad. We're focusing on meaning, mission, and discipleship this year. It was "servant leadership" just a few years ago, and it was "execution and financial acumen" when I was younger. According to most reports, there are hundreds of management and leadership characteristics that characterize performance, and each of us brings a slightly different and special combination of them to the table.

This can now be decoded with the aid of artificial intelligence. Three companies have developed "AI-based" coaching tools, which include programs that solicit feedback, read comments, and infer sentiment from employees and teams. They use this data to equate the problems of these individuals and teams to those of higher-performing teams, and to send managers and supervisors "nudges" on how to improve. One client reported that after just three months of using this method, their leadership teams had seen a 25% rise in organizational values simply by introducing tiny behavioral nudges. (Reflektiv, BetterWorks, Ultimate Software, Zugata, Humanyze, ADP, Impraise, and others are among the vendors in this space.)

The possibilities for fraud and enforcement are enormous. Employees who cheat or commit crimes are "contagious," according to one report (people who work with them pick up bad habits). AI will analyze organizational network data (email traffic, sentiment of comments) to identify areas of tension, potential ethical lapses, and a variety of other enforcement risks, and then alert HR or compliance officers to intervene before bad conduct occurs. TrustSphere, Keencorp, Volley, Cornerstone, and others are among the vendors in this space.)

2.13 Employee engagement and well-being

Artificial intelligence is now being used to classify habits that contribute to poor job efficiency. In the field of protection, AI can detect actions and interactions that contribute to mishaps. A new generation of survey tools may detect tension and bad behavior trends and warn HR or line managers. Limeaid, VirginPulse, Glint, Ultimate Tech, CultureAmp, TinyPulse, Peakon, and others are among the vendors in this space.)

2.14 Self-service for employees and applicant management

A new generation of intelligent chatbots can make communications smart and easy. (IBM, ServiceNow, Xor, Mya, Ideal, Paradox, and others are among the vendors in this space) [4].

3. Discussion

AI is a collection of algorithms and machine learning software that can quickly ingest data, recognize patterns, optimize, and forecast trends. The systems can recognize photos, understand expression, and use pattern matching to detect signals such as mood, sincerity, and even personality. These algorithms aren't as "simple" as humans, but they are fast, allowing them to analyze millions of pieces of data in seconds and quickly match them to patterns.

By plotting curves of potential outcomes and then optimizing decisions based on a variety of parameters, AI systems can statistically "predict" and "learn." As an example, consider an AI system that analyses a candidate's demographics, work experience, and interview questions and then "predicts" how well they will do on the job. (This is something that HiredScore, Pymetrics, HireVue, IBM, and others are working on.)

Many of these applications are brand new, and as exciting as they can appear, they come with a slew of risks. The most important is that AI cannot function without "Training info." To put it another way, the algorithms learn from their mistakes. If your current management methods are biased, racist, punitive, or unnecessarily bureaucratic, you may as well institutionalize everything you dislike. We need AI that is transparent and "tuneable" so that we can inspect the algorithms and ensure that they are performing as intended. Our early algorithms would need "bumpers" and "tuning knobs" to learn how to make them more accurate, just as early automobiles did not always drive straight.

Bias can be institutionalized across processes. Assume your organization has never employed a woman engineer and has a small number of African American engineers. Women and black engineers are less likely to succeed in management, according to the AI recruitment system. This form of bias must be carefully eliminated from algorithms, and doing so correctly will take time.

There is a chance of data leakage as well as inadvertent misuse. Consider a popular application of analytics: predicting the probability of a top performer leaving the business. We can inadvertently create the wrong behavior by telling managers that "this person has a high chance of leaving." For example, the manager may neglect or handle this person differently. We must carefully learn how to apply behavioral economics. Today, AI is a "tool" for advice and change rather than a self-contained decision-making method.

At Entelo, AI experts addressed the value of designing "interpretive" and "transparent" AI systems. To put it another way, if the machine makes a decision, it should clarify why it made it so that we, as people, can determine if the parameters it used are still relevant. This is one of the most critical requirements for new tools, and most AI systems today are completely opaque.

Consider what happens if a self-driving car crashes. We devote a considerable amount of time to evaluating how the accident occurred, what visual or algorithmic processes failed, and what circumstances might have contributed to the accident. What if AI makes a mistake in an applicant recommendation, a wage change, or a management intervention? Are we going to find out? Will we be able to work it out? Would we really be conscious of it before it's too late? We still have a lot of work to do in terms of instrumenting and learning how to "train" our management-based AI systems to work effectively.

The buzz around AI is at an all-time high right now. Any HR tech vendor claims to have a machine learning team and a best-in-class AI solution. Yes, these skills are critical to the industry, but do not be fooled by the hype.

The accuracy and completeness of an HR tool's algorithms, the ease of use of its programs, and, most importantly, its ability to offer "narrow AI" – or rather precise solutions that solve your problems – will all play a role in its success. Only when the provider has a large amount of data (to train the system) and a lot of feedback on how well it performs can this be achieved. So, rather than getting great engineers, I believe the barriers to entry would be concentration, business strategy, and client intimacy.

Also, do not buy a black box device unless you can demonstrate its value in your business. Since management and personnel decisions are always informed by a company's culture, we'll need to spend some time evaluating and fine-tuning these systems in the real world. For example, IBM has spent years fine-tuning its AI-based compensation and job strategies to suit the company's culture and business model. They're now taking these tools to corporate customers, and each one teaches IBM something different about the algorithms, allowing them to improve them for that market, community, or organizational need.

Despite these difficulties and dangers, the potential rewards are immense. Payroll accounts for 40–60% of a company's income, and much of this massive cost is motivated by management decisions based on gut instinct. I believe we will see drastic changes in efficiency, performance, and employee health as AI systems in HR become smarter, more proven, and more oriented on specific problems. What we need to do now is be patient, alert, and ready to put in the effort.

4. Consequences

The days of spending hundreds of man-hours sifting through thousands of CVs and online job-board profiles in search of new hires are over. For example, an AI recruitment firm claims on their blog that their AI candidate sourcing algorithm can "reduce time to hire from 34 days to 9 days." Using a non-biased process that eliminates prejudices from sourcing and finds applicants that are professionally suitable for the job, candidate sourcing and onboarding productivity increased by 73.53 percent.

Another role that AI technology can automate is candidate screening. Far more online data, such as information from social media accounts, previous online work records, and educational credentials, can be obtained using this intelligent-style approach, which will boost the ranking system of applicants for recruiters to choose from.

Given that AI technology can easily source and test a large number of applicants, the business's acceptance criteria and the applicant profile must be balanced in order to find and match the most promising candidates for the job. Using the information collected, AI systems will rate applicants on a scale based on experience, job history, skill sets, and salary requirements in order to find the right applicant. This method of data processing is becoming increasingly useful in today's market due to its ability to find passive candidates, who are usually the most sought after because they aren't actively searching for other jobs and are happy in their current role, suggesting that they are an asset to their organization and therefore face less competition to place them.

Interviewing is a big part of the hiring process until you have found the 'right match' for the position. Many expats are actively pursuing employment abroad in today's global work market, but they might not always be able to fly to the country of their choice for an interview. HireVue and Mya, for example, are two startups that specialize in AI interviewing apps. Through using video as a tool, these organizations are turning their emphasis to simplifying the interviewing process. Pre-made questionnaires are used in programs like HireVue, which the applicant can then film themselves responding. This enables the recruiter to perform generic interviews with a greater range of prospective applicants using pre-recorded recordings, which can then be sifted through to find those who will advance in the talent acquisition process.

The footwork is taken care of using AI technology, from sourcing to interviewing, significantly reducing the recruitment timeline. As a result, the talent management team is able to engage with potential applicants and assess their ability to succeed in the particular position, allowing them to make a placement much more quickly.

In today's economy, countless business dollars are expended on old-fashioned recruiting in addition to numerous man-hours. According to a 2016 report by the Society of Human Resource Management, "the total cost-per-hire is $4,129." That's a colossal sum of money to put single person in. Let us place it in context.

Amazon had "541,900 workers in the third quarter of 2017, up from a little more than 300,000 in the same period a year ago," according to CNN. This suggests that Amazon employed an estimated 241,900 new workers over the course of a year. Granted, Amazon still uses AI technology in its recruiting services, but let us assume they did not (as many large corporations do today) and that their cost of hiring one employee was the same as the average found by SHRM. The cost will be $4,129 (average cost to hire) multiplied by 241,900 (new employees) for a total of $998,805,100 in annual recruiting costs [5].

Amazon may have invested upwards of $1 billion USD on recruiting expenses alone over the course of a year in this case, according to reports. This is incredible and almost incomprehensible, yet it is possible. With many AI recruiting and Human Resources programs available that provide custom packages on a monthly, quarterly, or yearly subscription basis, it's easy to see how switching to AI technology solutions will save you a lot of money.

Richard Hughes, Senior Vice President of UnitedHealth Group, said at the recent IBM Think 2018 panel, "The future will be centered on the employee experience, with individual involvement being prioritized. We can't do it on any scale without using the best of what 'data science' has to offer." AI is not just about assisting humans with lower-level tasks; it's also about data. AI will collect massive quantities of data at a pace that is exponentially faster than humans could ever hope to achieve. This knowledge is what drives companies in general, not just HR teams.

Many workers of larger companies will feel disengaged and unappreciated by their bosses and HR departments. For most workers, anything from not being accepted for holiday requests to unenforced policies may be the turning point, resulting in high turnover rates. A high salary does not guarantee that an employee would be happy. Most people consider their work to be their lives, and who wants to live a life that is unhappy? Nobody.

Having access to a larger set of data ensures you can improve your workers' overall experience by analyzing the data and making appropriate changes to the working environment or internal processes. Hughes wrote in a recent tweet, "Having good data is comparable to being in good health. You take it for granted once you have it. You panic if you don't." Simply put, more data implies more data analytics, which means more advanced insights that lead to better working conditions for workers and lower turnover.

5. Digitizing HR functions

5.1 Recruiting and talent management

Ksenia Zheltoukhova, head of research at the Chartered Institute of Personnel and Development (CIPD), claimed in an article by Hagginbottom [6], which included excerpts from interviews with corporate experts from various organizations, that organizations are opting for video interviews to give candidates a personalized feel. Despite the fact that such new practices can jeopardize HR's value, some researchers claim that capabilities such as imagination, empathy, and a humanistic approach to problems have yet to be discovered by automation or AI. Alan Stukalsky, chief digital officer at Randstad US, agrees, believing that the use of chatbots in the recruiting process is still in its early stages. A robot cannot determine a candidate's cultural and behavioral characteristics. The most specialized role of HR, recruiting, profits the most from AI. Computer-assisted, automated systems handle everything from creating job descriptions to shortlisting the best candidates from a pool of applicants [7].

Onboarding After an employee has been on-boarded, a sequence of routine actions for the new hire begin. For HR department directors, directly handling newly recruited employees would be incredibly time consuming and draining. As a result, businesses employ user-friendly software that contains all of the necessary information for a new recruit. It contains simple answers to common questions posed by new employees. The HR manager will save time by getting involved with new hires later in the onboarding process. It is also assumed that AI's position in human resources is more of a facilitator, allowing human resources to complete tasks in less time, freeing up time for them to concentrate on studying and improving key positions such as "creative thinking," "design skills," and "psychological understanding," among others, in order to make strategic decisions for the company [8].

5.2 Development and learning

According to Jain [9] using AI-enabled software to design learning and development opportunities for employees would improve employee work satisfaction. Career growth programs that are tailored to the needs of workers result in lower absenteeism and higher productivity. We are already using AI as a learning tool, as Melissa Lamson, President and CEO of Lamson Consulting, points out in a post. Getting feedback from Alexa and Siri is nothing more than a form of learning. Today, we prefer to learn by flows rather than guidance through a digital experience. Focus learning through experience has been facilitated by AI, stressing design and critical thinking. AI has facilitated the production of individual employee charts, which is a new form of learning and development technique.

5.3 Mentoring and coaching

Coaching and mentoring are another important HR feature that is unlikely to be replaced by AI. Contrary to common opinion, apps such as "mobile coach" helps workers understand their needs and develop personalized learning and development programs. As a result, software will determine the employee's job requirements and guide them toward their preferred career paths. Creation of a party Various types of mini courses provide workers with ready-to-use coaching and mentoring resources. However, certain delicate issues involving employee actions and attitudes also necessitate the intervention of a human being to interpret the situation [10].

6. Future research prospects

Indeed, AI has provided for very systematic and precise HR business solutions. Employee record preservation, talent management, employee growth, employee appraisals, employee compensation distribution, employee selection, employee engagement, monitoring employee success and input, and other complex tasks are made easier by AI. HR managers must determine the extent to which technology is used in HR. Some researchers claim that AI will never be able to replace HR's valuable feedback, while others believe that AI will soon supplant HR's vital position because it has an advantage over HR in terms of error-free and fast responses. At this stage, when AI and HR are combined, it is up to HR managers to determine how much AI should be used in HR functions. A strong distinction between AI-controlled activities and HR-managed assignments must be made, and AI should be supplemented by HR influence in all functions. The current study examined the views of various corporate experts on the subject and concluded that AI plays a role in the efficient implementation of HR functions. Despite its ability to make work easier and more effective in different areas of HR, AI is still unable to substitute human participation in the implementation of HR functions. The HR department is primarily responsible for personal relations and critical behavioral knowledge of human minds. If all duties are delegated to robots, the company can never be able to retain its employees or their loyalty to the company. As a result, human resources must continue to do what they were doing before, but with AI's help, they can do it better. In numerous articles and research papers, the increasing use of technology in HR has been addressed, either in the context of HR digitization or the role of AI in HR. This paper aimed to cover various aspects of technology used in HR functions, but there is still space for future study. This research lays the groundwork for future research in the fields of AI and HR. Researchers should take advantage of the emerging stage of AI and HR in the future to contribute to the literature in the field by conducting empirical studies. Different perspectives of technology in HR functions, such as digitization of HR functions, the use of Expert Systems, technologically dominated work systems, technologically aided HR systems, the role of AI generated methods in HR, and so on, can be studied separately to understand HR's position in the evolving scenario. Researchers who are interested in comparing the ease of work before and after AI participation in HR functions should conduct a comparative analysis. In addition, the current study may provide food for thought for some researchers as they consider the different job profiles in the face of AI.

7. Conclusion

As much as AI manages to disrupt the HR technology environment. HR departments must strike a balance between cognitive technology advances and accountability. To avoid unintentionally incorporating prejudice into their services, HR leaders and practitioners must have a good understanding of how decisions are produced. This openness will be critical in ensuring that workers have confidence in the latest technologies.

As you may have guessed, there are many benefits of using AI technology for your human resources and hiring needs. However, nothing in life is perfect, particularly a new type of technology that has yet to achieve its full potential. Many of the services and programs available which lack features that people are used to in the non-AI world, such as the ability to leave feedback on an applicant after a video interview or clear CV search requirements. One big feature of AI technology that it lacks is empathy and human contact, or the ability to handpick an applicant and get to know them personally during the recruiting process, which cannot be done right now if you are relying on AI technology to do it for you. AI sees data, while humans experience emotion, and this will not change in the near future.

As a result, it is up to you to determine if AI technology is the best fit for your company's needs. Are you a large organization with thousands of workers that spends a lot of money on recruiting each year and is searching for a way to streamline the process and save money? Are you a small company with less than 15

DOI: http://dx.doi.org/10.5772/intechopen.97817

employees that takes pride in getting to know each employee as if they were family? Every organization has different priorities, budgets, and expectations, but the beauty of the AI industry is that there is a solution for everyone, regardless of size.

It's up to you to find out what works best for your business, whether it's adjusting to the ever-growing AI market, keeping things the same, or making incremental improvements over time. In any case, AI technology will continue to advance, and at some stage in the future, AI will be the standard, making conventional methods of recruitment and human resource management appear obsolete.

Author details

Mrinmoy Roy
Lovely Professional University, Punjab, India

*Address all correspondence to: mroy2612@gmail.com

References

[1] S. J. Russell and P. Norvig, Artificial Intelligence: A Modern Approach, 3rd ed., Upper Saddle River, NJ: Prentice Hall (2010).

[2] WirePiazza, L.N. (2018). How Can Artificial Intelligence Work for HR?SHRM

[3] Nicastro, D. (2018). 7 Ways Artificial Intelligence is Reinventing Human Resources. CMS

[4] Joshbersin. (2018). AI in HR: A Real Killer App. HR TECHNOLOGY

[5] Pay, V. B. (2018). How Artificial Intelligence Is Reinventing Human Resources. Entrepreneur

[6] Hagginbottom, K. (June, 2018). The Impact of AI on the HR Profession. In Forbes online magazine. Retrieved from https://www.forbes.com/sites/karenhigginbottom/2018/06/14/the-impact-of-ai-on-the-hr-profession/#7364c0e391ca on 21st November, 2018.

[7] Biswas, S. (March, 2018). Employee Experience, Jobs and Skills: How AI will impact HR. In HR Technologist. Retrieved from https://www.hrtechnologist.com/articles/digital-transformation/employee-experience-jobs-and-skills-how-ai-will-impact-hr/ on 20th November, 2018.

[8] John J. Lawler & Elliot, R. (1996). Artificial intelligence in HRM: An experimental study of an expert system, Journal of Management, 22(1), 85-111.

[9] Jain, S. (2016). Big data analysis: Changing the way. International Journal of Research in Advanced Engineering and Technology, 2(6), 34-36.

[10] Hooda, S. (April, 2018). 5 ways HR will be affected by Artificial Intelligence. In People Matters. Retrieved from on 21st November, 2018. https://www.britannica.com/technology/artificial-intelligence on 21st November, 2018.

Chapter 5

Agent Based Load Balancing in Grid Computing

Wided Ali and Fatima Bouakkaz

Abstract

Load-Balancing is an important problem in distributed heterogeneous systems. In this paper, an Agent-based load-balancing model is developed for implementation in a grid environment. Load balancing is realized via migration of worker agents from overloaded resources to underloaded ones. The proposed model purposes to take benefit of the multi-agent system characteristics to create an autonomous system. The Agent-based load balancing model is implemented using JADE (Java Agent Development Framework) and Alea 2 as a grid simulator. The use of MAS is discussed, concerning the solutions adopted for gathering information policy, location policy, selection policy, worker agents migration, and load balancing.

Keywords: load balancing, grid computing, agent migration, resource utilization, mobile agents

1. Introduction

Grid computing has appeared as an encouraging smart computing paradigm. Grid computing purposes to collect the power of geographically distributed heterogeneous, multiple-domain computational resources to offer high performance. To realize the encouraging potentials of grid computing, effective job scheduling, and load balancing algorithms are important. Such algorithms should be very scalable since these systems typically have thousands to millions of resources. They should also be flexible and be adaptive to task requirements.

The load balancing prevents the state in which some resources become overloaded while the others are underloaded or idle. Therefore, the use of a load balancing mechanism is expected to enhance reliability. The problem that can increase in this mechanism is related to the characteristics of the grid, which are resource variations, resource heterogeneity, application variety, and the dynamicity of grid environments. Multi-agent systems give encouraging features for resource managers. The scalability, reactivity, cooperation, proactivity, flexibility, autonomy, and robustness that characterize multi-agents system can help in the complex task of resource management in dynamic and changing environments.

Multi-agent distributed systems give an exciting solution to grid load balancing. An agent-based structure is developed to offer services for high performance-programming environments and applications that can be used on the grid computing environment. Software agents improve expandability, permitting the number of resources involved to rise easily, by providing services that include job scheduling, monitoring, and supervisory for the system.

Asynchronous communication, parallel actions, and autonomous operations of agents allow MAS to adjust to dynamic modifications of the grid environment, thereby enhancing the stability, fault tolerance, responsiveness, and reliability of the grid. Identifying key reasons to prove the convergence of MAS and grid is not an easy task. In this chapter, a new Agent-Based load balancing Model is presented. A hierarchical architecture with coordination is designed to ensure scalability and efficiency. Also, a multi-agent approach is applied to improve adaptability. Multi-agent system is implemented with the JADE (Java Agent Development) framework for grid load balancing. The chapter also discusses the difficulties and advantages surrounding the task of integrating multi-agent systems into grid computing.

The structure of the chapter is organized as follows: Section 2 describes Agent based load balancing architecture and implementation, Section 3 shows implemented algorithms. Finally, Sections 4 concludes the chapter with comments and discussion about current and future works.

2. Proposed agent based load balancing model

The proposed model is an extension of our previous works related to load balancing system [1, 2], which is integrated into our agent-based load balancing in a grid computing project.

In this section, we will introduce an Agent-based load balancing Model (ABLBM). We will mention the components of the system and the interaction between agents briefly. We will describe the new features we added to Agent- based load balancing Model in grid, UML Classes Diagram, UML Sequence Diagram, algorithms, and load balancing mechanism in detail.

2.1 The ABLBM framework

The UML Classes Diagram of the proposed model comprises fourteen connected classes as follows (**Figures 1** and **2**):

1. The Model class is linked by an aggregation relationship to the Level 2, Level 1, and Level 0 classes

2. The Level 0 class contains one and only one Grid Agent

3. The Level 1 class contains one or more cluster Agents

4. The Level 2 class contains one or more clusters and the cluster class contains one or more resources

5. A Resource can be associated with one or more users, and each user can submit one or more tasks.

6. The Resource class is linked by an aggregation relation to the cluster class

7. Grid Agent class can create one or more Cluster Agents

8. Cluster Agent can create one Migration Agent, one or more Resource Agents, LBC Agents, and Worker Agents.

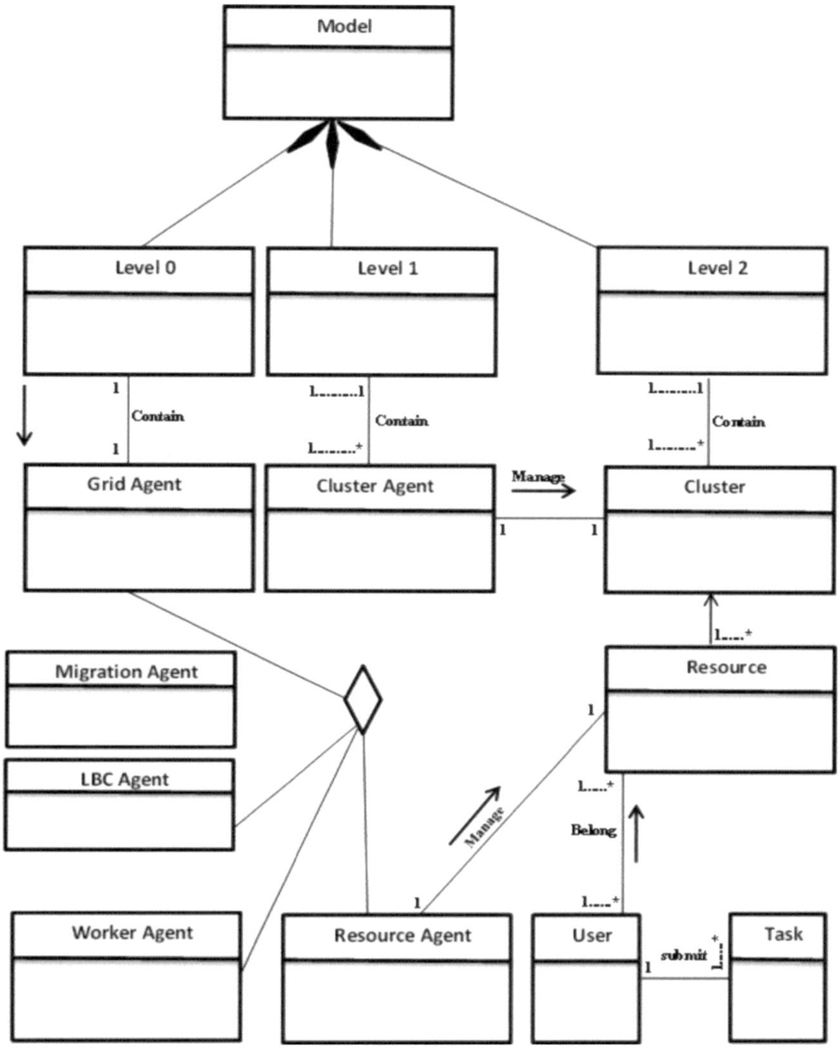

Figure 1.
UML classes diagram of ABLBM framework.

The proposed framework is intended to take advantage of the agent's characteristics to create a self-adaptive and self-sustaining load balancing system. The proposed system consists of six types of agents, in unbalanced situations, and if the Cluster Agent finds that there is a load imbalance between the resources under its control, it uses the Knowledge Algorithm to receive the load information from each Resource Agent. Based on this information and the estimated equilibrium threshold, it analyses the current load of the cluster. Depending on the outcome of this analysis, it decides whether to start a local balancing in case of an unbalanced state, or simply inform other Cluster Agent of its current load. Resource Agent sends the updated local load value to Cluster Agent, which updates its load information. Migration Agent is responsible for migrating Worker Agents to the selected underloaded resource. There is a Migration Agent in each Cluster, who expects acknowledgement of receipt from the receiving resource once it receives the migrated Worker Agent. The last agent is Grid Agent, it is the role of the distribution of jobs between clusters, and all Cluster Agents are started by this type of agents.

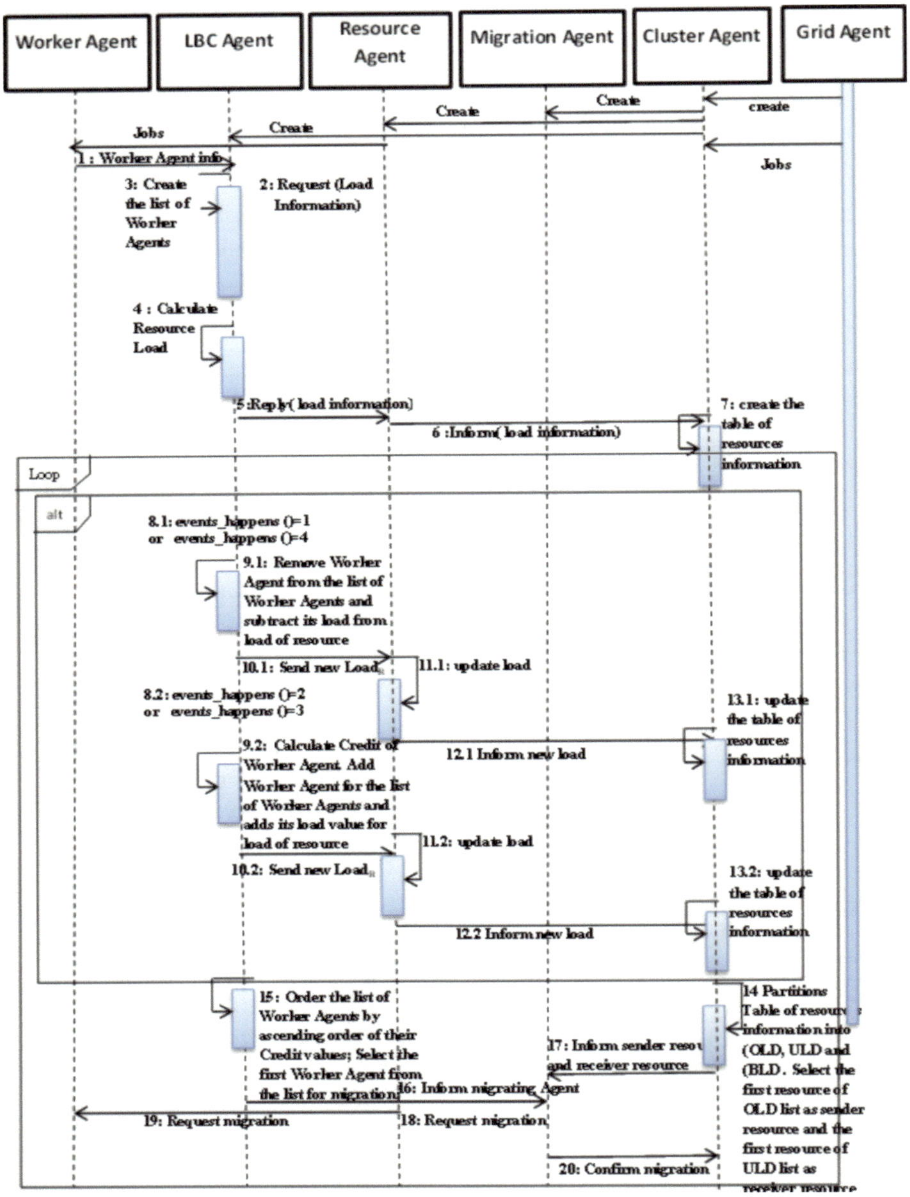

Figure 2.
UML sequence diagram describes agent interactions in intra cluster load balancing process framework.

2.2 Algorithms

We define two levels of load balancing algorithms: Intra-cluster load balancing and intra-Grid load balancing algorithm.

2.2.1 Intra cluster load balancing algorithm

This load balancing algorithm makes the imbalance situations can be resolved within a cluster. It is triggered when any Agent Cluster finds that there is a load imbalance between the resources which are under its control. To do this, the Agent

Cluster receives load information from each Resource Agent. Based on this information and the estimated balance threshold, it analyzes the current load of the cluster. According to the consequence of this analysis, it chooses whether to start a local balancing in the situation of imbalance state, or eventually just to notify other Agent Clusters about its current load. To implement this local load balancing, we propose the following three policies: load information gathering, agent selection policy, location policy, and Worker Agent migration.

2.2.1.1 Load information gathering

In the proposed algorithm, Agent Cluster decides to start a local balancing in the case of imbalance. There are some particular events that change the load configuration in a grid environment. The events can be categorized as follows:

1. Arrival of any new resource
2. Withdrawal of any existing resource.
3. Local Agent Worker Termination: a local Agent Worker's life cycle is ended
4. Local Agent Worker Start: a new local Agent Worker will be started
5. Incoming Migrating Agent: the local resource has been selected as a receiver for the migrating agent.
6. A Mobile Agent Departure: the local resource has been selected as a sender for the migrating agent.
7. Agent Worker ends the computation assigned to it, and becomes idle;

Whenever any of these activities happen the local load value is changed, Resource Agent sends the updated local load value to Agent Cluster who updates its Table of resources. Each Cluster Agent estimates its associated cluster capability by performing the following actions:

1. it estimates the current load of the cluster based on load information received from its Resource Agents;
2. it sends its load information to other Cluster Agents

The local host load is dependent on the Agent workers running on that host. A load of an agent executing on a machine is defined as the sum of its computational load and communication load in time unit [3].

A local host load can be defined as follows: The load L_k of a machine M_k is defined as the sum of its entire agents load on the host. More specifically

$$L_k = \sum_{M(ai)=k} (W_k + U_k) \tag{1}$$

A load of an agent executing on a machine is defined as the sum of its computational load and communication load $Load_{ij} = W_{ij} + U_{ij}$ Where: W_{ij} is Computational Load and U_{ij} is communication load.

2.2.1.2 Agent selection policy

The selection policy handles which Worker Agent is migrated whenever there is a necessity. We assign a numerical value, called credit, to every Worker Agent. The credit value designates the capacity of the agent to remain undisturbed in case of migration. For a Worker Agent, the higher its credit value, the higher its opportunity to stay at the same machine. In other words, its opportunity to be selected for migration is lower. The LBC Agent assigns credit to each Worker Agent and chooses which agent requests to be migrated using the credit. Any Worker Agent with high credit will be given more opportunity to preserve its current location (the resource the agent resides in) with less opportunity to be selected for migration.

The credit value of a Worker Agent is assumed to depend on two types of parameters, namely Worker Agent dependent parameters and System dependent parameters [4]:

2.2.1.3 Worker agent dependent parameters

1. Its computational load, as it represents the main source of resource loading.

2. Its communication load, as it represents another source of resource loading.

3. Agent's size, an agent migrates through the network to its new destination, thus an agent with big size is predictable to take more time to reach its destination resource.

4. Agent's priority, the interruption of a high priority agent running to perform a migration process should be prohibited.

2.2.1.4 System parameters

1. Reliability of the communication path between resources, the migrating agent delivery is not assured when the physical path reliability is low.

2. Availability of required resource on the source host, this factor represents the affinity between an agent and its running host.

3. Source Host's loading, the host with high load will be more subject to let some agents migrate.

The credit of a Worker Agent increases if the following situations [4]:

1. The Worker Agent's load reduces.

2. It communicates frequently with other worker Agents in other resources.

3. It has a high familiarity with the local machine. For example, it needs a special type of processors, I/O devices, or large volumes of data localized at the machine.

4. The agent's remaining execution time is short.

5. The agent's size is large.

6. The communication load is small.

7. The communication path between hosts is not reliable.

8. The needed Resource is available.

9. The agent has high priority.

In contrast, the credit value of Worker Agent reduces in the following situations:

1. The Worker Agent's load Increases

2. The communication with Worker Agents in other resources is increased.

3. Strong mobility or instant exchanges of messages (frequent message exchanges rises the Worker Agent's load.)

Using a multiple linear regression operation, we will try to gather all the mentioned factors into one equation, In linear regression, the relationship between a dependent variable, Y, and an independent variable X, is modeled by Y = a + βX. This interpretation of coefficient, it is appropriate only when the independent variable is continuous (quantitative). To incorporate qualitative independent variables into the regression model and formulate the model so the variables have interpretable coefficients, There are two commonly used methods for coding qualitative variables so they can be used in regression models, dummy coding and effect coding [4, 5]. To include the variables qualitative in the equation, we will use the simplest way which is the dummy coding, which assigns values "1" and "0" to reflect the presence and absence, For example, if we take a qualitative variable Resource availability R_i, we assigned value 1 when the resource is available and 0 if it is not available. The final equation can be written as:

$$\text{Credit } A_i = b_0 + b_1 W_i + b_2 U_i + b_3 R_i + b_4 Ld_{i1} + b_5 Ld_{i2} + b_6 H_{i1} + b_7 H_{i2} + b_8 P_{i1} + b_9 P_{i2} + b_{10} S_i \tag{2}$$

Having a big coefficient means that this variable will make the agent tends to stay rather than being migrated.

b1: Computation load Coefficient: if b_1 is a relatively large negative value then an agent having a big computation load is more likely to be migrated as its credit value will be reduced. If b1 is a positive value then the resource that has a big computational load value will be excepted from the list of receiver resources.

b_2: Communication load Coefficient: if b_2 has a negative value, then we can assume that an agent has a big communication load, it is more matter to migration as its credit value will be small. Since b_2 has the smallest weight among the regression coefficients then it has the weakest effect on the credit value and therefore the migrating agent selection. If b_2 is a positive value, so when it is multiplied by the communication load, a resource that has a big communication load value will be excepted from the list of receiver resources.

b_3: Resource Availability Coefficient: when R_i = 1, b_3 has relatively large values, that means that the agent finds the needed resource on the running host thus it is less subject for migration.

b_4, b_5: Host Load Coefficient: b_4 has a higher load than b_5 because when the running host is underloaded or balanced, it is less matter to select one of its agents to be migrated.

b_6, b_7: Reliability's Coefficient: if H_{i1}, H_{i2} = 1,1 then b_6, b_7 have relatively large values because that's means that the agent may not reach the destination node through the unreliable network, thus the migration frequency is less.

b_8, b_9: Priority's Coefficient: the high or moderate priority mean b_8 and b_9 have high weight because the high or moderate priority agent are less matter to be migrated.

b_{10}: Agent size Coefficient: a big size agent mean b_{10} has a positive sign which means that a medium-size agent will be less matter for migration as they will encounter more loads in the transmission.

2.2.1.5 Location policy

After a Worker Agent is determined to migrate, we have to select the receiving resource. The location policy defines to which destination resource the selected Worker Agent will be migrated to. The Cluster Agent selects the destination resource. For this purpose, it executes the following actions:

When the Cluster Agent receives the load information from its resources, it Partition cluster into an overloaded resources list (OLD), under-loaded resources list (ULD), and balanced list (BLD) and it sorts OLD by descending order of their load and ULD by ascending order of their load. The resource will be in an overloaded list if its load is high. The resource will be in the underloaded list if its load is low. The resource is not into the overloaded list or the underloaded, after that the Cluster agent sorts the overloaded resources list by descending order relative to their Load and sorts underloaded resources list by ascending order relative to Their Load. In the next step, Cluster Agent determines the sender resource and the receiver resource, where the sender resource is the first resource in the overloaded resources list and the receiver is the first resource in the underloaded resources list. Each Worker agent records the communication load between all the resources. If the receiver resource has the highest communication load with the migrated Agent then it is selected as the receiver resource else we must select another receiver resource from the list of underloaded resources. This is because, if a receiver resource is an external resource, the load of Worker Agent may not reduce due to large external communication. Instead, the load may rise.

2.2.1.6 Worker agent migration

The Worker Agent selection is related to its credit value while the receiver resource is the most under loaded resource. The migration decision is taken by a Cluster Agent that sends it for Migration Agent associated. The proposed MAS employs a mobile-agent system to support the migration of an agent. For migrating the Worker Agents, the status of the system and the agents currently operate or registered have to be considered. The receiver resource has to have more than one running agent. The Migration Agent sends a request message to the AMS agent. Then, the AMS sends an authentication message along with timestamp to it. The Migration Agent sends a request message of migration along with the authentication message to the DLA (Dynamic Library Agent) of the receiver resource. The DLA then sends the Worker Agent code after verifying the authentication and validation of the message. Finally, the Worker Agent migrates itself to the receiver resource or migrates a clone agent, in calling the doMove () method by the migrating agent with as parameter the receiver resource. The migrated agent is executed by the Dynamic Library Agent, and if the migrated one is a clone agent, it records itself to the platform by itself.

```
LBC Agent: Gathering Information Algorithm
Input: Worker Agents info
Output: LoadR = resource load
{
Creates the list of Worker Agents;
Calculates the total local load host LoadR by using Eq. (1) and sends it for Resource Agent
Send LoadR to its Resource Agent associated
Loop wait for load change//depends on happening of any of defined events
{
if (events_happens () = 2 or events_happens () = 3) then
        {
        Calculates Credits of Worker Agents (by using Eq. (2);
        Adds Worker Agents for the list of Worker Agents and adds their load
values for the load of resource.
Sends LoadR to its Resource Agent associated;
        }
if (events_happens () = 1 or events_happens () = 4) then
        {
        Removes Worker Agents from the list of Worker Agents and subtract their
load from the load of resource
Sends LoadR to its Resource Agent associated;
        }
End Loop
}
```

```
Function events_happens ()
output Type: integer
If (Worker Agent Termination) then events_happens () =1; End If
If (Worker Agent Start) then events_happens () =2; End If
If (Incoming Migrating Worker Agent) then events_happens () = 3; End If
If (Worker Agent Departure) then events_happens () = 4; End If
If (Arrival of any new resource) then events_happens () = 5; End If
If (Withdrawal of any existing resource in the local host) then events_happens () = 6;End If
If (Loadcluster > Sthreshold)then events_happens () = 7; End If//Sthreshold saturation threshold
If (Cluster.state = unbalanced) then events_happens () = 8; End If
```

```
Resource Agent: Workload Estimation
Input: receive LoadR from LBC Agent, Worker Agents info
Output:
{
Started up LBC Agent associated;
Started up Worker Agents associated;
Receives LoadR from LBC Agent associated;
Sends LoadR to its Cluster Agent associated;
Keeping track of the number of alive Worker Agents on the local host;
}
```

```
Cluster Agent: Knowledge Algorithm
Input: receives tasks from AgentGrille, LoadR, LoadC
Output: Cluster Load, table of resources information
{
sends tasks among Resource Agents;
create the table of resources information;
receive LoadR from the resource Agents under its control;
Updates the table of resources information;
if (events_happens () = 5) then
{
Create Resource Agent for the new resource;
Creates LBC Agent for the new resource;
Creates Worker Agents for new resource;
Sends tasks among Resource Agent of new resource
Adds information of the new resource for table of resources information
Updates the table of resources information;
}
if (events_happens () = 6) then
{
Kill Resource Agent of the destroyed resource;
Kills LBC Agent of the destroyed resource;
Kills Worker Agents for the destroyed resource;
Removes information of the destroyed resource from table of resources information
Updates the table of resources information;
}
Diffuses Cluster Load to other Cluster Agents;}
```

```
AgentLBC: Selection policy Algorithm
Input: AgentWorkers info
Output: AgentWorkers list are sorted by the ascending order of their credit value, selected
AgentWorker
{
   Orders the list of Worker Agents by ascending order of their Credit values;
   Selects the first Worker Agent from the list for migration;
   Sends this information for Migration Agent;
}
```

```
Cluster Agent: location policy algorithm
Input: table of resources information, LoadR,Loadcluster
Output: Sender Resource, Receiver Resource
{
if (events_happens () = 7)//cluster is saturated
intra-grid load balancing algorithm
Else
If (events_happens () =8) then
{
Partitions Table of resources information into overloaded resources table (OLD), under-loaded
resources table (ULD) and balanced resources table (BLD)
OLD ← φ; ULD ← φ; BLD ← φ
```

```
For every resource_i of cluster do
{
If (resource_i is saturated) then OLD ← OLD ∪ resource_i;
Else Switch
Case 1:
Load_R > B_threshold: OLD ← OLD ∪ resource_i; /* B_threshold is balanced threshold */
Case 2:
Load_R < B_threshold: ULD ← ULD ∪ resource_i;
Case3:
Load_R = B_threshold: BLD ← BLD∪ resource_i;
Sort OLD by descending order relative to their Load_R;
Sort ULD by ascending order relative to their Load_R;
Selects the first resource of OLD list as sender resource;
Selects the first resource of ULD list as receiver resource;
Sends this information for Migration Agent;
```

```
Migration Agent: Worker Agent Migration algorithm
Input: Sender Resource, Receiver Resource
Output: an Acknowledgment
Receives Sender Resource and Receiver Resource from its related Cluster Agent.
Sends migration request for AMS agent;
If receives an authentication message from AMS agent then
{
Sends a request message for Dynamic Library Agent of the receiver resource;
DL Agent sends code for the Worker Agent;
Worker Agent migrates itself to the receiver resource;
Waits for an Acknowledgment from the Dynamic Library Agent of receiver resource;
Sends an Acknowledgment for its related Cluster Agent;
}
```

2.2.2 Intra grid load balancing algorithm

Load balancing at this level is used if the Cluster Agent fails to balance its load among its related resources. In this case, each overloaded cluster migrates Worker Agents from its overloaded resources to underloaded clusters. In contrast to the intra-cluster level, we should consider the communication cost among clusters. Knowing the global state of each cluster, the overloaded cluster can send its Worker Agents for under-loaded clusters. The selected under-loaded clusters are those that require minimal communication cost for migrating agents from overloaded clusters. The agent can be transferred only if the sum of its latency in the source cluster and cost transfer is lower than its latency on the receiver cluster. This assumption will avoid making useless agent migration.

We associate a period to each Cluster Agent, during which each Cluster Agent sends its current load information to the other clusters. So, a Cluster Agent can receive new load information about another one at any time. This updated information will be considered in the next period.

```
Cluster Agent: intra-grid load balancing algorithm
Input: Load_cluster
```

```
Output: Sender Resource, Receiver Resource
{
If (events_happens () =7) then
{
Receives Load_cluster of other clusters of grid;
Collects Load_cluster in the table of clusters information
Sort table of clusters information by ascending order relative to their load
Select the first cluster as receiver cluster;
Sorts the resources of receiver cluster by ascending order of their load
Receiver Resource = the first resource of list of resources in receiver cluster
Sorts the resources of current cluster by descending order of their load
Sender Resource = the first resource of list of resources in sender cluster
Sorts Worker Agents of first resource of current cluster by selection policy and communication cost;
Sends this information for the Migration Agent
}
```

3. Implementation

We implemented a system prototype using JADE [6] (Java Agent Development Framework) for agent implementation, and Alea 2 [7] (Job Scheduling Simulator based on GridSim) as a simulator of the grid. Alea 2 is based on GridSim Toolkit [8] and represents an extension that contains better tools for scheduling algorithm implementation visualization competency and an upper speed of simulations.

To find the constant H for calculating the higher threshold, we execute our load balancing method 10 times for the different values of H = 0.5, 0.6, 0.7, 0.8, 0.9, and observed number of migration.

Figure 3 demonstrates the number of migration for the different values of H threshold. The number of migration augments with H threshold values but when the value of H threshold changes to 0.9 and 1, the number of migration is augmenting intensely. So we set the value of H threshold at 0.9.

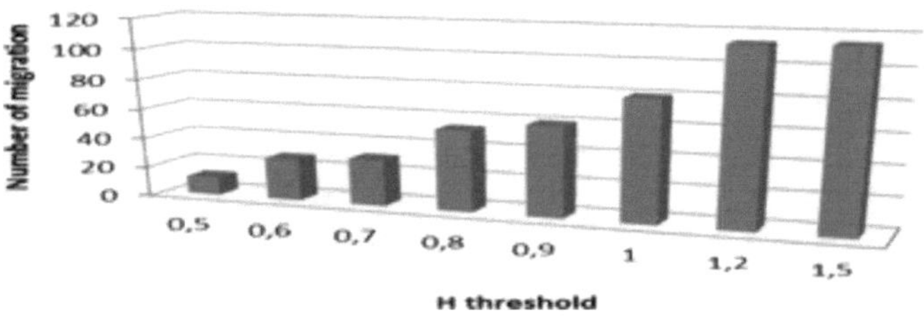

Figure 3.
Number of migration on different value of H.

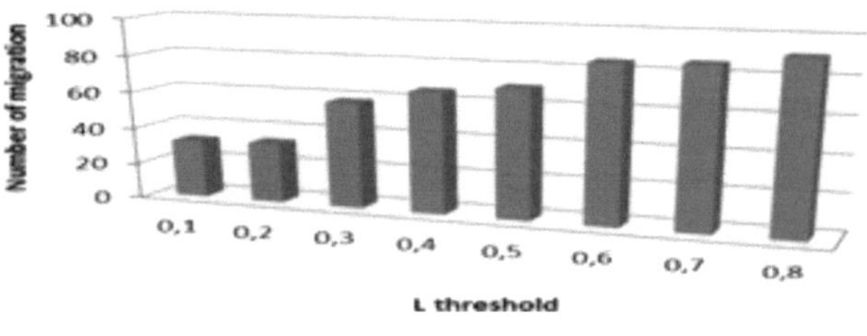

Figure 4.
Number of migration on different value of L.

In **Figure 4**, we are using the H threshold = 0.9. So, to find the best value of the lower threshold we executed our load balancing algorithm 10 times for the different values of the L threshold L = 0.1, 0.2, 0.3, 0.4, 0.5, 0.6, 0.7, 0.8, and we observed the number of migration. We found that number of migration augmented with the value of L threshold. It offers the best result at L = 0.3.

3.1 Workload

We modeled the complex data set from the National Grid of Czech republic MetaCentrum, these data permit us to implement very realistic simulations. Also, it offers information about machine failures and specific job requirements and that information influences the quality of solutions generated by the scheduling algorithms. Job description includes (Job ID, user, queue, number processors used, etc.). Also, the description of clusters includes complete information with RAM size, CPU speed, CPU architecture, operating system, and the list of supported properties (cluster location, allowed queue (s), and network interface, etc.). Additionally, information machines were in maintenance (failure/restart). Finally, the list of queues containing their time limits and priorities is provided. More details on the trace file used can be found at [9].

3.2 The simulation environment

A class library was developed that simulates the activities of an agent platform. This library, called ABLBM (Agent-based load balancing), includes the classes: Grid Agent, Cluster Agent, Migration Agent, LBC Agent, and Resource Agent. The simulation is initialized by the Grid Agent class which makes instances of resources, jobs, and other entities as required by the GridSim standard. Grid Agent reads information describing the grid resources and jobs from a data file, reads the jobs from the data_set file, and dynamically produces the job instances over time. **Figure 5** specifies the Grid Resource parameters such as resource ID, resource's CPU speed, and resource's memory capacity. Next, Grid Agent lists all the available grid resources within the grid environment. When the simulation time is equal to the job submission time, the Grid Agent starts the Cluster Agent and dynamically sends the jobs created for the Resource Agents over time.

Based on its own load and the estimated balance threshold, Cluster Agent analyzes the load state of the cluster. In the imbalance state, Cluster Agent defines the

Figure 5.
Grid agent interface.

Figure 6.
Cluster agent interface.

overloaded resources (sources) and the underloaded ones (receivers), depending on their load information by using the threshold values. Grid Agent and Cluster Agent interfaces are shown in **Figures 5** and **6**.

3.3 Model comparison with some works

Model	System configuration	Load information gathering policy	Selection policy	Location policy	Decision making	Migration condition	Implementation
ABLBM	The system contains a set of computing resources hierarchy of control, with six types of agents	Event-based information gathering	Credit -based concept	receiver resource is the most under loaded and it has the highest communication load with the migrated Agent	Migration decision is taken by Cluster Agent	Cluster state is unbalanced;	Jade [6] + Alea2 [7] simulator
VM, dynamic balancing [10]	The system contains entity, federate, VM, and host with migration management agent	periodic-based information gathering	computation and communication cost	receiver resource is the least loaded host	Migration decision is taken by migration management agent	host is over-loaded,	AST-RTI [11] version 2.0 + C+ +
LB in distributed MAS [4]	The system contains a set of nodes decentralized in control, with seven agents	Event-based information gathering	Credit -based concept	The destination node is the node with the least LC (Location Credit) value	Migration decision is taken locally by the LBC Agent	Local load value is greater than the load threshold value	Java + Jade
A2LB [12]	The system contains a set of VMs centralized in control, with three agents	periodic-based information gathering	Not cited	receiver VM having desired configuration	Migration decision is taken by Load agent	fitness value of a VM becomes less than or equal to threshold value	Java
N LB WITH STRONG MIGR ATION IN AN	The system contains a set of machines centralized in	periodic-based information gathering	task cost	receiver is available worker agent in	Migration decision is taken by	network traffic analysis	Jade

Model	System configuration	Load information gathering policy	Selection policy	Location policy	Decision making	Migration condition	Implementation
AGENT BASED GRID SYSTEM USING CSP APPROACH [13]	control, with five agents			the desired container	migration manager		

4. Conclusion

Recognizing key factors to prove the convergence of grid and MAS and models is not a simple task. We note that the current state of GRID and MAS research activities are necessarily developed to enable justifying the study of the path towards an integration of the two fields.

We have presented a theoretical comparison between some related works and the proposed model. The proposed model has some unique features. It is hierarchical, which facilitates the circulation of information through the tree and defines the flow of messages between agents. Also, the proposed Agent-based load balancing model uses an event-driven information gathering policy, the latter being especially beneficial in terms of economy of usage of network resources. Furthermore, it can achieve excellent performance with significantly less computational load and system instability than a periodic information gathering policy. To select the migrating agent, we use the credit-based concept, accordingly, some factors are considered to calculate the credit value. Moreover, in the selection of receiver resources, we take into consideration the resource loads and the communication between the receiver resources and the migrating agent for avoiding the migration for external resources and reducing the communication cost. The migration decision is taken locally by Cluster Agent, where each cluster agent to balance its load among its associated resources. If it fails, the Cluster Agent migrates worker agents to underloaded clusters based on the load information received by other clusters. Finally, it supports flexibility and expandability, thus, various intelligent agents have been deployed to decrease system complexity by modularization. Moreover, it is easy to modify its components, and add more features and functions to it.

In theory, the multi-agent architecture of load balancing systems introduces important improvements, such as better average performance when one computer is not working and a lower system-error probability. In terms of the development process, fault-tolerance, and scalability, the agent approach offered the expected improvements, both in objective real-world measurements and in the subjective observations of designers, developers, and users.

On another hand, we could not overcome several well-known problems when designing distributed systems. For example, handling failed entities, synchronization problems, and query-response-related issues turned out to be the same as in any distributed programming. It is important to be aware of the advantages and disadvantages of the agent and non-agent approaches, but the most important point is whether the advantages prevail. For load balancing systems, our theoretical analysis and practical experiences both indicate that the advantages of agent-based load balancing systems clearly be more than the observed disadvantages.

The system performance was not studied yet. Thus, there is a need to analyze execution efficiency and compare it to available Agent-based load balancing platform evaluations. Further research is going to concentrate on execution performance.

Author details

Wided Ali* and Fatima Bouakkaz
Larbi Tebessi University, Tebessa, Algeria

*Address all correspondence to: wided.ali@univ-tebessa.dz

References

[1] A. Wided, K. Okba, and B. Fatima. Load balancing with Job Migration Algorithm for improving performance on grid computing: Experimental Results. Advances in Distributed Computing and Artificial Intelligence Journal, 2019; 8(4): 5–18. DOI:10.14201/ADCAIJ201984518

[2] A. Wided, K. Okba . A new agent based load balancing model for improving the grid performance. Multiagent and Grid Systems Journal, 2020; 16(2):153–170. DOI: 10.3233/MGS-200326.

[3] Chow K-P, Kwok Y-K. On load balancing for distributed multiagent computing. IEEE Trans Parallel Distrib Syst ,2002;13(8):1153–61.

[4] A.M. Metawei, G. Salma,M.H. Sahar , M.N.Salwa .'Load balancing in distributed multi-agent computing systems', Ain Shams Engineering Journal,2012, 3(3):237–249.

[5] R. Gupta . Coding categorical variables in regression models: dummy and effect coding.Cornell Statistical Consulting Unit,2008,4(2):202–210.

[6] F.L. Bellifemine, G.Caire, and D. Greenwood, Developing Multi-Agent Systems with JADE. John Wi-ley & Sons,2007, NJ. ISBN: 978–0–470-05747-6

[7] D. Klusáček and H.Rudová. Alea 2 job scheduling simulator. In Proceedings of the 3rd International Conference on Simulation Tools and Techniques (SIMUTools 2010), Torremolinos, MalaMA, Spain. DOI: 10.4108/ICST.SIMUTOOLS2010.8722

[8] R.Buyya, and M.Murshed. Gridsim: a toolkit for the modeling and simulation of distributed resource management and scheduling for grid computing, The Journal of Concurrency and Computation: Practice and Experience (CCPE),2002, 14:13–15. DOI: 10.1002/cpe.710

[9] N. Li, X.-Y. Peng, M.-H. Zhang, M. Wang, and G.-H. Gong, Multimedia communication over HLA/RTI, SimulationModelling Practice and Theory,2006,14(2): 161–176. https://doi.org/10.1016/j.simpat.2005.03.003

[10] A.Singh,D. Juneja, M.Malhotra. Autonomous agent based load balancing algorithm in cloud computing. International Conference on Advanced Computing Technologies and Applications, 2015. DOI: 10.1016/j.procs.2015.03.168

[11] X. Song, Y. Ma, D.Teng. A load balancing scheme using federate migration based on virtual machines for cloud simulations, Mathematical Problems in Engineering, 2015,pp.1–11. https://doi.org/10.1155/2015/506432

[12] Z. A .Sayar and N.Erdogan. Network load balancing with strong migration in an agent based grid using CSP Approach. International Journal of Grid Computing & Applications (IJGCA),2012, 3(4),43–53. DOI: 10.5121/ijgca.2012.3404

[13] http://www.cs.huji.ac.il/labs/parallel/workload/l_metacentrum

Chapter 6

A Food Recommender Based on Frequent Sets of Food Mining Using Image Recognition

Thunchanok Tangpong, Somkiet Leanghirun, Aran Hansuebsai and Kosuke Takano

Abstract

Food recommendation is an important service in our life. To set a system, we searched a set of food images from social network which were shared or reviewed on the web, including the information that people actually chose in daily life. In the field of representation learning, we proposed a scalable architecture for integrating different deep neural networks (DNNs) with a reliability score of DNN. This allowed the integrated DNN to select a suitable recognition result obtained from the different DNNs that were independently constructed. The frequent set of foods extracted from food images was applied to *Apriori* data mining algorithm for the food recommendation process. In this study, we evaluated the feasibility of our proposed method.

Keywords: food recommender, food data mining, image recognition, deep neural network, data mining algorithm

1. Introduction

People are now consuming more high energy foods, fats and meat, and most of them do not eat enough fruit, vegetables and other dietary fiber. The make-up of a diversified and combined food will vary depending on individual characteristics such as age, gender, lifestyle and degree of physical activity, cultural context, locally available foods and dietary customs. While the increase of food services plays an important role in food market and business, the food service industry is a vital part of economy [1–3]. The business relies on its management to control costs, keep customers happy, and ensure smooth operations on a daily basis. There are many different types of food service types or procedures, but the major category of the food service is Buffet and Family style services.

Being an industry that serves the human needs, the food service is always the forefront of innovation. Even the food safety practices have been continuously updated along with legislation, the service is still facing a number of issues such as food technologies and consumer trends. For example, a customer wants to know the food information in order to have a set of food on the table. Foreigners who are not familiar with the local foods would like to enjoy having foods in a common style in those countries. In addition, a food designer is seeking a new decoration idea for the beautification of foods on plate. Food recommendation therefore is an important tool to enrich our life. It can be defined as a system that will recommend items to the users/customers within an environment depending on their past activities.

There was demonstration that digital imaging could estimate food information in many environments and it had many advantages over other methods [4, 5]. However, to derive the food information such as food type, food combination and portion size from food images remains uncertainty.

Accordingly, to achieve better food recommendation, it would be useful to analyze foods that people are actually eating in daily life. POS (Point of Sale) is a large-scale transaction data relevant to the customer's purchase tendency [6]. The data is used only by individual store and not open for public. Therefore we cannot analyze the food purchase data among different stores, restaurants, canteens, and so on. *Amazon Go* is a smart store where a purchase transaction can be detected by a camera. Comparing with the POS system, the *Amazon Go* provides an automatic management of information about the foods that people bought, including the items that associated with those products and the appearance of each item with individual preference [7]. In addition, the system can predict the expectation of the market. Note that this kind of *Amazon-Go-like* system has similar constraint for collecting big data. The obtained database from different sources thus is varied. Therefore we can say that there is a limitation of integrating the purchase transaction over different database as shown in **Figure 1**.

From the diagram, it seems to be meaningful to create a system that analyzes the big data of food-images from various communities including companies, restaurants, and groups in social network system for extracting the people's preference of food combination, food design, and food appearance by applying the image recognition technology. In the field of learning representation, there are many established models such as Artificial Neural Network (ANN), Convolutional Neural Network (CNN) and Recurrent Neural Network (RNN).

ANN is a broad term that encompasses any form of deep learning model. It can be either shallow or deep depending on the number of hidden layers. CNNs are designed specifically for computer vision. They are different from standard layers of ANNs as they are constructed to receive and process pixel data. RNNs are the "time series version" of ANNs. They are meant to process the sequences of data. They are at the basis of forecasting models and language models. The most common kind of recurrent layers are called LSTM (Long Short Term Memory) and GRU (Gated Recurrent Units). They contain a series of small, in-scale ANNs that are able

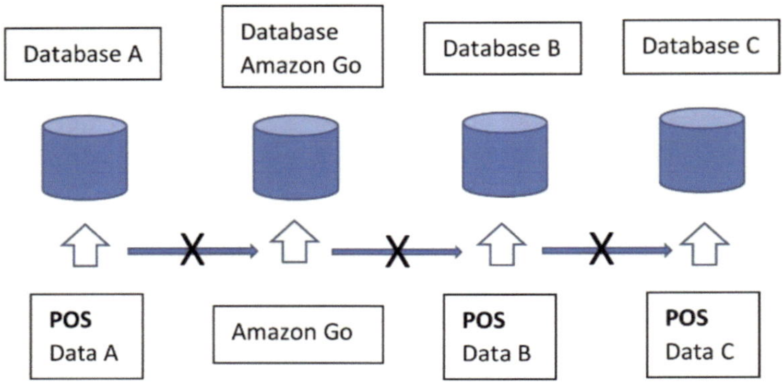

Figure 1.
Limitation of integrating the purchase transaction over different database.

to choose the existed information they want to let it flow through the model. That is how they establish the "memory".

However, some problems for food recognition by these models may occur as there are tremendous number of foods. In addition, it remains a challenging issue due to the complexity of emotional expressions, arising from the food variety, gender differentiation, cross culture and age-related differences [8, 9]. Thus, it is hard to find the proper model that can recognize all of them.

2. Related work

Food image recognition is one of the promising applications of visual object application, as it will help estimate food characteristics and analyze people's eating choices for daily life. Many research works represented food recognition more practical by using the convolutional neural network (CNN) model [10–12]. CNN was applied to the tasks of food detection and recognition through parameter optimization. A dataset of the most frequent food items was constructed in a publicly available food-logging system. The CNN showed significantly higher accuracy than a conventional method did. In addition, the color feature is not always helpful for improving the accuracy by comparing the results of two group of controlled trials. It was reported that the achievement of CNN model was at 70–80% on one dataset and 60% on the multi-food dataset. The improvements could be expected by collecting more images and optimizing the network architecture and hyper-parameters.

For example, Deep Convolutional Neural Network (DCNN) was introduced for food recognition based on a combination of CNN-related techniques such as pre-training with the large-scale ImageNet data, fine-tuning and activation features extracted from the pre-trained CNN [13, 14]. Another approach was based on two main steps: firstly, to produce a food activation map on the input image (i.e. heat map of probabilities) for generating bounding boxes proposals and, secondly, to recognize each of the food types or food-related objects presented in each bounding box [15]. Interestingly, the Max-Pooling function was used for the data and the features extracted from this function were used to train the network. An accuracy of 86.97% for the classes of the FOOD-101 data set was recognized [16]. It was found that the image classification could be extended using prominent features that could categorize food images. Note that the feature-based approach and the multi-level classification approach (hierarchical approach) were highly appreciable to avoid mis-classifications when the number of classes was increased. However, these methodologies consumed high computational time.

2.1 Concept of convolutional neural network (CNN)

Convolutional neural network is a network that employs a mathematical operation called convolution. There are two main processes in CNN architecture – Learning extraction and Classification [17].

Step-1: Learning extraction

This process executes feature extraction from images through the following three layers -

a. Convolution layer: this is the first layer to extract features from an input image. There are matrix filters (feature map) that multiplies with image in order to extract some features such as edge, blur, and color.

b. Activation layer: this layer is used to increase non-linearity of the network without affecting receptive fields of convolution layer. The output is $f(x) = \max(0,x)$.

c. Pooling layer: this layer reduces the number of parameters when the images are too large. This operation means that the layer reduces the dimensionality of each map but keeps the important information.

Step-2: Classification
This process executes image classification. There are two main layers as follows:

a. Fully connected layer (FC layer): to connect every neuron in one layer to every neuron in another layer. We flattened our matrix into vector and feed it into a fully connected layer like neural network.

b. Softmax layer: A special kind of activation layer, usually at the end of FC layer outputs. It produces a discrete probability distribution vector.

At this stage, the pretrained models such as *AlexNet, VGGNet, GoogLeNet*, and *ResNet* will be applied in order to integrate the CNNs. The procedure is to merge the multiple CNNs with fixed number of CNNs and trained them after merging.

2.2 Association rule

Association rule is utilized in data mining phase as it is a machine learning method which finds the relationship between the items based on the frequency of item sets [18, 19]. To do this, a mathematical algorithm is needed to arrange the frequent item sets, for extracting association rule of food sets.

There are three measures in association rule task as shown in **Figure 2**:

a. Support: It indicates how often the items appear in the data-set.

b. Confidence: It indicates how often a rule is found to be true.

c. Lift: It indicates how the *antecedent* and the *consequent* are related to one another. If the Lift value is 1, it means that the *antecedent* and the *consequent* are independent. If the Lift value is less than 1, it means that the *antecedent* has negative effect on occurrence on the *consequent*. In addition, if the Lift value is more than 1, it means that the *antecedent* and the *consequent* are dependent.

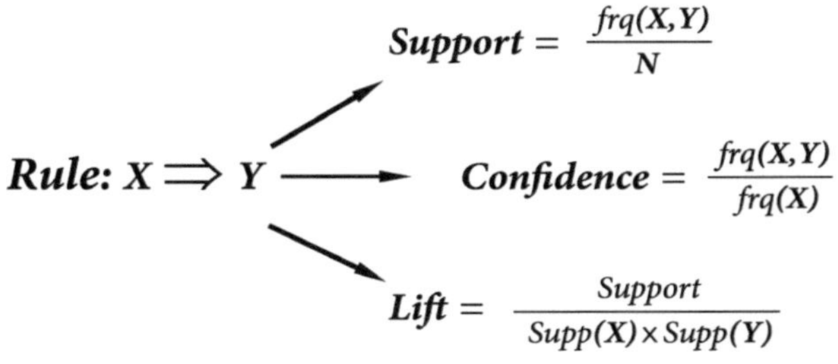

Figure 2.
Basic terminologies of association rule measure.

3. Proposed method

As the uncertainty of convolutional architecture due to the fix number of CNNs and the interpretability after merging of CNNs [20]. Simpler and more highly scalable method to integrate the multiple networks is necessary and therefore there are three features in consideration - liability score for the system, no further training after integration, and high scalability. Deep neural network (DNN) may be an alternative choice to solve this problem [21]. It provides the neural basis for efficient visual object recognition in humans. Its architecture comprises more than three layers. Each of layers contains a combination of convolution, max-pooling and normalization stages, whereas these layers are fully connected. It inherently fuses the process of feature extraction with classification into learning using Fuzzy Support Vector Machine (FSVM) and enables the decision making [22, 23]. Many efforts were made to speed up both the training time as well as inference time of DNNs. Since the flexibility and the performance scalability to deal with various types of networks are crucial requirement of the DNN accelerator design [24], we therefore proposed a scalable architecture for integrating different deep neural networks with a reliability score to increase the probability to return correct class as the result of food recognition. The reliability score allowed the integrated DNN to select a suitable recognition result obtained from the different DNNs that were independently constructed. In this study, we evaluated the feasibility of our proposed method.

The frequent set of foods extracted from food images was applied to a data mining algorithm such as the *Apriori* algorithm for the food recommendation process. **Figure 3** shows the schematic diagram of food recommender. This system would recommend a set of foods suitable for users based on association rule, which were extracted by food set mining from food images.

The process of food recognition and extraction of association rule is given in **Figure 4**. Firstly, the food set images from database were collected. Secondly, the reliability score was calculated by Eq. (1). Then the food recognition and

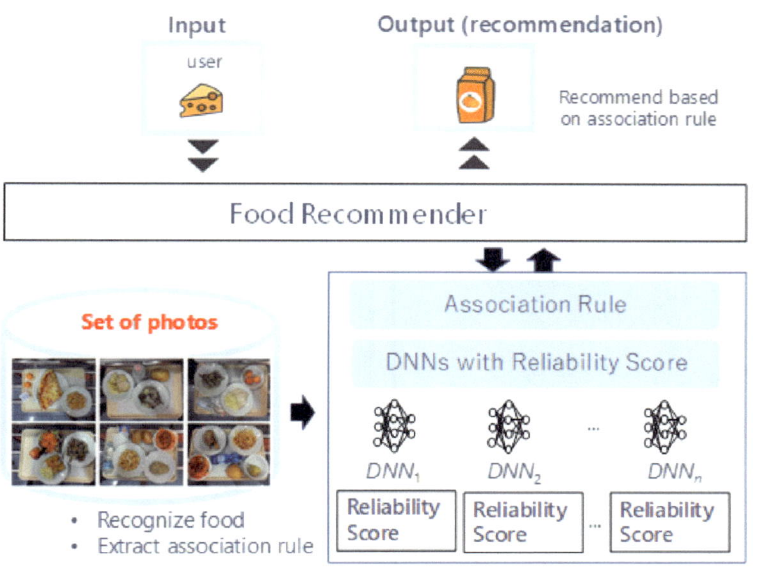

Figure 3.
Schematic diagram of food recommender.

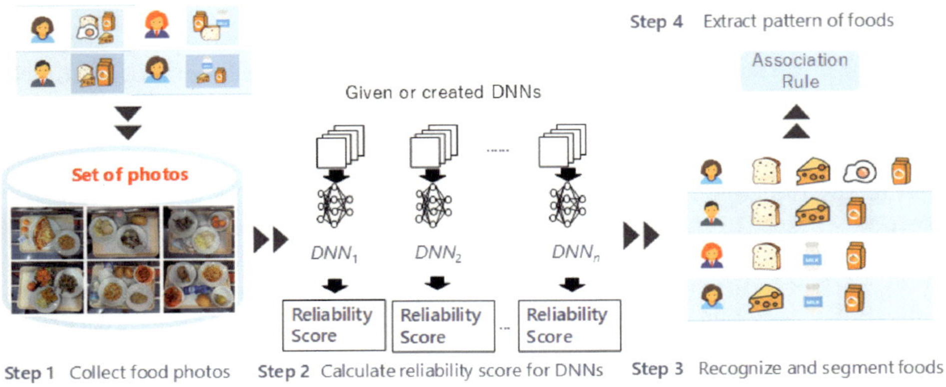

Figure 4.
Process of recognition of food set images and extraction of association rule.

segmentation from the images were operated using DNNs. Finally, the extraction of association rule was obtained as the frequent food sets.

$$\text{Reliability score} = \text{A} \times \text{C} \times \text{I} \times \text{D} \tag{1}$$

where A, C, I, and D represented the accuracy of the learning process, number of classes, number of leaning images, and difference between learning data and test data, respectively.

We combined several DNNs and calculated new probability with reliability scores as shown in **Figure 5**. Each DNN has different reliability score depending on following factors:

- accuracy of the learning process
- number of classes
- number of learning images
- difference between learning data and test data

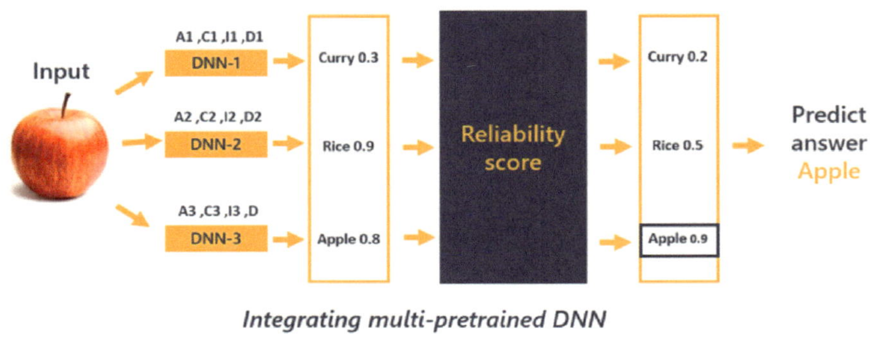

Figure 5.
The feature of proposed method.

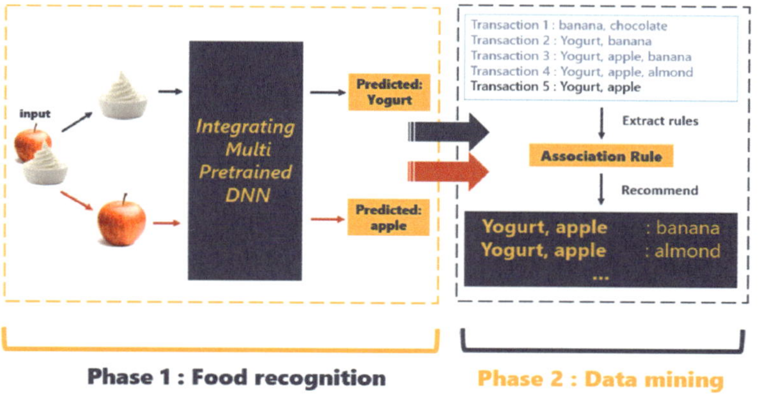

Figure 6.
Workflow of proposed food recommender.

If the learning data and the test data are similar, the accuracy will be high but it may be not reliable. As we test with the unseen data, the DNN may predict wrong answer. Therefore, the difference between the learning data and the test data is necessary.

We calculated the reliability score and the weight output (W) of fully connected layer as the new probability using Eq. (2). The label of the new probability as the predicted result was provided.

$$\text{New probability} = \text{W} \times \text{Reliability score} \tag{2}$$

Accordingly, the food set could be recognized from food images using different DNNs with the reliability scores as shown in **Figure 6**. Based on the recognition results, transactions of food were formed and applied to conventional association in the phase of data mining.

4. Experimental and evaluation

We implemented our prototype of merging the results from different DNNs using MATLAB. The performance of recognition accuracy and the relationship between the recognition accuracy and the number of classes were evaluated. We used the dataset of food images for creating the DNNs and evaluated them as shown in **Table 1**. Three DNNs with different number of recognition classes for each data-set were created as given in **Table 2**. In addition, we made each DNN from *Scratch* by applying the transfer learning using *GoogLeNet*. Accordingly, we totally had 18 DNNs in this experiment.

Recognition accuracy was calculated using the following equation:

$$\text{Accuracy} = (\text{TP} + \text{TN}) / (\text{TP} + \text{TN} + \text{FP} + \text{FN}) \tag{3}$$

where TP, TN, FP, and FN were True Positive, True Negative, False Positive, and False Negative respectively.

Type of dataset	Dataset	Number of classes	Number of images
Pretrained	Food-101	101	101,000
Pretrained	UEC-256	256	31,395
Pretrained	Fruit-360	81	77,917
Test	UNIMIB2016	33	1,047

Table 1.
Dataset of food images.

Dataset	Number of classes	*Scratch*	*GoogLeNet*
food-101	34	DNN_1^{food}	DNN_1^{food*}
	50	DNN_2^{food}	DNN_2^{food*}
	101	DNN_3^{food}	DNN_3^{food*}
uec-256	85	DNN_1^{uec}	DNN_1^{uec*}
	128	DNN_2^{uec}	DNN_2^{uec*}
	256	DNN_3^{uec}	DNN_3^{uec*}
fruit-360	27	DNN_1^{fruit}	DNN_1^{fruit*}
	40	DNN_2^{fruit}	DNN_2^{fruit*}
	81	DNN_3^{fruit}	DNN_3^{fruit*}

Table 2.
Deep neural network with different number of classes.

No.	Number of DNNs	Type of DNN	Dataset
1	1	*GoogLeNet*	Food-101
2	2	*GoogLeNet*	Food-101 + UEC-256
3	3	*GoogLeNet*	Food-101 + UEC-256 + Fruit-360
4	1	*Scratch*	Food-101
5	2	*Scratch*	Food-101 + UEC-256
6	3	*Scratch*	Food-101 + UEC-256 + Fruit-360

Table 3.
Integrated deep neural network.

	Types of food label
1	Predicted label by integrated DNN using *GoogLeNet*
2	Predicted label by integrated DNN made from *Scratch*
3	Corrected label (no prediction)

Table 4.
Food labels used for association rule.

To evaluate the performance of integrated deep neural network, we created two single DNNs and four integrated DNNs as shown in **Table 3**. The *UNIMIB2016* dataset for the test was employed. Recognition accuracy then was calculated using Eq. (3).

DOI: http://dx.doi.org/10.5772/intechopen.97186

To evaluate the accuracy of extracted frequent food set, we employed three food labels as shown in **Table 4** for extracting the association rule.

5. Results and discussion

Figure 7 shows the recognition accuracy of DNN by food-101 dataset, uec-256 dataset, and fruit-360 dataset respectively. There was a relationship between the recognition accuracy of DNN and the increase of the number of class for each database. It was found that the recognition accuracy of DNN slightly decreased according to the increase of the number of recognition classes. In addition, the performance of DNNs where *GoogLeNet* applied was higher than the DNNs made from *Scratch*.

Figure 8 shows the result of integrated deep neural network. It implied that if the number of networks was increased, the recognition accuracy of the integrated

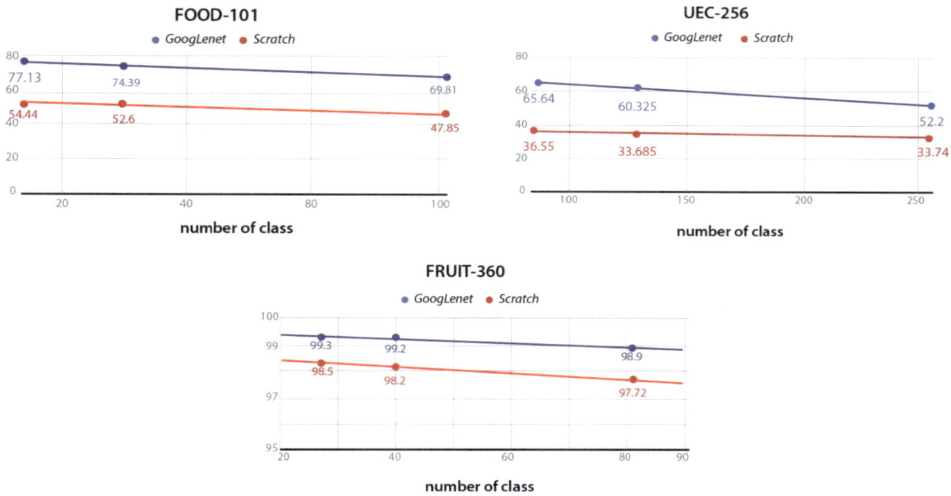

Figure 7.
Recognition results of food-101, uec-256 and fruit-360.

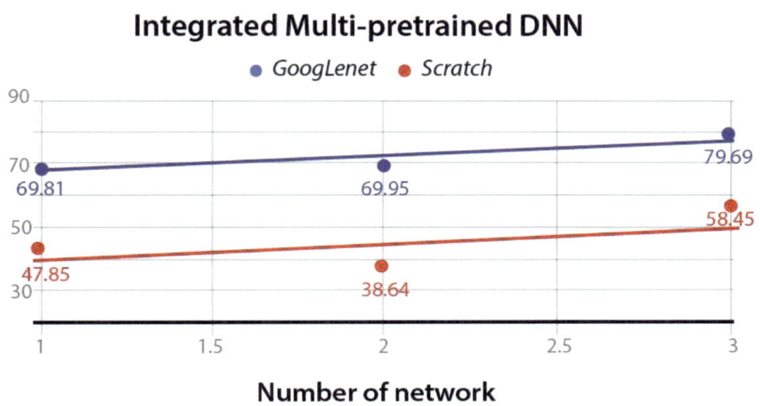

Figure 8.
Result of integrated deep neural network.

DNNs would be enhanced. In addition, it was found that the performance of DNNs where *GoogLeNet* applied was higher than the DNNs made from *Scratch*. It is because the proposed reliability score allowed the integrated DNNs to select a suitable recognition result obtained from the three different networks, which were constructed from the food-101, the uec-256 and the fruit-360 dataset. Note that although the DNN constructed from the fruit-360 dataset showed the high accuracy of 97.72% for 10 classes recognition, it could not return a suitable result for an image of general food other than a fruit. This is the disadvantage of a DNN constructed from a specific image dataset.

Tables 5–7 show the results of food labels where the association rules were sampled from the whole results. It was found that the number of bad and good results for "Kiwi, Doughnut" was almost equal. While "Pineapple mini and Ice-cream" in **Table 6** gave better results. It was confirmed that the number of good results in the integrated networks using *GoogleNet* was preferable. In **Table 7** "Steak and French fries" showed good result relevant to the test data.

Antecedents	Consequents	Result
Kiwi, Doughnut	Pineapple, Orange	Good
Kiwi, Doughnut	Orange, Miso soup	Bad
Kiwi, Doughnut	Spaghetti Bolognese, Orange	Good
Kiwi, Doughnut	Orange, Spam musubi	Bad
Kiwi, Doughnut	Pineapple, Miso soup	Bad
Kiwi, Doughnut	Pineapple, Spaghetti Bolognese	Good
Kiwi, Doughnut	Pineapple, Spam musubi	Bad
Kiwi, Doughnut	Spaghetti Bolognese, Miso soup	Bad
Kiwi, Doughnut	Spam musubi, Miso soup	Good
Kiwi, Doughnut	Spaghetti Bolognese, Spam musubi	Bad

Table 5.
Results of integrated DNNs made from Scratch.

Antecedents	Consequents	Result
Pineapple mini, Ice-cream	Apple red/yellow	Good
Pineapple mini, Ice-cream	Cantaloupe	Good
Pineapple mini, Ice-cream	Cocos	Good
Pineapple mini, Ice-cream	French loaf	Good
Pineapple mini, Ice-cream	Granadilla	Bad
Pineapple mini, Ice-cream	Grapefruit pink	Good
Pineapple mini, Ice-cream	Kiwi	Good
Pineapple mini, Ice-cream	Peach flat	Good
Pineapple mini, Ice-cream	Peach abate	Good
Pineapple mini, Ice-cream	Pitahaya Red	Good

Table 6.
Results of integrated DNN using GoogLeNet.

Antecedents	Consequents	Result
Steak, French fries	Banana, Roll bread	Good
Steak, French fries	Baklava, Orange	Good
Steak, French fries	Roll bread, Orange	Good
Steak, French fries	Spaghetti, Orange	Good
Steak, French fries	Baklava, Roll bread	Bad
Steak, French fries	Spaghetti, Baklava	Good
Steak, French fries	Spaghetti, Roll bread	Good
Steak, French fries	Yogurt, Roll bread	Good
Steak, French fries	Spaghetti, Yogurt	Good
Steak, French fries	Spaghetti	Good

Table 7.
Results of corrected labels.

6. Conclusion

In food recognition phase, integrated networks (DNNs) showed higher recognition accuracy (80%) than a single network. Since the proposed reliability score allowed the integrated networks to select a suitable recognition result obtained from the different network with different domains. The performance of networks where *GoogLeNet* applied gave higher recognition accuracy. In addition, it was found that when we used the test dataset different from the trained dataset, we could not get the suitable results.

In Data mining phase, we could extract some meaningful rules by applying the *Apriori* algorithm to recognize the results of canteen image dataset. In our future work, we will modify this system in recognition phase and will increase the performance of the networks. We will evaluate the effectiveness of modified system using bigger size of food data. In addition, we are developing visual food mining using mixed model of DNN and RNN (recurrent neural networks) for continuing our research.

Acknowledgements

This research is a part of academic cooperation between Chulalongkorn University, Thailand and Kanagawa Institute of Technology (KAIT), Japan. Authors would like to thank KAIT for providing scholarship and deeply appreciate Professor Kosuke Takano for his advice and facility in his Laboratory at KAIT.

Conflict of interest

The authors declare no potential conflict of interest.

Author details

Thunchanok Tangpong[1], Somkiet Leanghirun[2], Aran Hansuebsai[2*]
and Kosuke Takano[3]

1 Department of Mathematics and Computer Science, Faculty of Science,
Chulalongkorn University, Thailand

2 Department of Imaging and Printing Technology, Faculty of Science,
Chulalongkorn University, Thailand

3 Department of Information and Computer Sciences, Faculty of Information
Technology, Kanagawa Institute of Technology, Japan

*Address all correspondence to: aran.h@chula.ac.th

References

[1] Johns N., Pine R. Consumer behavior in the food service industry: a review. Int. J. of Hospitality Management. 2002;21(2):119-134

[2] Gwo-Hshiung T., Hung-Fan C. Applying Importance-Performance Analysis as a Service Quality Measure in Food Service Industry. J. of Technology Management & Innovation. 2011;6(3). DOI: 10.4067/S0718-27242011000300008

[3] Abdullah F., Abdurahman, A., Hamali J. Managing Customer Preference for the Foodservice Industry. Int. J. of Innovation, Management and Technology. 2011;2(6):525-533

[4] Zubair Hasan H.M., Khan H., Asif T., Hashmi S., Rafi M. Towards a transfer learning approach to food recommendations through food images. In: Proceedings of the 3rd International Conference on Machine Learning and Soft Computing. January 2019. Da Lat, Viet Nam, p. 99-105

[5] Liu C., Cao Y., Luo Y., Chen G., Vokkarane V., Ma Y. DeepFood: Deep Learning-Based Food Image Recognition for Computer-Aided Dietary Assessment. In: Proceedings of Int. Conference on Smart Homes and Health Telematics. May 2016, p. 37-48

[6] Inman J.J., Nikolova H. Healthy Choice: The Effect of SimplifiedPoint-of-Sale Nutritional Information on Consumer Food Choice Behavior. Journal of Marketing Research. 2015;52(6):817-835

[7] Polacco A., Backes K. The Amazon Go Concept: Implications, Applications and Sustainability. Journal of Business and Management. 2018;24(1):79-92

[8] Ding N., Sethu V., Epps J., Ambikairajah E. Speaker variability in emotion recognition-an adaptation based approach. In: Proceedings of the 2012 IEEE International Conference on Acoustics, Speech and Signal Processing (ICASSP), IEEE 2012. p. 5101-5104

[9] Mill A., Allik J., Realo A., Valk R. Age-related differences in emotion recognition ability: a cross-sectional study. Journal of Emotion. 2009:9(5):619

[10] Zhang W., Zhao D., Gong W., Li Z., Lu Q., Yang S. Food Image Recognition with Convolutional Neural Networks. In: Proceedings of 2015 IEEE 12th Intl Conference on Ubiquitous Intelligence and Computing. Beijing, China, 10-14 August, 2015.

[11] Kagaya H., Aizawa K., Ogawa M. Food Detection and Recognition Using Convolutional Neural Network. In: Proceedings of the 22nd ACM international conference on Multimedia. November 2014. p. 1085-1088

[12] Ng Y.S., Xue W., Wang W., Qi P. Convolutional Neural Networks for Food Image Recognition: An Experimental Study. In: Proceedings of the 5th International Workshop on Multimedia Assisted Dietary Management. October 2019. p. 33-41

[13] Kowano Y., Yanai K. Food image recognition with deep convolutional features. In: Proceedings of the 2014 ACM International Joint Conference on Pervasive and Ubiquitous Computing: Adjunct Publication. September 2014, p. 589-593

[14] Yanai K., Kawano Y. Food image recognition using deep convolutional network with pre-training and fine-tuning. In: Proceedings of 2015 IEEE International Conference on Multimedia & Expo Workshops (ICMEW). June 2015

[15] Bolanos M., Radeva P. Simultaneous Food Localization and Recognition. In: Proceedings of 23rd International

Conference on Pattern Recognition (ICPR). December 2016

[16] Attokaren D.J., Fernandes I.G., Sriram A., Srinivasa Murthy Y.V., Koolagudi S.G. Food classification from images using convolutional neural networks. In: Proceedings of 2017 IEEE Region 10 Conference (TENCON), Malaysia, November 2017, p. 2801-2806

[17] Saha S. A Comprehensive Guide to Convolutional Neural Networks – the ELI5 way. Available from: http//www.towardsdatascience.com [Accessed: 2020-06-12]

[18] Ziauddin Z., Kammal S., Khan K.Z., Khan M.I. Research on Association Rule Mining. Journal of Advances in Computational Mathematics and its Applications. 2012;2(1):226-236

[19] Traore B.B., Kamsu-Foguen B., Tangara F. Deep Convolution Neural Network for image recognition. Journal of Ecological Informatics. 2018;48:257-268

[20] Wickstrøm K., Kampffmeyer M., Jenssen R. Uncertainty and interpretability in convolutional neural networks for semantic segmentation of colorectal polyps. Journal of Medical Image Analysis. 2020; 60: 101619

[21] Zhou L., Zhang C., Liu F., Qiu Z., He Y. Application of Deep Learning Food: A review. Journal of Comprehensive Reviews in Food Science and Food Safety. 2019;18(6):1793-1811

[22] Cichy R.M., Khosla A., Pantazis D., Torralba A., Oliva A. Comparison of deep neural networks to spatio-temporal cortical dynamics of human visual object recognition reveals hierarchical correspondence. Journal of Scientific Reports. 2016; 6(1):27755

[23] Verma J.K., Paul S., Johr P. In: Book - Computational Intelligence and Its Applications in Healthcare. Academic Press. 2020. ISBN 978-0-12-820604-1

[24] Sakamoto R., Takata R., Ishii J., Kondo M., Nakamura H., Ohkubo T., Kojima T., Amano H. The Design and Implementation of Scalable Deep Neural Network Accelerator Core. In: Proceedings of 2017 IEEE 11th International Symposium on Embedded Multicore/Many-core Systems-on-Chip (MCSoC). Seoul, Korea. September 2017

Chapter 7

The Prospects for Creating Instruments for the Coordination of Activities of International Organizations in the Regulation of Artificial Intelligence

Valentina Petrovna Talimonchik

Abstract

The objective of the research is identifying the prospects for the development of instruments for coordinating the activities of international organizations on the regulation of artificial intelligence and elaborating proposals in relation to the mechanisms of cooperation of international organizations on the universal level on issues related to artificial intelligence. A complex of general scientific and philosophical methods, including the logical, comparative-legal, formal-legal, systemic-structural, problematic-theoretical methods, as well as methods of analysis and synthesis were used in the research. In the research it was found that Action Lines of the World Summit on the Information Society are working on issues that are discussed at the AI for Good Global Summit. The activities of the World Summit on the Information Society such as ICT regulation are more general in nature while those of the AI for Good Global Summit are more special. The problem of "international institutional competition" of the two discussion platforms can be resolved by ITU's efforts to coordinate the two discussion platforms and by supplementing the competence of UNGIS with issues of artificial intelligence. The findings can be used in activities of international organizations in execution of their functions of unification and harmonization of the international information law.

Keywords: international law, international organizations, artificial intelligence, information and communication systems, international institutional competition

1. Introduction

The theory of the information society was initially developed by researchers in social studies, and in the 21st century, its practical implementation began in the activities of international organizations.

There is currently no common opinion in the doctrine on the moment when the theory of the information society appeared. A. Matterlart [1] noted early origins of the theory of the information society. He began exploring theories of the information society from Leibniz (1646–1716) who was the first to arrange the set of numbers and gave it a strict hierarchy. Leibniz is also the author of the idea of a universal mathematical language, the so-called binary system, which was later used in cybernetics.

Christopher May began exploring the concept of the information society with the work of Fritz Machlup "The Production and Distribution of Knowledge in the United States", which was published in 1962 [2].

Without denying the achievements of thinkers of the 17th – 19th centuries, one should note that the first studies of the information society date back to the 1960s (Y. Hayashi, F. Machlup, and T. Umesao) [3].

One can use the following periodization of the development of the information society concept as proposed by C. May:

1. from 1962 to the mid-1970s, the analysis of the concept was focused solely on the USA;

2. from the second half of the 1970s to the early 1990s, information and communication technologies (ICT) began to develop intensively in rich and developed countries, and the scope for analysis expanded;

3. at present, analysis is focused on the potential and capabilities of the Internet and leads to widespread interest in the global information society [2].

At present, the theory of the information society has been reflected in a number of international documents. In particular, such documents include the Okinawa Charter on Global Information Society of July 22, 2000, the Declaration of Principles "Building the Information Society: a Global Challenge in the New Millennium", and the Plan of Action of the World Summit on the Information Society of December 12, 2003.

The problem of systematization of ideas about the information society is complicated by the fact that researchers often made assumptions of an ideal information society and social predictions, the reliability of which is too early to discuss.

In order to demonstrate the diversity of theories of the information society, let us use the classification by F. Webster [4]. He distinguished five groups of theories of the information society, namely, technological, economic, occupational, spatial, and cultural.

The diversity of theories of the information society is explained by the fact that there are many factors and phenomena interacting in the information society.

In our opinion, contemporary relations in the creation, distribution, receipt, and other acts for the circulation, storage, and destruction of information are characterized by the transformation of the object of such relations. Information and communication systems have appeared that include artificial intelligence, Big Data, neural networks, and distributed ledgers. It is hard to predict what information and communication systems will appear in the future.

Earlier, in the Plan of Action of the World Summit on the Information Society it was stated that the information society is an evolving structure that has reached different levels across the world, reflecting the different stages of development. At the present stage of development of the information society, one can speak of the widespread use of qualitatively new and in many respects 'revolutionary' information and communication technologies, the main of which is artificial intelligence.

The transformation of the object of information relations should lead to a review of the concept of the information society. Along with the review of the concept of the information society, there is the development of flexible instruments of the unification with the purpose of regulation of information and communication systems. While formerly drafts of international acts were developed by expert groups and adopted by resolutions of international organizations, nowadays the international organizations develop broad public discussion before establishing any expert groups.

The International Telecommunication Union (ITU), under whose auspices the World Summit on the Information Society was previously held, is already redefining the concept of the information society. As the specialized UN agency for information and communications technologies, ITU brings together stakeholders from governments, industries, academic organizations, and civil society groups from around the world, having since 2017 launched a new initiative named the Artificial Intelligence (AI) for Good Global Summit.

The activities of particular international organizations in the regulation of ICT use were discussed in fundamental research of information technology law by D.I. Bainbridge [5], D. Campbell and C. Ban [6], D. Rowland and E. Macdonald [7], I.J. Lloyd [8], A. Murray [9], D. Rowland, U. Kohl, A. Charlesworth [10], B. Craig [11], A. Schwabach [12], S.K. Black [13], T.J. Shaw [14], J. Kulesza [15].

David I. Bainbridge examined matters of e-commerce in view of EU and UNCITRAL acts, intellectual property and personal data protection in EU, and the application of the 1950 European Convention for the Protection of Human Rights and Fundamental Freedoms [5]. The EU and UNCITRAL acts were also considered in the research by Diane Rowland and Elizabeth Macdonald [7].

In 2008, Ian J. Lloyd examined initiatives in data protection that were considered by the Council of Europe, the Organization for Economic Cooperation and Development, the UN, and states of the Pacific region, as well as issues of information security in accordance with the Council of Europe Convention on Cybercrime and OECD and EU acts, and the regulation of intellectual property in accordance with treaties administered by WIPO [8]. The Council of Europe Convention on Cybercrime and EU acts were also analyzed in the research by Andrew Murray [9], Diane Rowland, Uta Kohl, and Andrew Charlesworth [10]. Issues of international protection of intellectual property in relation to the Internet were considered in the research by Brian Craig [11], Aaron Schwabach [12].

The regulation of the telecommunication market within WTO and EU acts were examined by Sharon K. Black [13].

In a fundamental study edited by Dennis Campbell and Chrysta Ban, there is an analysis of the 1886 Berne Convention for the Protection of Literary and Artistic Works, the 1996 WIPO Copyright Treaty, TRIPS, and EU acts relating to personal data protection, data on activities related to the Internet regulation at UNCITRAL, ASEAN, APEC, ICANN, WIPO, and The Hague Conference on Private International Law, and discussion of the activities of the World Summit on the Information Society [6].

In general, it should be noted that the abovementioned studies on IT law belong to the field of comparative jurisprudence and only involve international law aspects to the extent necessary for the purpose of the study.

Matters of international law are discussed in greater detail in the works of Thomas J. Shaw [14], Joanna Kulesza [15]. However, they do not take account of the special features of the functioning of information and communication systems that include artificial intelligence, Big Data, neural networks, and distributed ledgers.

At the same time, international organizations that formerly regulated ICT have just started working on the regulation of information and communication systems, the international documents in this field are scarce, and, therefore, more profound research of the mechanisms of activities of international organizations and drafts of their acts is required.

The author has proposed a concept of international legal regulation of information and communication systems, and this paper develops one of its aspects, namely, the activities of international organizations in the regulation of artificial intelligence.

The personal contribution of the author to the study of the problem of the international legal regulation of information and communication systems made by this chapter is that the author noted radical changes in the global information society associated with the emergence and development of information and communication systems, analyzed current initiatives of international organizations in the field of the international legal regulation of the artificial intelligence and identified prospects in this area, and proposed a new mechanism for coordinating of activities of international organizations to regulate the artificial intelligence, based on the existing mechanism for coordinating of activities of international organizations on the creation of the global information society with the application of "traditional" information and communication technologies.

2. Concept headings

2.1 The activities of international organizations at the universal level in the regulation of artificial intelligence

The objective of the research is identifying the prospects for the development of instruments for coordinating the activities of international organizations on the regulation of artificial intelligence and developing proposals in relation to the mechanisms of cooperation of international organizations on the universal level on issues related to artificial intelligence. In order to achieve the objective of the research, it is first of all necessary to analyze the activities of international organizations with regard to the regulation of artificial intelligence and draft acts of international organizations that they develop.

In the legal doctrine, the first publications on the use of artificial intelligence in law enforcement and the legal profession appeared in the 1980s [16, 17].

At present, there are hundreds of publications on legal matters relating to artificial intelligence, and there is discussion on issues of legal personality and liability relating to problems of the theory of law as well as branch sciences of domestic law, and the application of artificial intelligence in judicial and other legal activities.

The contribution of experts in international law to the problems under consideration is not as significant. Thomas Burri analyzed the problems that arise for international law in relation to the use of artificial intelligence for peaceful and military purposes [18]. John Weaver examined the status of artificial intelligence in international law [19].

There are particular studies aiming to understand the impact of artificial intelligence on the global world order [20, 21].

There are publications on specific problems of international law including human rights in binary economics [22] and problems of international humanitarian law [23].

In the framework of this research, it is necessary to answer the question of what institutional and treaty mechanisms would be effective for cooperation between international organizations for the regulation of artificial intelligence.

The statutes of a number of international organizations entitle them to deal with issues of scientific and technological cooperation and development, which includes the regulation of artificial intelligence.

The Charter of the United Nations of June 26, 1945, stipulates that the purpose of the United Nations is to achieve international co-operation in solving international problems of an economic, social, cultural, or humanitarian character, and in promoting and encouraging respect for human rights and for fundamental freedoms for all without distinction as to race, sex, language, or religion. Basically, the United Nations is the center of cooperation in any issues affecting the international legal order. The UN deals with issues of information and communication technologies in the aspect of its program document, namely, the UN Millennium Declaration, which was adopted by UN General Assembly Resolution 55/2 of September 8, 2000. To that end, on July 12, 2018, the UN Secretary-General established an advisory and expert subsidiary body, namely, the High-level Panel on Digital Cooperation. In its report entitled "The Age of Digital Interdependence", the High-level Panel on Digital Cooperation explored digital technologies as such without distinguishing artificial intelligence.

According to the Constitution of the ITU, its purpose is to promote the extension of the benefits of the new telecommunication technologies to all the world's inhabitants. As the specialized UN agency for information and communications technologies, ITU brings together stakeholders from governments, industries, academic organizations, and civil society groups from around the world, having since 2017 launched a new initiative named the Artificial Intelligence (AI) for Good Global Summit. The 2019 Summit brought together more than 30 UN agencies and other global stakeholders to identify strategies to ensure that AI technologies develop in a reliable, secure, and inclusive way with fair access to their benefits. The Summit presented 30 innovative proposals for the AI for Good Global project to expand and improve healthcare, to improve monitoring of agriculture and biodiversity using satellite images, and to develop smart cities and trust in artificial intelligence. At the 2019 Artificial Intelligence (AI) for Good Global Summit, a call was made for more attention to standardization in healthcare, which led to the establishment of the Focus Group on "Artificial Intelligence for health" (FG-AI4H), which intends, among other things, to establish a standardized assessment framework for the evaluation of AI-based methods for healthcare applications.

ITU maintains an AI data storage center where anyone working with artificial intelligence may submit important information on how AI can be used for the benefit of humanity. It is the only global data center that identifies AI-related projects, research initiatives, research centers and organizations that commit to accelerate progress towards the 17 Sustainable Development Goals of United Nations.

The ITU Focus Group on Machine Learning for Future Networks including 5G is investigating where technical standardization could support emerging applications of machine learning in fields such as big data analytics and security and data protection in the upcoming 5G era.

The ITU holds regular meetings of the heads of ICT regulatory authorities from various countries of the world to exchange views and information on AI and other relevant issues of regulation, solving management problems, and strengthening cooperation for the use of AI for the good of mankind.

Therefore, the ITU uses only institutional instruments for the regulation of artificial intelligence including international conferences such as the AI for Good Global Summit as well as the establishment of international bodies (Focus Groups).

According to the UNESCO Constitution of November 16, 1945, the purpose of the Organization is to contribute to peace and security by promoting collaboration among the nations through education, science and culture in order to further universal respect for justice, for the rule of law and for the human rights and fundamental freedoms which are affirmed for the peoples of the world, without distinction of race, sex, language or religion, by the Charter of the United Nations. UNESCO is a specialized agency of the United Nations. UNESCO has embarked on a two-year process to elaborate the first global standard-setting instrument on the ethics of artificial intelligence following the decision of UNESCO's General

Conference at its 40th session in November 2019. Towards the end of 2020 and in 2021, the focus will be on an intergovernmental process and on negotiation on the draft text to produce a final version of the Recommendation for possible adoption by UNESCO's General Conference at its 41st session at the end of 2021. UNESCO is currently using the Preliminary Study on the Ethics of Artificial Intelligence prepared by UNESCO experts. The Preliminary Study includes such issues as (1) education including the social role of education, the AI in teaching and learning, training AI engineers; (2) artificial intelligence and scientific knowledge including artificial intelligence and scientific learning, artificial intelligence and sciences on life and health, artificial intelligence and science on the environment, AI and social science, decision-making on the basis of artificial intelligence; (3) culture and cultural diversity including creativity, cultural diversity, and language; (4) communication and information including misinformation, data journalism, and automated journalism; (5) AI in international order and security; (6) AI and gender equality; (7) Africa and issues of artificial intelligence. The Preliminary Study proposes legal forms of a global act on the ethical aspects of artificial intelligence, such as a UNESCO declaration or recommendation, which does not impose international legal obligations on states but become binding only if the state consents to be bound by the international treaty or an international custom is established.

The Preliminary Study is currently a detailed analytical document that expresses the opinion of the international expert community on important issues of the regulation of artificial intelligence, which can become a basis for an international act. This document proposes solutions to the international community on the issues in the competence of UNESCO as well as on issues that are of interest for the entire mankind, which a number of international organizations are dealing with.

Issues that are significant for the entire mankind are issues of peace and international security. In these matters, artificial intelligence plays both a positive and a negative role. On the one hand, artificial intelligence with its ability to analyze large data arrays could become a powerful tool for preventing and resolving conflicts. A learning 'proactive intelligence' could anticipate the development of social unrest and social instability and suggest ways to prevent them. States could detect social pathologies at an early stage, find out what actions can de-escalate threatening situations, and find ways to combat threats for the national and international security. AI can lead mankind to a more sustainable society and help it move towards a peaceful and conflict-free world.

On the other hand, AI transforms the nature and practice of conflict, and its impact on the society goes far beyond purely military matters. AI promises to significantly improve the speed and accuracy of everything from military logistics, intelligence and situational awareness to the planning and execution of operations on the battlefield. The very system of AI can be used to develop its own suggestions on the action that should be taken; it can create a set of orders using the enemy's weakness, which it will identify based on its own analysis, or find patterns in the enemy's acts and develop countermeasures against predicted aggression.

The resolution of matters of peace and international security does not depend on UNESCO alone. The UN and regional collective security organizations play a key role in these issues.

Another issue that affects the interests of the entire mankind is gender equality. Artificial intelligence systems have significant consequences for gender equality, because they can reflect existing social biases and potentially exacerbate them. Most artificial intelligence systems use sets of data that reflect the real world, which can be misleading, unfair and discriminatory. A recruitment tool used by Amazon has been recognized as sexist because it gave priority to male candidates for technical jobs. Matters of gender equality are dealt with by the UN, its specialized agencies (UNESCO, ILO), and international judicial institutions for human rights.

Not only UNESCO but above all the UN has always paid attention to problems of developing countries including African states. Like other developing regions, Africa is facing the need to expand the use of information technologies and artificial intelligence. From the point of view of infrastructural relations, Africa has a great deficit and falls short of other developing regions significantly; domestic communications, regional communications, and limited access to electricity are significant problems. Infrastructure services are expensive even though more and more Africans (even in urban slums) have mobile phones. The common problems of developing countries include underdeveloped infrastructure, inadequate skills, knowledge gaps, and insufficient availability of local data.

Therefore, UNESCO is dealing with issues that could be resolved more efficiently in the framework of the United Nations and the entire UN system including its specialized agencies.

The World Intellectual Property Organization (WIPO) has achieved significant progress in the regulation of artificial intelligence. According to article 3 of the Convention Establishing the World Intellectual Property Organization of July 14, 1967, the object of the organization is to promote the protection of intellectual property throughout the world through cooperation among States and, where appropriate, in collaboration with any other international organization. In September 2019, WIPO held the first session of the Conversation on IP and AI. Governments, corporations, academic organizations and civil society groups may participate in the Conversation. On December 13, 2019, the WIPO published a draft concept document designed to provide a framework for developing a common understanding of the key issues to be discussed and addressed in the context of AI and IP policy. On July 9, 2020, the revised concept document was published, which has the status of a draft concept of an international act. The discussion resulted in the development of a second version of the concept of an international legal act, which will regulate such issues as (1) patents including authorship and ownership of inventions, patentability of objects, and guidelines for determining patentability, inventive step and non-obviousness, disclosure of information about the invention, general policy considerations regarding the patent system; (2) copyright and related rights, including authorship and ownership, violations and exceptions, digital fabrication, general issues of a political nature; (3) additional rights regarding data; (4) authorship and ownership of samples; (5) trademarks; (6) trade secrets; (7) capacity building.

2.2 The activities of regional international organizations in the regulation of artificial intelligence

Issues of artificial intelligence are also dealt with by regional international organizations.

In the EU framework, the Communication from the Commission to the European parliament, the European council, the Council, the European economic and social committee and the Committee of the regions "Artificial Intelligence for Europe" of April 25, 2018, has been adopted. The document covers three important aspects of AI development in Europe. Firstly, Europe should become the leader in technology developments and their implementation in the public and process sectors. The EU Commission increases its annual investments in AI by 70% in the framework of the Horizon 2020 research and innovation program. In 2018–2020, it will reach 1.5 billion Euro. The objectives of the investments are (1) support of

AI research centers throughout Europe; (2) support of the development of the "AI-on-demand platform", which will provide access to relevant AI resources in the EU for all users; (3) support of the development of AI applications in key sectors of the economy.

Secondly, there are also preparations in process in Europe for the socio-economic changes caused by AI. To support the efforts of Member States responsible for the labor and education policy, the Commission: (1) supports business and education partnerships to attract and retain more talents in the field of artificial intelligence in Europe; (2) develops specialized training and retraining programs for specialists; (3) monitors changes on the labor market and qualification mismatches; (4) supports digital skills and competencies in the field of science, technology, engineering, mathematics (STEM), entrepreneurship, and creativity; (5) encourages Member States to modernize their systems of education and professional training. This area of EU activities affects the competence of the ILO and UNESCO. In its activities, the EU Commission could use the experience of UNESCO.

Thirdly, the EU pays attention to the ethical and legal framework for artificial intelligence. On February 19, 2020, the European Commission published the White Paper for the development of the European ecosystem of best practices and trust for AI, and a report on the aspects of security and responsibility of AI. The White Paper proposes (1) measures that will allow to organize research, to strengthen cooperation between Member States, and to increase investments in the development and implementation of artificial intelligence; (2) policy options for the future EU regulatory framework, which will define the types of legal requirements that will apply to the respective entities.

After publication, the White Paper is open for public consultation. All European citizens, Member States, and relevant stakeholders (including the civil society, industry, and academic organizations) have been invited to take part in the consultations by responding to an online survey and presenting their position papers on the subject.

Matters of artificial intelligence in the EU are a responsibility of a special expert group, namely, the High-Level Group on Artificial Intelligence (AI HLEG). The first Draft Ethics guidelines for trustworthy AI were presented by the expert group in December 2018. After further discussion and in the light of consultations with the stakeholders and meetings with representatives of the Member States, the guidelines were revised and published in April 2019. At the same time, AI HLEG prepared a revised document, which sets out in detail the definition of artificial intelligence, which is used for the purposes of its results. At present, the interim results of the expert group's work are the final Ethics Guidelines for Trustworthy Artificial Intelligence prepared by the High-Level Group on Artificial Intelligence and published on 8 April 2019: the Report on liability for Artificial Intelligence and other emerging technologies prepared by the Expert Group on Liability and New Technologies – New Technologies Formation and published on 21 November 2019.

The EU Commission also released the Communication on Building Trust in Human-Centric Artificial Intelligence of April 8, 2019 (COM(2019)168 final). Guaranteeing that European values are the basis of the development and use of AI, the Commission highlighted the key issues, namely, (1) human agency and oversight; (2) technical robustness and safety; (3) privacy and data governance; (4) transparency; (5) diversity, non-discrimination and fairness; (6) societal and environmental well-being; (7) accountability.

The Declaration of Cooperation on Artificial Intelligence, signed by 25 European countries on 10 April 2018 builds further on the achievements and investments of the European research and business community in AI and sets out the basis for the Coordinated Plan on AI.

The experience of the EU is a benchmark for other integration associations. For example, in the framework of the Caribbean Community (CARICOM) there is a subgroup on science and technology. The organization has proposed the STEM (science, technology, engineering, mathematics) concept. CARICOM is also implementing the concept of a single ICT space. An intersectoral and very complex entity, the single ICT space is the digital layer of the CARICOM Single Market and Economy (CSME). The single ICT space will make it possible to harmonize legislation, abolish roaming fees, stimulate digital entrepreneurship, provide all citizens with digital personalities, and consider financial solutions in ICT. In February 2017, the leaders of CARICOM countries approved the roadmap of the single ICT space.

In general, it should be noted that international organizations have not yet adopted any resolutions in respect of artificial intelligence, which are provided by their constitutions. The work of international organizations has the format of discussing draft documents and setting up international expert groups.

3. Results

3.1 Problems of the regulation of artificial intelligence that need to be resolved at the international level

There are two problems that can only be solved by joint efforts of international organizations as a result of coordination of their activities, namely, (1) the development of a unified concept of artificial intelligence in international law; (2) the development of unified international legal approaches to liability for acts committed with the use of artificial intelligence. The most effective instrument for solving these problems would be an international treaty containing the principles of use of artificial intelligence for the good of mankind as well as the rules of civil, administrative, and criminal liability for acts involving the use of artificial intelligence. However, discussion of these matters in the framework of international organizations has just started, and no work groups for the preparation of draft international treaties have been created, which is due to the complicacy of legal problems related to artificial intelligence.

Artificial intelligence is quite a difficult concept to unify. WIPO's Revised Issues Paper on Intellectual Property Policy and Artificial Intelligence contains the following definition of artificial intelligence, ""Artificial intelligence (AI)" is a discipline of computer science that is aimed at developing machines and systems that can carry out tasks considered to require human intelligence, with limited or no human intervention. For the purposes of this paper, AI generally equates to "narrow AI" which is techniques and applications programmed to perform individual tasks. Machine learning and deep learning are two subsets of AI. While the AI field is rapidly evolving it is not clear when the science will advance to higher levels of general artificial intelligence which is no longer designed to solve specific problems but to operate across a wide field of contexts and tasks." Therefore, one definition comprises two different concepts, namely, "a discipline of computer science" and "techniques and applications programmed to perform individual tasks". However, such an imperfect definition was provided for discussion only and not for inclusion in the glossary as a part of an international legal act. At the same time, the WIPO Revised Issues Paper did not raise the key issue for defining artificial intelligence as an object of international legal regulation, which is whether artificial intelligence will be considered equivalent to 'ordinary' software.

The object that is protected at the universal level that is closest to artificial intelligence is computer programs.

Legal protection of computer programs arose before the advent of electronic communication technologies and developed in stages from patent to copyright.

Patent protection of computer programs has been used since the 1960s in the USA. At first, the Patent and Trademark Office refused to patent computers programs, regarding them as mental objects. But in 1968, the Court of Customs and Patent Appeals, in several judgments, concluded about the patentability of algorithms, computers, and coding methods.

In the 21st century, the US courts of the United States have a similar attitude as they are faced with a qualitatively new technical object. This conclusion is confirmed by the practice of national courts in the recognition of the patentability of artificial intelligence, which was summarized by Mizuki Hashiguchi [24].

In the USA, the McRO.Inc. v. Bandai Namco Games America Inc. case is an example of the recognition of patentability of a method for automatically animating lip synchronization and facial expressions of animated characters in computer graphics. Federal court ruled that this method was patentable because it did not lead to an abstract idea. The court considered the specifics of the automatic method, which covered individual operations with specific characteristics. The method, which includes individual operations, is intended to translate information into a specific format that is used to create characters. The features of the industrial applicability of this invention were also considered. Firstly, it is not just the methodology as such that is applied. Secondly, the invention cannot be used without a computer technology. Overall, the court concluded that processes which automate human tasks are patentable.

US courts are primarily guided by the criterion of usefulness of inventions with elements of artificial intelligence.

Considering the experience of legal protection of computer programs, it is unlikely that the idea of patentability of inventions with elements of artificial intelligence will be supported at the universal level.

A copyright regime for computer programs has been established at the universal level. The WIPO Copyright Treaty of December 20, 1996, states that computer programs and databases are copyright protected. Moreover, Article 1 of the Treaty stipulates that this Treaty is a special agreement within the meaning of Article 20 of the Berne Convention for the Protection of Literary and Artistic Works. Article 4 of the Treaty stipulates that computer programs are protected as literary works within the meaning of Article 2 of the Berne Convention.

The specificity of computer programs is taken into account in Article 11 of TRIPS. In respect of at least computer programs, a Member shall provide authors and their successors in title the right to authorize or to prohibit the commercial rental to the public of originals or copies of their copyright works. In respect of computer programs, this obligation does not apply to rentals where the program itself is not the essential object of the rental.

It is obvious that artificial intelligence cannot be considered an equivalent of a 'simple' computer program in the meaning of the abovementioned international legal acts. TRIPS stipulates that computer programs, whether in source or object code, shall be protected. Thus, TRIPS has demonstrated the structure of a computer program, which is the source text and the object code. At the same time, WIPO's Revised Issues Paper on Intellectual Property Policy and Artificial Intelligence states that the machine learning and deep learning are two subsets of AI. Artificial intelligence has a different structure as compared to 'ordinary' software.

According to Directive 2009/24/EC of the European Parliament and the Council of the European Union on the legal protection of computer programs (codified version) of April 23, 2009, the object of legal protection is the program as such and the preparatory work leading to the development of the program. This rule differs significantly from the rule in the WIPO Model Provisions on the Protection of Computer Software. Under the Model Provisions, protection applied not just to the abovementioned objects but also program use manuals, which are not objects of protection in Europe. These international documents do not disclose the concept of a 'program', but in their interpretation one should consider the historical period when those documents were developed and adopted. Their 'modernized' interpretation as applied to artificial intelligence is hardly admissible.

It should be noted that artificial intelligence is a more complex object in its structure than 'ordinary' software. It is an information and communication system that can synthesize creative activities in the literary, artistic, and industrial fields.

It should be noted that the "information system" category in its traditional understanding has been established in scientific literature as a database controlled by algorithmic computer programs [25–27]. With the emergence of logic programming, a need to rethink the "information system" category has arisen. We use the term "information and communication system" that means an information object with complex structure that has unity and multifunctionality and, at this stage of scientific and technical development, relative autonomy from the operator of such a system.

UNESCO experts have explored issues of responsibility of artificial intelligence and came to a number of important conclusions. Firstly, noting the broad scope of AI use (transport, medicine, communication, education, science, finance, law, military, marketing, customer services or entertainment), the UNESCO experts noted numerous concerns ranging from the disappearance of traditional jobs, over responsibility for possible physical or psychological harm to human beings, to general dehumanization of human relationships and society at large.

Secondly, a solution was proposed for the problem of liability for possible physical or mental damage to humans. "The development of future technologies is in the hands of technical experts. Traditionally, engineers are educated to develop products to optimize performance using minimum resources (power, spectrum, space, weight etc.), under given external constrains. Over the past decades, the ethics of technology has developed various methods to bring ethical reflection, responsibility and reasoning to the design process. In the context of AI, the term 'ethically aligned design' (EAD) has been developed to indicate design processes that explicitly include human values."

Finally, the UNESCO experts proposed wordings for the principles of AI use, in particular:

1. Human rights: AI should be developed and implemented in accordance with international human rights standards.

2. Inclusiveness: AI should be inclusive, aiming to avoid bias and allowing for diversity and avoiding a new digital divide.

3. Flourishing: AI should be developed to enhance the quality of life.

4. Autonomy: AI should respect human autonomy by requiring human control at all times.

5. Responsibility: Developers and companies should take into consideration ethics when developing autonomous intelligent system.

6. Accountability: Arrangements should be developed that will make possible to attribute accountability for AI-driven decisions and the behaviour of AI systems.

7. Good governance: Governments should provide regular reports about their use of AI in policing, intelligence, and security.

Consequently, the new UNESCO act will assign the liability for actions of artificial intelligence to developers and companies which develop autonomous intelligent systems. States will be imposed an implementation obligation to provide regular reports about their use of AI in policing, intelligence, and security.

The matter of liability for actions related to artificial intelligence has been elaborated thoroughly by the EU experts in the Report on liability for Artificial Intelligence and other emerging technologies prepared by the Expert Group on Liability and New Technologies – New Technologies Formation and published on 21 November 2019. The reports of the EU experts gives a clear definition of the prospects (challenges of emerging digital technologies for liability law, operator's strict liability, producer's strict liability, fault liability and duties of care, vicarious liability for autonomous systems) and mechanisms of implementation of liability for actions related to artificial intelligence (logging by design, safety rules, redress between multiple tortfeasors, insurance, compensation funds). However, the progressive experience of the EU has not found support on a universal level.

At the same time, in the EU document attention should be paid attention to the multiplicity of persons in charge, which is due to the adaptation of traditional institutions of contractual and tort liability to the conditions of AI use. In our opinion, this problem cannot be solved without the introduction of a legal fiction, namely, a single subject responsible for the actions of artificial intelligence. We prefer the approach of UNESCO, which establishes the liability of developers and companies which develop autonomous intelligent systems for any acts committed with the use of artificial intelligence.

3.2 Proposals on the development of a universal mechanism for the coordination of activities of international organizations in the regulation of artificial intelligence

Given the complexity of the problems faced by mankind, there is the question of whether the existing mechanisms for the coordination of activities of international organizations on the development of a legal framework for the global information society can play the same role in respect of the regulation of artificial intelligence?

In the international institutional system in the field of information, there exist established system relations. Various institutional entities are trying to coordinate their efforts in the development of a global information society. At the level of an institutional mechanism of cooperation, the concept of a global information society has been supported. The World Summit on the Information Society has taken place largely thanks to the initiative of the ITU. Back in 1998, the International Telecommunication Union instructed its Secretary-General to include the issue of holding the World Summit on the Information Society in the agenda of the UN Administrative Committee on Coordination and to report to the ITU Council about the results of this consultation. In his 1999 report to the Council, the ITU Secretary-General noted that the Administrative Committee reacted positively to the idea of such a forum and that most other organizations expressed interest in preparing and participating in it.

At the World Summit on the Information Society, a Plan of Action was developed, and the task of building the information society has moved into the practical field.

The ideas of the World Summit on the Information Society have been supported by many international organizations, both intergovernmental (UN, OAS, OAU, and others) and non-governmental. International organizations are developing the concept of a global information society paying particular attention to certain issues of the application of new technologies including information security, computer crime, privacy, etc.

In particular, a special body was established within the UN, namely, the UN Group on the Information Society (UNGIS). UNGIS was established in April 2006 by the UN Chief Executive Board for Coordination (CEB). The main objective of UNGIS is to coordinate substantive policy issues facing the United Nations system's implementation of the measures adopted by the World Summit on the Information Society. Members of UNGIS are not only organizations of the UN system but also several regional organizations such as OECD. UNGIS: (1) contributes towards the implementation the Geneva Plan of Action and Tunis Agenda for the Information Society, primarily at the international level, by mainstreaming them into the activities and programs of CEB members; (2) facilitates synergies between organizations belonging to the UN system in order to maximize joint efforts, avoid duplication and enhance effectiveness in achieving the WSIS outcomes; (3) promotes public awareness about how the UN system is implementing WSIS. As part of its activities, UNGIS prepares information for CEB on relevant issues of building the information society (e.g., cybersecurity) and helps CEB in identifying key issues related to UN activities in the field of ICT use.

In order to assess the efficiency of the World Summit on the Information Society and UNGIS with regard to the regulation of artificial intelligence, one should address the relevant issues of their activities.

At present, the World Summit is acting via 11 international bodies for different areas of the development of the information society. One can note a trend of its gradual transformation into an international organization, as it did not stop its activities after the Tunis meeting. Further, the World Summit is a platform for cooperation between the UN, UNESCO, ITU, and other international organizations, which has the function of coordinating cooperation of international organizations in the development of the information society. At the WSIS 2018 forum in the Outcome Document, attention was paid to the work of such groups as WSIS Action Line C7: ICT applications: benefits in all aspects of life (Multi-Hazard Early Warning Systems and the Role of ICT; Digital Health - Status and Roadmap & WHO eHealth activities); WSIS Action Line C4: Capacity Building (Building ICT Skills for Social Entrepreneurs); WSIS Action Line C6: Enabling Environment (Sharing Collaborative Regulatory Approaches for Digital Transformation); WSIS Action Line C5: Building Confidence and Security in the use of ICTs (Blockchain as an Enabler of Security and Trust); WSIS Action Line C9: Media (Strengthening the role of media and social media in relation to the SDGs); WSIS Action Lines C1 (The role of governments and all stakeholders in the promotion of ICTs for development), C11 (International and regional cooperation).

It should be noted that the issues of the World Summit on the Information Society in relation to ICT 'overlap' with issues that are discussed at the AI for Good Global Summit and in the framework of UNESCO in relation to artificial intelligence. However, the World Summit on the Information Society has not included artificial intelligence in its agenda.

UNGIS Technical Meeting on 11 July 2019 discussed the issue of rebranding the group to include "digital transformation" in the name, it was agreed that a tag line of "UNGIS for Digital Transformation" will be added to the UNGIS activities and website. Therefore, the key issue of UNGIS activities is digital transformation.

Assessing the allocation of the regulation of artificial intelligence in a separate area of international cooperation in connection with the AI for Good Global Summit, we have a positive opinion about the development of a new discussion platform for discussing issues of artificial intelligence. However, WSIS Action Line C6: Enabling Environment could develop common approaches to the legal regulation of information and communication systems as such and not just artificial intelligence.

Issues of regulation of information and communication systems could be discussed at the annual forums of the World Summit on the Information Society as a result of the activities of such work groups as Access to information and knowledge (C3), E-learning (C7), E-science (C7), Cultural diversity and identity, linguistic diversity and local content (C8), Ethical dimensions of the Information Society (C10), in which UNESCO participates with its significant achievements in the field of artificial intelligence.

At present, the World Summit on the Information Society could begin developing a new Plan of Action taking into account the functioning and development of the information and communication systems (currently, the 2003 Plan of Action is being implemented). The result of the new Plan of Action would be the establishment of new work groups (with preservation of some of the existing and efficient ones) and the change in the competence of UNGIS to include issues of regulation of information and communication systems.

4. Discussion

4.1 The concept of "international institutional competition"

The identified phenomenon of the 'overlapping' of the competence of international organizations and international institutions that coordinate their activity requires theoretical analysis.

In the doctrine of international law, we can find an explanation of this phenomenon in the work by Ruth Okediji "WIPO-WTO Relations and the Future of Global Intellectual Property Norms" [28] in relation to competition between the WTO and WIPO. For the analysis of competition between the WTO and WIPO, the special term "forum proliferation" is proposed, which is used in this context to characterize the situation arising with the proliferation of international organizations with intercrossing scopes of activities and the possibility to choose the most suitable one for solving a particular issue. Another term used is "international institutional competition".

WIPO deals with the most pressing issues of the protection of intellectual property arising from the development of both economic and social sectors as well as scientific and technical progress. WIPO also deals with issues that are indirectly related to the protection of intellectual property including the regulation of artificial intelligence, the implementation of the sustainable development agenda in the period up to 2030, the WIPO Traditional Knowledge Program that also covers traditional expressions of culture and genetic resources, the WIPO Global Challenges Program, which aims to raise awareness and understanding of the complex relations of the global healthcare system and issues of access to medical technology and innovation, technology transfer and trade, and research in the field of competition.

The WTO deals with similar issues. Since 1994, an alternative mechanism for the protection of intellectual property has begun to establish in the framework of the WTO. It is related to the adoption of the Agreement on Trade-Related Aspects of Intellectual Property Rights (TRIPS). This agreement has led to the development of a specialized body, namely, the Council for TRIPS, which mainly deals with intellectual property issues in the framework of the WTO. The WTO also deals with current issues related to the protection of intellectual property, namely, the implementation of the 2001 Doha Declaration on the TRIPS Agreement and Public Health, the relation between TRIPS and the UN Convention on Biological Diversity, the issue of protection of traditional knowledge and folklore, and technology transfer. Looking at current issues of the WIPO and WTO activities, it is easy to see that a number of issues are being developed in parallel by both organizations.

4.2 The application of the concept of "international institutional competition" to issues of the regulation of artificial intelligence

Developing the concept of "international institutional competition", let us turn to the issues that were discussed at the AI for Good Global Summit in 2019. At the 2019 summit, the main attention was paid to the meaning of AI in the development of education, healthcare, and well-being, in achieving social and economic equality, space research, and 'smart' and safe mobility. Unforeseen consequences of AI were discussed as well as the relationship of AI with art and culture. "The learning day" gave potential AI users an opportunity to communicate with leading experts and educators in the field of AI.

Issues of education, art, and culture, and gender equality were discussed by experts of UNESCO in the Preliminary Study on the Ethics of Artificial Intelligence, which will be the basis for the future UNESCO resolution to be adopted in 2021. Issues of art and culture from the point of view of the protection of intellectual property were considered by WIPO experts in a concept paper, which is intended to become the basis for the development of a common understanding of the key issues that require discussion and decisions in the context of AI and policies in the field of IP. However, the the 'overlapping' of the competence of international organizations and the discussion platform for the discussion of common issues does not cause negative consequences provided that the international stakeholders are involved in the discussion.

At the same time, the WSIS Action Lines (E-learning (C7), E-science (C7), Cultural diversity and identity, linguistic diversity and local content (C8), Ethical dimensions of the Information Society (C10), etc.) deal with issues that are discussed at the AI for Good Global Summit. "International institutional competition" of the two discussion platforms may overtime cause a decline of their efficiency unless the ITU provides proper coordination of such activities. It should be taken into account that the activities of the World Summit on the Information Society are more general in nature while those of the AI for Good Global Summit are more special. However, special issues cannot be resolved without consideration of the solutions that are offered for the general issues.

5. Conclusion

There is no unified conventional definition of artificial intelligence in international law. An international custom for a uniform understanding of artificial intelligence for the purposes of its legal regulation has not yet established. We propose the following definition of artificial intelligence: it is an information and communication system that can synthesize creative activities in the literary, artistic, and industrial fields. In view of the above, the current concept of an information system that exists in the legal doctrine should be revised. An information and communication system is an information object with complex structure that has unity and multifunctionality and, at this stage of scientific and technical development, relative autonomy from the operator of such a system. Information and communication systems include artificial intelligence, Big Data, neural networks, distributed ledgers, and their combinations.

International organizations (ITU, UNESCO, WIPO, EU) are currently developing approaches to the regulation of artificial intelligence by establishing expert groups and using broad public discussion. The activities of some international organizations affect issues that are in the competence of other international organizations. Thus, all of the above international organizations are simultaneously developing the concept of artificial intelligence and issues of its liability. UNESCO is working on issues of international peace and security, gender equality, and problems of developing countries, which could be resolved more efficiently in the framework of the United Nations. The 'overlapping' of the competence of international organizations raises a need for international mechanisms of coordination of their activities.

In the international institutional system in the field of information, the system interrelations have been established by the present time. Various institutional entities coordinate their efforts for the establishment of a global information society. Coordination is achieved thanks to the activities of the World Summit on the Information Society. At present, the World Summit is acting via 11 international bodies for different areas of the development of the information society, being a transitional institutional entity from an international conference to an international organization. The issues of the World Summit on the Information Society in relation to ICT 'overlap' with issues that are discussed at the AI for Good Global Summit and in the framework of UNESCO in relation to artificial intelligence. However, the World Summit on the Information Society has not included artificial intelligence in its agenda.

The Action Lines of the World Summit on the Information Society (E-learning (C7), E-science (C7), Cultural diversity and identity, linguistic diversity and local content (C8), Ethical dimensions of the Information Society (C10), and others) deal with the issues that are discussed at the AI for Good Global Summit. At the same time, the World Summit on the Information Society works on ICT regulation, while the AI for Good Global Summit works on the more special issue of the regulation of artificial intelligence. The problem of "international institutional competition" of the two discussion platforms can be resolved by ITU's efforts to coordinate the two discussion platforms and by supplementing the competence of UNGIS with issues of artificial intelligence so that the resolutions of both forums would be implemented by the same international body.

Acknowledgements

The author is an employee of the St. Petersburg State University. This research was performed as a result of an initiative using the resources of the library of the St. Petersburg State University.

Declaration of competing interest

The authors declare that they have no known competing financial interests or personal relationships that could have appeared to influence the work reported in this paper.

Author details

Valentina Petrovna Talimonchik
Saint Petersburg State University, Russia

*Address all correspondence to: talim2008@yandex.ru

References

[1] Matterlart A. The information society: an introduction. London: SAGE Publication Ltd; 2003. 182 pz.

[2] May C. The Information Society: a sceptical view. Cambridge: Polity Press; 2003. 189 p.

[3] May C, editor. Key Thinkers for the Information Society. London: Routledge; 2003. 194 p.

[4] Webster F. Theories of the Information Society. 3rd ed. London: Routledge; 2006. 317 p.

[5] Bainbridge DI. Introduction to Information Technology Law. 6th ed. Edinburg: Pearson Education Limited; 2008. 665 p.

[6] Campbell D, Ban C, editors. Legal Issues in the Global Information Society. New York: Oceana Publications Inc.; 2005. 758 p.

[7] Rowland D, Macdonald E. Information technology law. 3rd ed. Abingdon: Cavendish Publishing Ltd; 2005. 573 p.

[8] Lloyd IJ. Information Technology Law. 5th ed. Oxford: Oxford University Press; 2008. 597 p.

[9] Murray A. Information Technology Law: Law and Society. Oxford: Oxford university press; 2010. 596 p.

[10] Rowland D, Kohl U, Charlesworth A. Information Technology Law. 5th ed. London: Routledge; 2017. 549 p.

[11] Craig B. Cyberlaw: the Law of the Internet and Information Technology. Boston: Pearson Education Inc.; 2013. 262 p.

[12] Schwabach A. Internet and the Law: Technology, Society and Compromises. Santa Barbara; ABC-CLIO Inc.; 2006. 395 p.

[13] Black SK. Telecommunications Law in the Internet Age. San Francisco: Morgan Kaufmann Publishers; 2002. 516 p.

[14] Shaw TJ. Information and Internet Law: Global Practice. Createspace Independent Publishing Platform; 2016. 454 p.

[15] Kulesza J. International Internet Law. 2nd ed. London: Routledge; 2013. 194 p.

[16] Lashbrooke EC. Legal Reasoning and Artificial Intelligence. Loyola Law Review. 1988; Vol. 34: P. 287-310.

[17] Blodget N. Artificial Intelligence Comes of Age. ABA Jornal. 1987; N 1.

[18] Burri T. International Law and Artificial Intelligence. German Yearbook of International Law. 2017; Vol. 60: P. 91-108.

[19] Weaver JF. Abhor a Vacuum: The Status of Artificial Intelligence and AI Drones under International Law. New Hampshire Bar Journal. 2013; Vol. 54; Iss. 1: P. 14-21.

[20] Polido P, Bertini F. Artificial Intelligence between National Strategies and the Global Regulatory Race: Analytical Routes for an International and Comparative Reappraisal. Revista da Faculdade de Direito da Universidade Federal de Minas Gerais.2020; Vol. 76: P. 229-256.

[21] Maas M. International Law Does Not Compute: Artificial Intelligence and the Development, Displacement or Destruction of the Global Legal Order. Melbourne Journal of International Law.2019; Vol. 20; Iss. 1: P. 29-57.

[22] Fleissner C. Inclusive Capitalism Based on Binary Economics and Positive

International Human Rights in the Age of Artificial Intelligence. Washington University Global Studies Law Review. 2018; Vol. 17; Iss. 1: P. 201-244.

[23] Shuller AL. At the Crossroads of Control: the Intersection of Artificial Intelligence in Autonomous Weapon Systems with International Humanitarian Law. Harvard National Security Journal. 2017; Vol. 8: P. 379-425.

[24] Hashiguchi M. The Global Artificial Intelligence Revolution Challenges Patent Eligibility Laws. Journal of Business & Technology Law. 2017; Vol. 13; N 1: P. 1-35.

[25] Wolff MA. Missouri's Information-Based Discretionary Sentencing System. Symposium: Blakely and the States. Ohio State Journal of Criminal Law. 2006; Vol. 4; Iss. 1: P. 95-120.

[26] van der Vinne J. A Sentencing Information System Named NOSTRA. International Journal of Law and Information Technology. 1998; Vol. 6; Iss. 2: P. 230-234.

[27] Milojevic I. Accounting Information System and Information in the Defence System. ODITOR - Journal for Management, Finance and Law. 2017; N 2: P. 54-66.

[28] Okediji RL. WIPO–WTO Relations and the Future of Global Intellectual Property Norms. Netherlands Yearbook of International Law. 2008; Vol. 39: P. 69-125.

Chapter 8

Artificial Intelligence Assisted Innovation

Gideon Samid

Abstract

Artificial Intelligence Assisted Innovation (AIAI) is a technology designed to improve innovation productivity by helping human innovators with all the support tasks that kindle the creative spark, and also with sorting out innovative propositions for their merit. Innovation activity is mushrooming and hence innovative history is an ever growing data accumulation. AIAI identified a universal innovation map, which is processed like the tape in a Turing machine, only here in the Innovation Turing machine, marking an innovation pathway. By mapping innovative history onto these maps, one enables the growing record of innovation history to guide current innovation as to merit, expected cost, estimated duration, etc. Using Monte Carlo and Discriminant Analysis, an Artificial Innovation Assistant runs a dialog with the human innovator with a net effect of accelerated innovation. Users of AIAI are expected to exhibit a commanding lead over innovators guided only by their creativity.

Keywords: innovation, AI, innovation challenge, innovation solution protocol, Monte Carlo

1. Introduction

AI -- artificial intelligence -- per se is human innovation, all its achievements should then be credited to its human creators, therefore, by Gödelian reasoning, in a very deep level, the artificial entity is subservient to the natural entity, however more efficient AI is in countless specific tasks. One would then wish to combine the in-depth human superiority to the avalanche of superficial superiority exhibited by intelligence that is computational and artificial, and speaks in binary and no more.

We propose a framework for natural and artificial intelligence collaboration in pursuit of an innovative (R&D) objective. We envision a human innovator (HI), interacting with a computerized entity: Artificial Innovation Assistant (AIA). The HI (i) poses questions, (ii) submits information to the AIA, and the AIA in return (i) poses questions, (ii) replies to questions. The AIA is comprised of (i) a dialog part (D), a processor part (P), and an environmental part, (E). The dialog part uses modern AI technique to appear as human-like as possible for its human operator, the processor part is running the powerful AI search and discover algorithms, and operates the underlying innovation framework (the Innovation Solution Protocol -- Innovation^{SP}), while the environmental part (E) interacts with (i) innovation partners, (ii) propriety innovation sources, and (iii) public domain sources.

In addition to the AIA running a dialog with the human innovator, HI, it also runs a dialog with the other innovation stakeholders: (i) the financial investors, (ii) the beneficiaries, and with anyone impacted by the project.

This AIA configuration is geared towards a single innovator working alone, or to a team of small or large size. It applies to local, or global effort, to cases of one private investor, or to many socially minded investors, and to any number of beneficiaries or impacted parties.

This chapter first describes the underlying innovation solution protocol, (Innovation^{SP}), then depicts the AIA configuration, followed by a description of the various AIA parts, concluded with an outlook and a prospective view of the future of artificial intelligence assisted innovation.

For a good review of established innovation thinking see [1–10].

2. The innovation solution protocol

The Innovation Solution Protocol refers to an innovative challenge for which one has no apparent direct solution. The procedure identifies three possible routes of action:

1. **Divide the challenge to components** -- solve, or generate insight about the components, then return to the original challenge.

2. **Re-define the challenge in a more abstract fashion** -- solve, or generate insight about the abstract version, then revisit the original challenge.

3. **Extend the challenge to a larger one including related challenges** -- solve or generate insight about the extended challenge, then revisit the original challenge.

Whichever road the innovator takes, they end up with one or more new challenges. These new ones may be solved in a direct manner, but if not -- and here comes the iterative aspect -- each of these challenges can be likewise tackled through the same three-way solution procedure. Doing so would create a third generation (now front and center) of challenges, which again can each be treated the way the original challenge was -- applying the three-way solution. See **Figure 1**: B-A-X.

This ongoing procedure would keep generating new challenges, until such time that the new ones can be resolved in a direct manner. And if not completely resolved, then partially resolved. When this happens the attention backtracks to the parent challenge, and if that challenge is resolved (completely or partially) then it would point to its parent challenge, and so on, until the backtracking process would

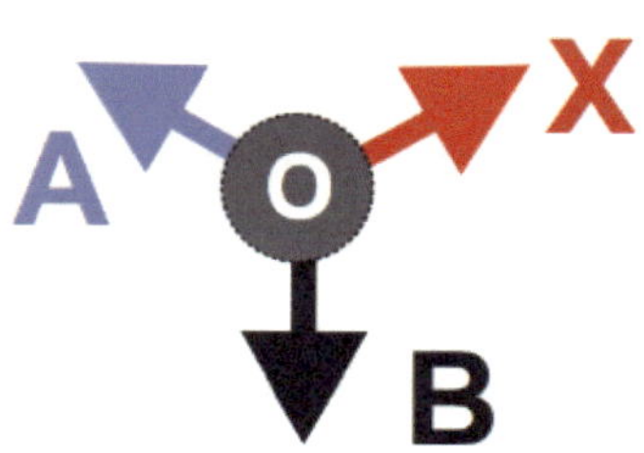

Figure 1.
B-a-x.

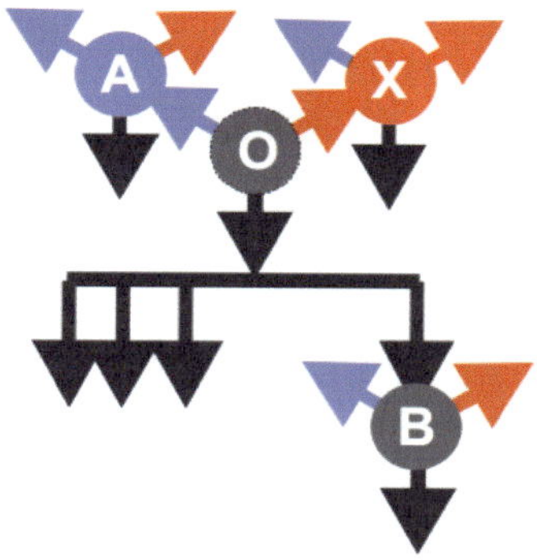

Figure 2.
The innovation solution map.

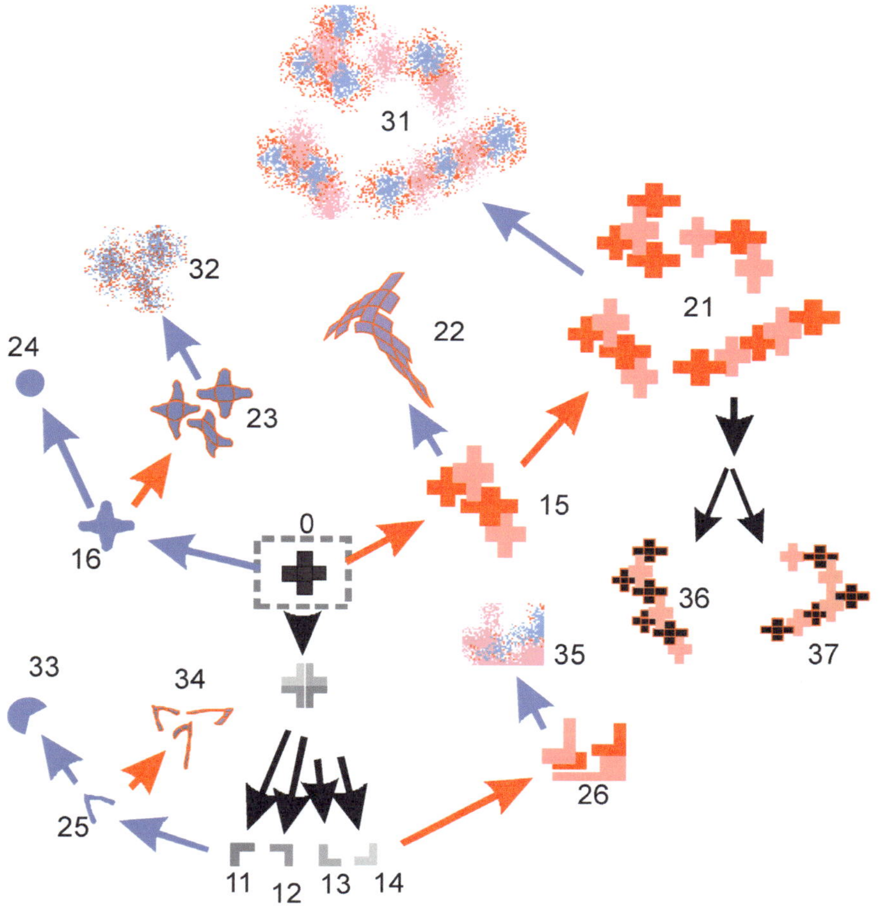

Figure 3.
An evolved ISP map.

refocus on the original challenge. The solution seeker has always something concrete to do. There is always a next step. See **Figure 2**: The Innovation Solution Map.

This procedure is captured as the Innovation Turing Machine (ITM). Its operation moves the innovator's attention from one innovation challenge to the next. It is iterative, open-ended; it spreads further and further until it hits a negotiable innovation challenge. Once this challenge is negotiated (resolved), the innovator's attention shifts back to its parent challenge. Applied repetitively, this "Innovation Machine" ends up with a resolved original challenge. Check out an evolved map in **Figure 3**.

3. The innovation Turing Machine

The innovation process can be described via a generic machine. Its operation is designed to express any innovation sequence. The machine is dubbed The Innovation Turing machine, citing its analogy to the famous Turing Machine that became the generic framework for all computers (up to the emerging quantum computers). The Innovation Turing Machine, ITM, operates on the fundamental innovation object: the innovation challenge, IC. The innovation challenge may be viewed as the gap between two states: a desired state, and an existing state. The states define a technological situation. The fundamental dilemma of innovation is the mystery of that gap, the difficulty to measure it, and to eliminate it. Measuring the gap constitutes a quantitative definition of the effort to close it, where effort is measured in time, cost or any individual or combinations of resources. To resolve, or to solve an IC is to eliminate its gap. The fundamental rhythm of the ITM is a combination of foretracking and backtracking, defined as follows: If an IC is too difficult to resolve, then advance (foretrack) to another, -- hopefully, but not necessarily -- simpler IC, and when it is resolved, backtrack to the former IC, and try again. Repeat and re-apply the sequence of foretracking-backtracking. By re-applying the foretracking-backtracking sequence to each IC that was defined to help out with a former IC, one generates an indefinite sequence of ICs -- an IC track. And since every IC may have more than one simpler IC associated with it, these tracks expand into a tree structure. And, since some of the ICs so defined may be identical, the tree structure transforms into a network, referred to as the ITM-WEB.

According to the ITM model there are only three types of "simpler ICs": those that may be defined as components of the IC, those that may be defined as an abstraction of the IC, and those that may be defined as an extension of the IC. By way of convention, the number of components may be two or more, while all possible extensions are summarized into a single "master extension challenge," and similarly all possible abstractions are summarized into a single "master abstraction challenge". Hence, every innovation challenge gives rise to m + 2 next generation of challenges, where m is the number of components.

One's attention is focused on a single challenge. If that challenge is not the very original one then, following the attempt to resolve it, one's attention moves to another; either to the "next" challenge or to the "before" challenge. This is analogous to the motion of the tape under the read/write head in the original Turing machine. This process continues until the original challenge is resolved, or the system halts. Like with the original Turing machine the single read/write head may be expanded to two or more heads working in parallel. This expansion will reflect the work of a large R&D team working in parallel. See ahead a sample of the IC map:

THE TRIANGULAR OPTIONS: The three triangular options B-X-A (Breakdown, Extension, and Abstraction), along with the nominal (direct solution) option, represent the full spectrum available for the innovator wrestling with an innovation challenge. This is essentially a dialectic range: If you cannot solve a problem directly, you can opt downward -- breaking the problem down to smaller parts, or upward -- considering a 'higher' problem where insight may be easier to come by. The 'higher' option divides to abstraction and extension, while the 'lower option' divides to at least two parts. The nature of these options is explained below.

BREAKDOWN CONFIGURATION: We distinguish between three types of configurations, which can be pieced together to form a complex configuration:

- serial breakdown configuration
- parallel breakdown configuration
- concentric breakdown configuration

SERIAL BREAKDOWN CONFIGURATION: An innovation challenge (problem), IC, may be broken into n serial breakdown units: S_1, S_2, S_3, ...S_n, such that a sequential solution of these units, constitutes a solution to the former challenge, IC.

$$IC = \{S_1 \to S_2 \to S_3 \to .....S_n\} \tag{1}$$

If any one of the n serial units remained unsolved, then IC remains unsolved. **Figure 4**.

PARALLEL BREAKDOWN CONFIGURATION: An innovation challenge (problem) IC, may be broken down into n distinct parallel breakdown units: L_1, L_2, L_3, ...L_n, such that solution to any one of the parallel breakdown units would constitute a solution to the former problem, P. In order to insure completeness, one of the n solution options (solution scenarios) would have to be: "a solution different from the other (n-1) scenarios". This implicit scenario would be associated with a probability rating, and treated computationally as the others. **Figure 5**.

CONCENTRIC BREAKDOWN CONFIGURATION: An innovation challenge (problem), IC, may be broken down to n concentric breakdown units: C_1, C_2, C_3, ...C_n, such that the first unit provides a solution to IC_1 a simplified model of IC, the second unit provides a solution to IC_2, a bit less simplified solution to IC, and in general C_i provides a solution to IC_i, a simplified model of IC. For all $j > i$ IC_i is more simplified than IC_j and $IC_n = IC$. For each IC, it may be that C_i $i = 1,2,...(n-1)$ would be practically sufficient for the purpose at hand. There are several typical formats for concentric breakdown. For instance: theory-practice sequence, shedding constricting assumptions.

It's quite common to formulate an IC as 'build contraption X'. One could then define the following children challenges: (1) prove or disprove theoretical feasibility; (2) find a practical feasibility. (If the IC is not zero-generation then the first and second consecutive steps may be sufficient); (3) develop a construction option. There are circumstances when an innovation objective cannot be carried out under a set of some constricting assumptions. In that case, one might break down that challenge into concentric components. The first component is comprised of parallel

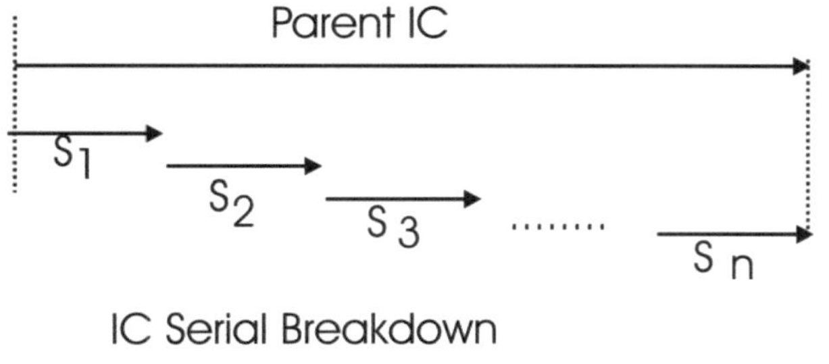

Figure 4.
IC serial breakdown.

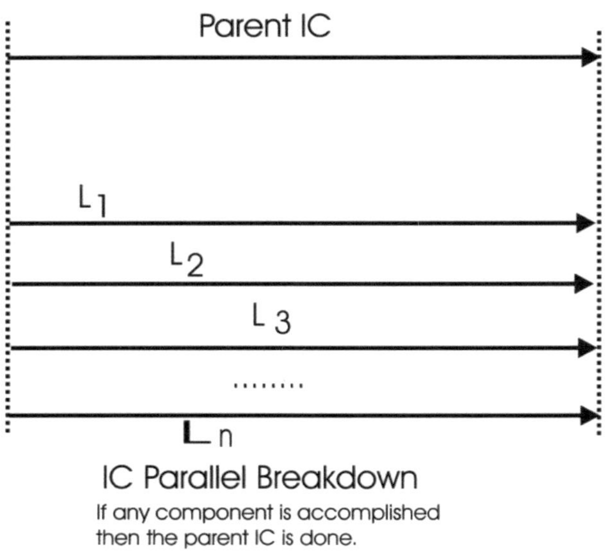

Figure 5.
IC parallel breakdown.

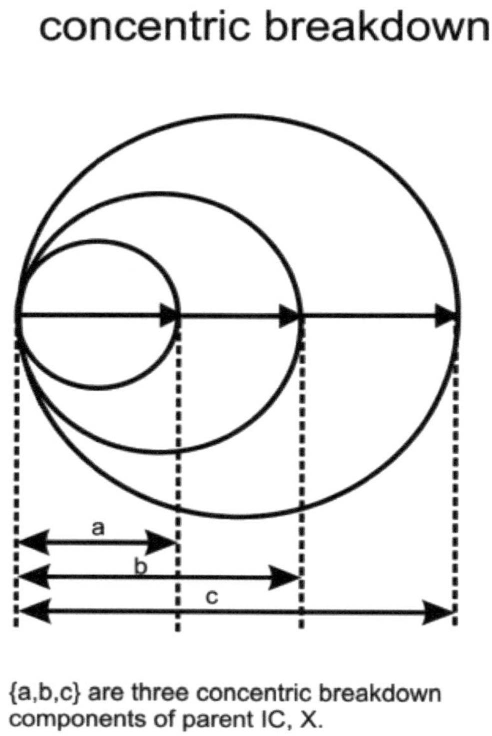

Figure 6.
Concentric breakdown.

ICs, each defined as accomplishing the parent IC by circumventing one assumption. The second concentric component would be to accomplish the same circumventing two assumptions, etc. It would be the same if the assumptions are worded to alleviate the construction: the first component would assume all these relaxing assumptions; the second would assume the same minus one assumption, then minus two assumptions, etc. **Figure 6.**

ABSTRACTION: This R&D route amounts to an effort to redefine the challenge at hand with fewer confusing details, and more fundamental principles, with the hope that the new view would bring to the fore some insight that was hidden when the issue was presented with all its "gory details". Filtering out less important particulars might be helpful by reducing the emotional impact of those details.

ENLARGING THE CIRCLE OF PROBLEM SOLVERS: Abstraction has the inherent benefit of allowing for a larger number of people to think of a solution to the R&D challenge. By stripping the former challenge to its essence, its difficulty can be appreciated by intelligent people who are not necessarily versed with the particular discipline of knowledge of the formal R&D. They may offer a solution that escapes the narrow professional. The more readily communicated abstracted version of the problem, also allows for the challenge to be considered by people who are not cleared to know the details of the original problem. It's a confidentiality issue. For so many cases this aspect severely limits the number of potential problem solvers.

EXTENSION: This option amounts to identifying related challenges, and defining a master challenge that would encompass them all. The underlying idea is that every challenge at hand has some "neighbors" -- challenges that bear certain similarities with it. Some of these challenges are associated with a solution or a partial solution, and this can inspire or suggest a solution to the former problem. The pioneer of the extension approach to innovation practice is the Russian scientists Altshuller [10–12].

IDENTIFYING RELATED CHALLENGES: The quality of this step determines the prospects of the extension route. Some similar challenges are obvious, and readily listed. Others need a more formal effort to be flushed out.

SEARCH STATUS: The search parameters are generally:

- Any-Fit/Best-Fit
- Needle in a Haystack
- Grouping
- Bayesian

A search may be conducted to find one fit instance among many, and it matters not which. Alternatively, the case may be where one is searching for the best fit, and second best will not do. This is a critical search parameter. When a search is characterized as a needle in a haystack, it implies that both the needle and the haystack are well defined. Once the needle is found, there is no confusion about it being the needle and not a strand of hay. The challenge here is simply the size of the stack compared to the size of the needle. Some search cases may be conducted by grouping individual instances into a single group and somehow concluding whether the target is, or is not, in that group. Such searches share a strategy for how to define the most efficient groups. Some searches develop new information as the search goes on. Even failed searches are thus helpful. This is expressed through the revised probability profile for the unchecked instances based on the search so far (Bayesian probabilities). In attempting to diagnose a disease, generally the results from failed tests help reshape the probabilities for the remaining options. By contrast, searching for the right cryptographic key is a case where all the futile searches are probably unhelpful in terms of better searching the remaining options. These search parameters will help identify similar ICs to exercise the extension step with the IC at hand.

SYMMETRY: Symmetry refers to the relationship of an innovation challenge towards its counter-challenge (a precise definition of counter challenge is given ahead). In the symmetric case both challenges are difficult, in the a-symmetric case the counter-challenge is easy, or no challenge at all. To suppress some gene expression may be as difficult as it would be to express the same (symmetry), but to construct a gene sequence from inorganic building blocks is infinitely more difficult than the opposite job (a-symmetry). A-symmetric challenges enjoy some similarities that may be exploited in the extension step. Generally the counter-challenge of an a-symmetric challenge represents a verification metrics for performance or even progress of the original challenge. Also, a-symmetric challenges may allow for incremental R&D work. Trying to cure an ailment, one may wonder if some measures taken have been helpful or not. Since it is generally easy to induce a disease, it opens the possibility for some animal trials where infected specimens are compared (statistically) as to any distinction between treated and untreated cases. It is therefore that the symmetry status of an IC is an important factor in trying to round up similar challenges for the extension step.

METRIC DEVELOPMENT: Challenges can be sorted out based on how easy it would be to measure success and progress towards success. Consider a researcher trying to develop a dye that would not be shaded or faded for one hundred years. How would one measure a successful accomplishment of that challenge (without waiting one hundred years)? Challenges that face such metric difficulty have some attributes in common. They all have to come up with some metric-substitute. Such substitutes have innate similarities. They may be mathematical models, some indirect metric, or extrapolated incremental measurements. By reviewing such similar challenges together, these similarities are likely to generate resolution ideas for the challenge at hand. Progress metric is also an important parameter. In a search challenge suppose one tries to find a single target within a field of search candidates. If the number of candidates is not known, then one lacks any measure of progress after having checked (and not found) m candidates. However if the number of search candidates, n, is known, then the ratio m/n represents progress rating [0:1]. If the search is also Bayesian, then the information skimmed from the m tests would change the probability profile for the remaining (n-m) candidates, and potentially accelerate the R&D progress. For that reason, it is generally helpful to identify the metric status of the IC at hand, and to identify similar ones to help develop solution ideas.

COUNTER-RESEARCH: Generally, an IC may be matched with a counter-IC, IC*, such that the two ICs in a series void each other:

$$IC + IC^* = 0 \text{ [the null IC].} \tag{2}$$

If the IC under consideration is to find something, then IC* is to lose the same. Configured in a series, they pose no challenge at all. Same for reduction and increase, mixing, and separation, etc. Recalling the symmetry attribute, an IC would be either a "one way" or a "zero way" case where the former is defined as an IC where the counter-IC is an easy one, not really much of a challenge, while a zero-way challenge is one where the counter challenge is also intractable. While it may be difficult to separate two similar liquids, it's rather easy to mix them (one-way). While it is difficult to increase the amount of rain in a given area, it is also difficult to decrease the same (zero-way). In either way it may be very helpful to define the counter-IC for the IC at hand, and handle the two challenges together, learning from each other. It is therefore a recommended extension option to match a given challenge with its counter.

TRIANGULAR CHAINING: Any challenge that is not resolved directly is eventually being replaced by one or more different (but related) challenges, taking one of the three routes: breakdown, extension, or abstraction. The new challenge or challenges may be solved in a direct manner or may opt again to one of the three replacement routes, and so on. An innovator unable to find a direct solution to the problem at hand may choose to bet all his time and resources on one of the three replacement options. The new challenge may be solved directly, or branch out again in one and only one direction. In the simplest version the innovator would branch out n times, and face (n + 1) challenges. When the (n + 1)-th challenge is eventually resolved in a direct manner, the process returns, and after n back-branching (backtracking) the innovator is facing the original challenge. If one of the branching is a breakdown, then the number of challenges is larger. If the innovator, considering a given challenge is unsure about which is the best branching option, and thus he divides his resources to two or three options in parallel, then the number of challenges becomes much larger yet. If we assume that every breakdown step produces m subdivision challenges, then a single branch option would lead to (m + 2) new challenges, and n steps would lead to $(m + 2)^n$ challenges. Even for modest values of n, the number of challenges to consider becomes astronomical and impractical. It is necessary then, at some point, to rank-order the three branching options to limit the number of attacked challenges. An innovator may pick one of the three options at a given challenge, and proceed accordingly, chaining more triangles to the web. At some point, the innovator would conclude that this route is futile, and s\he might return to the original challenge and pick a different branching option. Since this can happen at every challenge, the actual "travel route" of the innovator over this so called Turing Web may be quite complicated. Complicated or not,

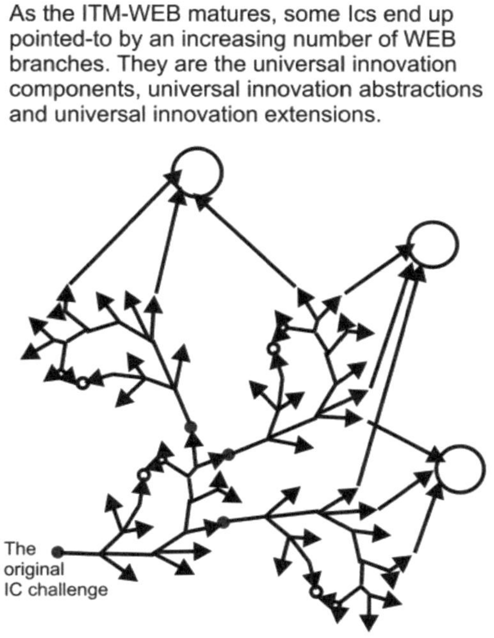

Figure 7.
ITM-web.

the travel route of the innovation process over the Turing web of triangles is a formal codification of the innovation process. It can be documented, analyzed, compared, and learned-from for the benefit of future innovative processes. The accumulating history of innovation processes mapped on the Turing web leads to the identification of innovation invariants that would be helpful for future R&D.

UNIVERSALITY: Is the Innovation Turing Machine universal? That is, is it possible to map every innovation process onto the Turing web? Historic innovation processes, to the extent they were tested, could all be mapped onto the web. It serves as no proof with respect to future innovation tasks, but at least this is a positive indication. The generality of the model can be argued from the following analysis: The three triangular options to handle a challenge that cannot be solved directly are well defined, distinct and thus valid. However, these options may not be complete. In other words, a technological challenge may be faced with the three options: A (abstraction), B (breakdown), and X (extension), plus a forth one, Y, not recognized by the model. To be distinct, Y must not be a component of the current challenge, and may not be an abstraction thereto. It may not be some reverse-abstraction challenge, which means it is a breakdown component. It may be a different description of the current problem, at the same level of abstraction. In such case, the Y option would qualify as a challenge to be listed abreast of the current one by selecting the extension option. See **Figure** 7.

4. AIA configuration

The Artificial Innovation Assistant is comprised of:

1. The Dialog Element, D

2. The Processor Element, P

3. The Environmental Element, E

This configuration is emerging from prior configurations, see [1].

The Dialog element communicates primarily with the human innovator, (HI), but also with the Innovation Underwriter (IU), and with the Innovation Beneficiary (IB). It employs the most advanced man–machine interface techniques to maximize communication efficiency. The Processor element is running the innovation related databases (AI-DB), the innovation processing procedures, and the respective calculations. The environmental part, (E), reaches out to parties in cyber space: innovation partners, paid data and information services, as well as to public domain sources. See **Figure 8**: AIA Configuration.

4.1. State of the innovation challenge

The state of the innovation challenge is comprised of:

1. Current definition of the R&D objective

2. Assessment of cost-to-complete and time-to-finish

3. Credibility Measure of (2)

4. Time since Kick-off

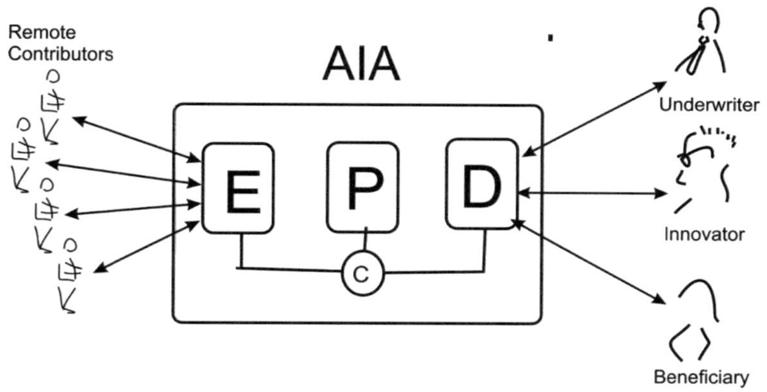

Figure 8.
AIA configuration.

5. Expenditure since Kick-off

6. List of Key Documents

7. List of the R&D team

8. Competing Models and Theories

9. Display of the Innovation^{SP} map

10. Brief history of the innovation project

At any moment the Innovation^{SP} map is comprised of some t specified innovation challenges (IC) configured as tree structures where the original IC is the root. Upon user request the map may be marked by the innovation pathway: how attention shifted from one IC to another.

If the map is comprised of a large number of ICs then the map will be displayed with the standard dynamic focus technology where the default is the full map with small IC indicators, and upon touch screen, or mouse-click the clicked or touched area swells into the center of the screen.

Upon further clicking on a given IC, a side screen displays the important information regarding that IC.

4.2 Next steps suggestions

Next steps suggestions are comprised of:

1. Strategic pathways to achieving the current R&D objective

2. Assessment of (1)

3. Specific next step suggestion

4. Assessments of (3)

4.3 The dialog module

The conversation with the human innovator (HI) will range from pre-defined forms in which the HI just enters specific parameters, up to full free conversational mode emulating human to human innovation discussion.

Emulating Human to Human Innovation Discussion: For this module one applies the current technology for human conversation emulation, complete with colorful words and expressions familiar to the HI. The conversation will be replete with "Hmm....", "I am not sure", and "How about that?" etc. The add-on of the AIA is to deploy randomness options; accordingly the AIA will suggest randomized ideas, emulating 'brain storming'.

The AIA may be programmed to participate in a conversation where more than one HI speak together, and even to accommodate other AIA modules.

An important part of this conversational module is to imprint warnings and alarms, and do so in a perfectly conversational manner.

4.4 The processor element

This module will include the AI computation power, mainly:

1. The AI engine
2. Monte Carlo State Evaluation
3. BiPSA operation
4. multi-variate analysis
5. The AI database
6. Innovation^{SP} map processing

See **Figure 9**.

Challenge Based Process Overview: The human innovator will query the AIA with a particular innovation challenge (The innovation challenge of reference,

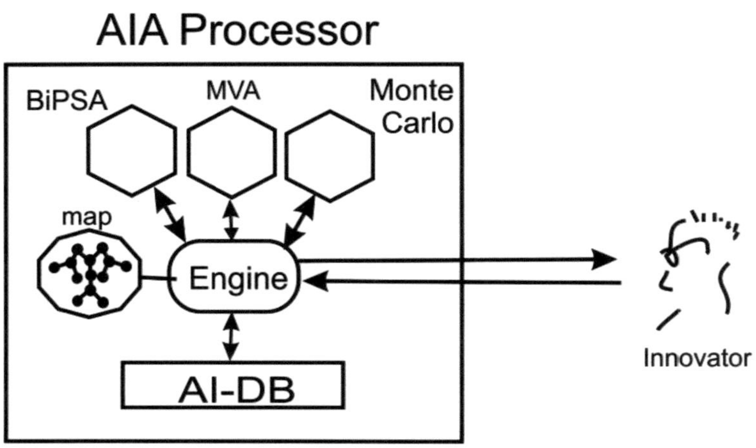

Figure 9.
AIA processor.

ICR). The AIA engine will evaluate the ICR and issue (i) a probability statement for the ICR to be solved directly within a preset time and within preset resources; (ii) resource requirements (time, budget) for identifying (B) breakdown ICs, (X) extension IC, and (A) abstraction IC. Each estimated resource requirement will be accompanied by a credibility metrics of that estimate. Each of the resultant 'switched IC' (ICS) will be estimated per its chance to be resolved directly, and the chance to resolve the ICR given the ICS was resolved, will also be estimated, along with a credibility assignment. This AIA report will be evaluated by the innovator who will decide on the next step based on the following conditions:

1. **Nominal Situation:** the option with the highest estimate credibility will be selected, regardless of its resource consumption.

2. **Stressed Situation:** the option estimated for minimum requirement of resources (time, budget) will be selected.

3. **Exploratory Innovation:** the option with the lowest credibility assessment will be selected, since it is expected to present more productive innovation load.

Following his or her decision, the innovator will do one of the following:

1. Address the ICR directly.

2. Address the most promising ICS directly.

3. Re-Query the AIA over the most promising ICS.

If option 1 is successful, the process terminates. If option 2 is successful, the innovator backs off to the ICR. The dynamics is depicted in **Figure 10**: (map pathway dynamics).

The figure shows the ICR on the left, branching out to a set of switch ICs as the AIA indicates. One of the pointed ICs, is selected for another AIA round, identifying a second set of switched (2nd generation) ICs, and so on until the switched IC can be directly solved. Once so, the process backs up, all the way to the ICR.

When drawn on the map, the process may look as follows (**Figure 11**).

The figures depict a path forward on the Innovation Map leading from the ICR to the last IC (ICL), which is easy enough to resolve directly. This terminates the initial forward path (see the left side of the figure). On the right side the backwards path is depicted where the innovator climbs back from the ICL, tracing the forward path. Upon arriving at a particular IC (ICB), the innovator runs into difficulties. ICB cannot be solved directly (although all the ICs from ICL to ICB were properly solved). In that case the innovator branches off from ICB, and starts another

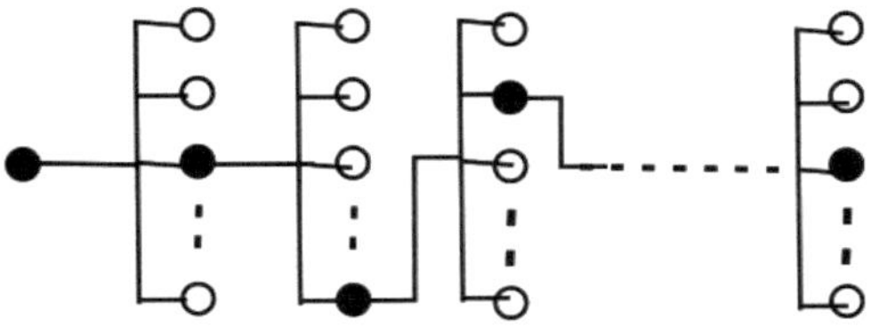

Figure 10.
Map pathway dynamics.

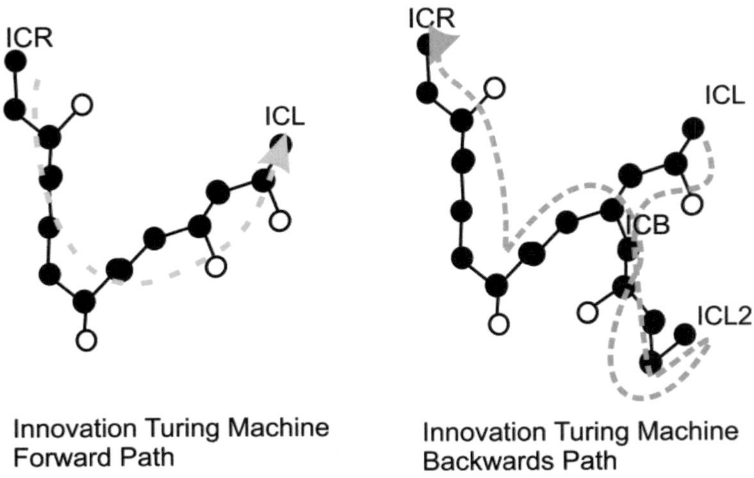

Figure 11.
Innovation Turing machine forward and backwards path.

forward path. As depicted the new forward path progresses to a second last IC: ICL2. From there it regresses to ICR where the process terminates.

Monte Carlo State Evaluation: The Monte Carlo Procedure is the central activity of the AIA processor. It is used to estimate cost-to-complete and time-to-finish, and its credibility. Its results are used to judge 'next steps' options.

In describing the Monte Carlo method for this purpose we adopt the integral sign over the cost probability function. We regard f(x) as the cost probability function of cost-bearing entity x, where the chance for x to cost between a low level, L, and a high level, H is given by:

$$C(L \le X \le H) = \int_L^H f(X)dx \tag{3}$$

Thereby f reflects both the estimated cost and the credibility of the estimate. We also 'steal' the integral sign to denote Monte Carlo integration of two or more probability functions:

$$\mathrm{f}(x+y) = \int_0^\infty MC(f(x)+f(y))dc \tag{4}$$

where the integration in special cases can be taken over different boundaries across the cost parameter, c. In this Monte Carlo context the limit of the integral sign will reflect the interval of values from where a randomized selection is made. Given a query regarding the ICR = "o", the AIA will respond with a cost probability function f'(o). If f'(o) is too high for the innovator, then the innovator will prompt the AIA to estimate the cost probability functions for the three derived IC: $O \to x$, $O \to b$, $O \to a$: $f(x), f(b), f(a)$, and the corresponding cost probability functions for the resolution of o, given the respective derived IC was resolved: f(o|x), f(o|b), f(o|a). x, b, o designates extension, breakdown, abstraction respectively. The derived estimate for o will then be computed based on f(o||x), f(o||b) and f(o||a) where:

$$f(o \| e) = \int_0^\infty MC(f(e)+f(o|e))dc \tag{5}$$

where e stands for x, a, or b, and the derived cost for o will be:

$$f(o) = \int_0^\infty MC(f(o||x) + f(o||b) + f(o||a))\,dc \qquad (6)$$

The innovator will choose among the x,b,a options according to the innovation mode, as described above (nominal, stressed, exploratory). More on R&D cost estimation in [13–16].

BiPSA Operation: BiPSA (Binary Polling Scenario Analysis) is a discriminant analysis tool engineering to accommodate large number of discrimination factors. The BiPSA processor is working both for human respondents and for functional respondents. It is responsible for "Bipsizing" all questions to a series of binary options, the results for which progress into the answer for the original question. This is readily proven through Gödel numbers. A solution to any complex problem can be expressed via some set of elements and their relationships. Gödel has shown that such set can be represented arithmetically by an integer, G. One can then construct a series of binary questions: is G smaller or larger than some arbitrary value R. The answer limits the interval for G. The next question will ask whether G is located in the lower half of that interval or the higher half thereto. And the resultant half can again be halved again with a binary question, until G is pin pointed, and the answer to the complex question is given. Based on this premise AIA will use a BiPSA network to answer complex innovation questions. Because each question is binary, it will be readily possible to integrate the various answers coming from different knowledge sources in the system. Questions regarding path choices, cost to complete, time to finish, etc., are readily answered through progressive binary questions where each question is answered by any element of relevant knowledge in the system. As the binary questions progress the detailed answer surfaces.

The BiPSA processor includes the randomized sub processor to devise new innovation scenarios to be BiPSA processed. BiPSA is an adaptive network comprised of BiPSA elements. A BiPSA element is an operation that accepts n inputs, x_1, x_2, ... x_n, all in a form of integers in the range {-N:+N}, where N is an arbitrary integer. The BiPSA element responds to such input tuple with a single integer y in the same range: $-N \leq y \leq +N$. The BiPSA operator is symmetrical for change of signs. Its prime output is the sign of y. Its secondary output is the absolute value of y, which is regarded as the confidence measure of the prime answer. The prime answer is binary (positive or negative), or 'no answer' (y = 0).

BiPSA output can be threaded as an input to a next BiPSA element, and thereby a given set of BiPSA inputs may be processed through a network of BiPSA elements.

The BiPSA network is adaptive, and can be constructed as any adaptive algorithm. It reflects the growing wisdom of the system based on its expanding innovation database. **Figure 12** "BiPSA Network" depicts a network comprised of 6 BiPSA elements: B1, B2, B3, B4, B5, B6 processing n BiPSA inputs: x_1, x_2, ... x_n into a BiPSA output, y. The network can be defined algebraically as (x_{ij}, B_k), to indicate that input x_i is threaded through element B_k at position j. In **Figure 12** if x_1 is the top input then we write: (x_{11},B1), (x_{12},B4), (x_{13},B6) and the same for all the inputs. This algebraic definition can be adapted to best reflect the accumulated knowledge. Also note that for any value of n, there can be infinite number of BiPSA elements to "play with". **Figure 12**: "BiPSA Network".

BiPSA lends itself to genetic adaptation with increasing network complexity. One common expansion for BiPSA is to break the input tuple to confidence levels, to be subsequently integrated, as illustrated in **Figure 13**: "BiPSA Confidence Mapping":

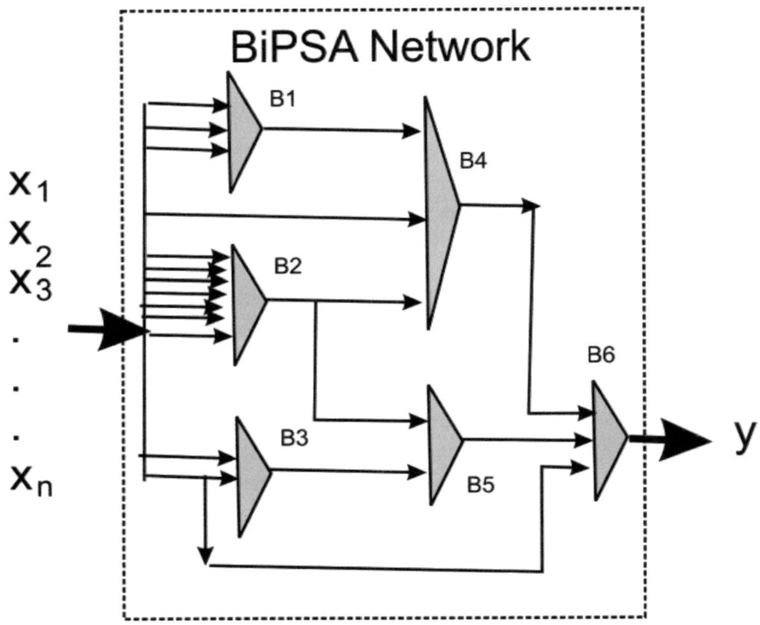

Figure 12.
BiPSA network.

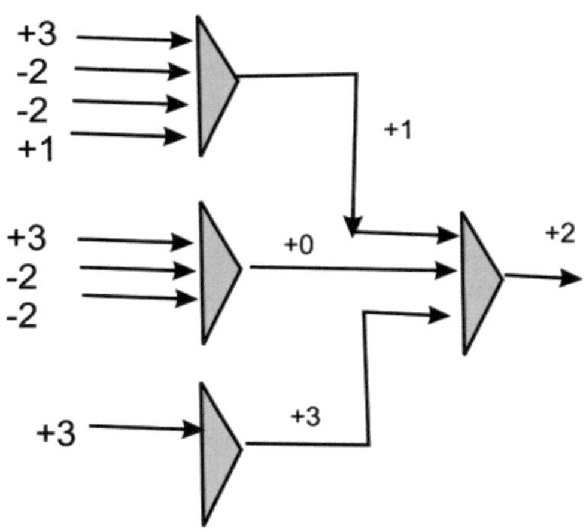

Figure 13.
BiPSA confidence mapping.

The input tuple {+3, −2, −2, +1} is processed as is in the upper element with an output of +1. A second element is processing only input values of confidence level 2 or above, resulting with an output of +0, and the third BiPSA element is processing only input values of confidence level 3. All the three respective output values are further BiPSA integrated to an outcome of +2.

Note: the BiPSA methodology is documented in various references [17].

Multivariate Analysis: Innovation is an ever growing practice, millions of innovation effort hours are being recorded worldwide. Every innovation effort can be mapped onto a pathway on the innovation map. Innovation challenges may be characterized by a very large number of parameters. This ever-increasing database is the raw material for a potent multivariate analysis (or rather maga-variate analysis). This worldwide database is not openly shared, and thus large organizations that can assemble the entire innovation history into a database will have a distinct advantage. However, there is a considerable amount available on the public domain. Technical papers may be used to map a solution on the innovation map. Every published patent can be matched with an innovation challenge it solves. One may envision future service companies that would map public domain and some private innovation pathways onto a standard data platform (the innovation map). This database will serve as a guide for any current innovation challenge. This approach is inspired by the surprising success achieved by language translators that rely not on complex man-elucidated rules of linguistics, but on an ever larger database of properly translated text between the two languages of reference. The very large number of analyzed parameters suggest the BiPSA methodology as an effective multivariate analysis tool. We consider some n arguments x_1, x_2, ... x_n which are used as input to determine the value of an output variable y.

$$y = f(x_1, x_2, \ldots . x_n) \tag{7}$$

Typically f is not known. What is given is some k data points where in case i = 1,2...k the values of the arguments is x_{1i}, x_{2i},..... x_{ni} and the respective output is known as y_i:

$$y_i = f(x_{1i}, x_{2i}, \ldots . x_{ni}) \tag{8}$$

The function f can be approximated through one of the many techniques developed for the purpose. However, most of the common solutions are based on high dimensional metric spaces and complex cluster analysis. These are methods that get prohibitive when the value of n increases. Not so with BiPSA.

Interval Based Operation: let the k y values be organized by increasing order, so that $y_i \leq y_{i+1}$ for i = 1,2,...(k-1). Let y_0 be the median, or the average of the k y values, or sufficiently close to it, and let $y_0 \neq y_i$ for i = 1,2,...,k then the k data points are divided between those pointing to y values above the median and data points pointing to y values below the median. Given any new set of n input parameters, not listed in the k points database, then the binary question would be, is the corresponding y value above or below the median. Once answered the roughly k/2 points in the section of the y range pointed to by the first BiPSA question, will be used for in the same way to further pinpoint y in the upper or lower half of the established y range, and so on, pinpointing y as needed. The credibility of the answers will decrease as each successive BiPSA question uses about half of the data points used before. The larger y intervals will be stated with greater confidence.

Fuzzy logic neural network tools are a good alternative to BiPSA, as discussed in [18].

4.5 The environment element E

The environment element will connect to the environment comprised of:

1. Collaborating Teams

2. Proprietary Sources

3. Public Sources

Collaborating Teams: The given AIA will benefit from exchange with AIA machines operated by collaborating teams. The various AIA will agree on a sharing protocol that may be based on free updating of a shared access database, or on a push or pull configuration. Issues of cyber security will play a role in the selection of the right sharing solution.

A sophisticated AIA will use Homomorphic encryption to handle the division of confidentiality within the team members. This will account for collaborating teams who keep some proprietary information confidential while sharing the rest of the material.

Proprietary Sources: Companies like R. S. Means are selling innovation related data for a price. Mostly they are subscription based, but some international purveyors offer pay-as-you-go, requiring the AIA to use digital money to pay per services rendered real time.

Public Sources: The share of global information freely available to the public is growing exponentially. The efficiency of the major search engines like Google and Bing is improving daily. Yet, the utility of these search engines depends largely on the selected search keywords. It is the responsibility of the AIA software to translate the need for information into proper key words string.

A critical source of innovation related information is government. By law most democratic governments publish a wealth of data regarding public projects. This data is very useful for an effective AIA. One important government source is the patent office which publishes new patents in very searchable forms.

5. Outlook

Thomas Edison, Bill Gates, Alexander Graham Bell are examples of top tier innovators who changed our lives in a fundamental way. However societal progress is taking place via a myriad of non-famous innovators, each making a small innovative step forward. These run of the mill innovators are the target beneficiaries of AIAI. The Steve Jobs and the James Watts among us do not need the help offered by AIAI, but most of us are better served by advanced guidance to channel our creativity into a productive pathway.

We see AIAI making great progress in the dialog part with the innovator, and the other innovation stakeholders, in the interaction with innovation contributors from the outside.

The profound contribution of AIAI to the innovation process is in (i) a comprehensive exploitation of rich innovation history, and (ii) in advanced Monte Carlo computation of credible estimates of cost to complete and time to finish the innovation process. We witness a world with a "global library" as exemplified via Google, Bing, Yahoo, and Baidu and proprietary systems like R. S. Means offer a rich "digging ground" for sophisticated AIAI systems. Also, innovation is an ever-growing enterprise and invariably there are more research ideas than there are resources for them all. A competition ensues. The AIAI methodology centered around credible cost estimates leads to rational allocation of these scarce resources, all for the benefit of society at large.

The solution to most of the pressing and universal problems of humanity is to be found in the promise of innovation, and hence a tool to make the innovation effort more productive, is a welcome addition to the tool-box we use to meet our future.

Acknowledgments

This work owes its existence to my old teacher, Professor Ephraim Kehat, who encouraged me to pause my full-steam engineering practice, and dig deep into

DOI: http://dx.doi.org/10.5772/intechopen.96112

generic engineering principles of innovation, which became my PhD dissertation, and was subsequently boosted with artificial intelligence tools to mature into "Artificial Intelligence Assisted Innovation" (AIAI), summarized herein. My father Ya'acov, and my brother Amnon, both engineers, supported this daring track, and my beloved partner, Dolores, has kept me going, and still does.

Author details

Gideon Samid
Case Western Reserve University, Cleveland, OH, USA

*Address all correspondence to: gideon.samid@case.edu

References

[1] Basadur, M., 1995, "The Power of Innovation: How to Make Innovation a Way of Life and Put Creative Solutions to Work" Financial Times Prentice Hall.

[2] Battelle, 1964, "The Process of Technological Change " Battelle Technical Review, April 1964

[3] Beattie C. J. , Reader R. D. ,1971, "Quantitative Management in R&D " Chapman & Hall Ltd London

[4] Berg, P et al, 2001 Assessment of Quality and Maturity Level of R&D Portland International Conference on the Management of Engineering and Technology

[5] Berridge T ,1977, "Product Innovation and Development " Business Books London

[6] Bess J. L. 1995 "Creative R&D Leadership" Quorum Books

[7] Burgelman R. A. 2003, Christensen M. C., Wheelwright S. C. "Strategic Management of Technology and Innovation" McGraw Hill

[8] Burns ,1975, "Innovation, The Management Connection " Lexington Books

[9] Burns, Stalker ,1961, "The Management of Innovation " Tavistock, London

[10] Cuhls K. Blind et al Ed. 2002 "Innovations for Our Future: Delphi '98 New Foresight on Science and Technology" Physica Verlag "Simplified TRIZ: New Problem Solving Applications for Engineers & Manufacturing Professionals" Saint Lucie Press.

[11] Altshuller, G. 1999 "TRIZ, Systematic Innovation and Technical Creativity" Technical Innovation Center, Publisher, 312 pp, ISBN: 0964074044

[12] Kalevi R., Domb E., 2002 "Simplified TRIZ: New Problem Solving Applications for Engineers & Manufacturing Professionals" Saint Lucie Press

[13] Samid, G., 1996, (b) "Can you predict R&D costs?", CHEMTECH, American Chemical Society, July '96.

[14] Samid, G., 1996, (e) "R&D Cost Estimation - The Credibility Issue", INFORMS Annual Meeting Proceedings, May '96.

[15] Samid, G. "The Innovation Turing Machine" DGS Vitci Press 2007

[16] Samid, G. "Computer Organized Cost Engineering", CRC Press, e-version, July 2020

[17] Samid, G. "The Unending CyberWar" DGS Vitco Press, 2012

[18] Jian Cheng, G. et al, 2001 "Neural Network Approach to R&D Projects Termination Decision and Its Application" Portland International Conference on the Management of Engineering and Technology

Chapter 9

Quest for I (Intelligence) in AI (Artificial Intelligence): A Non-Elusive Attempt

Kumar S. Ray

Abstract

This chapter essentially makes a non-elusive attempt in quest of 'I' (Intelligence) in 'AI' (Artificial Intelligence). In the year 1950, Alan Turing proposed "the imitation game" which was a gaming problem to make a very fundamental question — "can a machine think?". The said article of Turing did not provide any tool to measure intelligence but produced a philosophical argument on the issue of intelligence. In 1950, Claude Shannon published a landmark paper on computer chess and rang the bell of the computer era. Over the past decades, there have been huge attempts to define and measure intelligence across the fields of cognitive psychology and AI. We critically appreciate these definitions and evaluation approaches in quest of intelligence, which can mimic the cognitive abilities of human intelligence. We arrive at the Cattell-Horn-Carroll (C–H–C) concept, which is a three-stratum theory for intelligence. The C–H–C theory of intelligence can be crudely approximated by deep meta-learning approach to integrate the representation power of deep learning into meta-learning. Thus we can combine crystallized intelligence with fluid intelligence, as they complement each other for robust learning, reasoning, and problem-solving in a generalized setup which can be a benchmark for flexible AI and eventually general AI. In far-reaching future to search for human-like intelligence in general AI, we may explore neuromorphic computing which is essentially based on biological neurons.

Keywords: general AI, crystallized intelligence, fluid intelligence, deep learning, meta learning, deep-meta learning, neuromorphic computing

1. Introduction

In this chapter, we look for I (Intelligence) in AI (Artificial Intelligence). Still today the term "Intelligence" is not well-quantified for machine implementation. According to the definition of the Oxford dictionary, it is stated as:

"The ability to acquire and apply knowledge and skills."

We assume rationality as Human Intelligence used in our day to day activity for planning, problem-solving, reasoning and others. With the tremendous growth and development of human civilization, different branches of science and technology are developed. Artificial Intelligence is one such branch which tries to mimic human intelligence through programs implemented into Human-made machines (computers).

IntechOpen

In 2007, Legg and Hutter provided a survey of definitions of Artificial Intelligence/Intelligence with methods of evaluation. A decade later, in 2017, José Hernández-Orallo reported an extensive survey on evaluation methods. In this chapter, we describe AI as an attempt to imitate human intelligence in algorithmic form [1, 2].

Normally the rational behavior of an individual indicates his/her basic element of intelligence. Aristotle held the belief that the man is a rational animal. But a growing body of research suggests otherwise. From ancient times, philosophers have been proposing theories of human rationality. There are, however, many definitions of rationality and these change over time. For Plato and Aristotle, man has both a rational and an irrational soul in different proportions. According to Bertrand Russel, "Man is a rational animal. So at least we have been told. Throughout a long life, I have searched diligently for evidence in favour of this statement. So far, I have not had the good fortune to come across it." The term rationality has a handful of interpretations.

With the gradual growth of science and technology people try to adopt sophisticated computing facilities, which may be an attempt to substitute complex mental computation at any particular situation at hand. Thus life becomes smarter and faster to face different challenges of the universe. If we look back at the history of computing facilities for intelligent decision making we observe as follows:

In the year 1942, physicist John Mauchly proposed ENIAC (Electronic Numerical Integrator and Computer). ENIAC project was completed in 1945. It was the first operational computer in USA developed by Army ordinance to compute ballistic firing table during world war II.

In the year 1950, Alan Turing, a British Mathematician and Logician, who broke the German Enigma code during world war II, proposed "The Imitation Game" which was a gaming problem to make a very fundamental question "can machine think?"; which was an informal announcement of Artificial Intelligence. The question raised by Turing was not essentially concerned about an abstract activity like playing chess [3, 4].

In 1950, Claude Shannon published a landmark paper on computer chess and rang the bell of the computer era. At that instant ENIAC was a newborn baby. But visionary people like Shannon, Alan Turing could realize the tremendous potential for computer science and technology. During that period computers were mainly used for ballistic calculations for missiles whereas games appeared to be a natural application for a computer which average people could appreciate. The first working checkers' program was published in 1952. Chess programs followed shortly after that. Arthur Samuel published a strong checker-playing program based on machine learning concept. Samuel used a signature table together with an improved book learning procedure which was a superior approach compared to the earlier one. "alpha-beta" pruning and several forms of forward pruning were used to control the spread of the movement over search tree and allow the program to look ahead to a much deeper depth than it otherwise could do. Though it could not outplay checker masters, the program's playing capability was highly appreciated.

The early effort of Alan Turing, Claude Shannon, Arthur Samuel, Allan Newell, Herbert Simon and others generated tremendous impetus in researching computer-performance at games which could be a testbed for ultimate "intelligence" generated artificially (through computer program) to "exhibit" human-level "intelligence". In the year 1955 J. Mccarthy, Marvin Minsky, N. Rochester and C.E. Shannon proposed to study "Artificial Intelligence" during the summer of 1956 at Dartmouth College in Hanover, New Hampshire. The basic objective of the study was to proceed based on the conjecture that every aspect of learning or any other feature of intelligence can in principle be so precisely described that a machine can be made to simulate it. Their basic ambition was to build a machine which can deal with the problems that are essentially reserved for humans. In those early days of "Artificial Intelligence" (AI), in 1958. Herbert A. Simon and Allen Newell published a paper titled, 'Heuristic problem solving: the next advance in operations research'. At the banquet of the Twelfth National Meeting of the Operations Research Society of America, Pittsburgh Pennsylvania, November 14, 1957, Simon presented the content of the paper as stated above. He brought the term "Heuristic" in practice. At that time it appeared to be an over-optimistic prediction, but its impact is still far-reaching. To establish the need for 'Heuristic' in real-life problem solving he precisely categorized two types of problems; well-structured problems and ill-structured problems. Well-structured problems can be solved explicitly by known existing computational techniques; whereas ill-structured problems are not well-structured. For instance, first, the variables are not numerical, but symbolic or verbal (linguistic), second, the truth status is vague multivalued, instead of precise two-valued, third, there are many practical problems where, in a time-critical situation, variables are not directly measurable (observable) and 'most practical problems' computational algorithms are not available under such circumstances. "Heuristic" can play a significant role to resolve some of the above mentioned ill-structured problems. The term "Heuristic" is essentially domain-specific information which can roughly quantify the perception and/or intelligence of an individual by estimating the intuition, experience and common sense in general for any judgemental decision process that cannot be reduced to systematic computational routine. The parameter 'Heuristic' is an added advantage for solving ill-structured practical problems associated with several environmental uncertainties. Under environmental uncertainty for any judgemental procedures, several 'hunches' and/or wild guess at random are consider as heuristic. The heuristic function may help find a feasible/reasonable (not necessarily optimal) solution of an ill-structured practical problem. Though the necessity for randomness is not proven, there is much evidence in its favor, as stated by Craik's model.

In May 1997 when the chess machine DEEP BLUE defeated world chess champion Garry Kasparov in an exhibition match, it was an indirect silent reply, "YES", to the very fundamental question "can machine think?" raised by Alan Turing in the year 1950. Of course, the thought process of DEEP BLUE machine is not comparable to that a human being, but definitely, the DEEP BLUE machine very efficiently imitated the thoughtful mind of a world champion of chess. Thus, game-playing became a roseta stone of Artificial Intelligence (AI).

Programming computer to play games is definitely a step towards understanding the methods that may be employed for machine implementation of human intelligent behavior. We still have much to learn from the study of games, and these newer techniques may be applied in future to real-life situations to imitate human intelligence. But the basic question remains that how human becomes so intelligent.

In this chapter, however, we try to explore the cognitive abilities of human being through psychrometric models of human intelligence. We observed that the present state of art of artificial intelligence can mimic human intelligence in a crude sense of approximation. At present AI cannot reach the top level of three stratum of Cattell-Horn-Carroll (C-H-C) theory of intelligence. AI can only model few lower level activities of fluid intelligence and crystallized intelligence. The present state of art of artificial intelligence is implemented through Von-Neumann computing. To breakout of Von-Neumann way of thinking, we also explore the possibility of neuromorphic computing. To develop new learning methods with the characteristic of biological brain it is necessary to learn from cutting edge research in neuroscience. As a part of this process there should be a theoretical understanding of "intelligence". Without the theoretical underpinning, we cannot implement intelligence through neuromorphic computing. Under the present scenario of understanding "intelligence" and mimicking human intelligence in an artificial manner we should further move towards the understanding of native/natural intelligence (NI) which is organic/biological and which is essentially based on biological model of human brain.

2. Evaluation of human intelligence: a brief exposure

Research in the fields of psychology, cognitive science, anthropology, and biology cultivates a sophisticated study on how human intelligence evolved. Understanding about the brain of living humans and great apes and the intellectual abilities they support are enabling us to assess what is unique about human intelligence and what we share with our primate relatives. Examining the habitats and skeletons of our ancestors gives cues as to environmental, social and anatomical factors that both constrain and enable the evolutional of human intelligence.

Many methods are used to assess human intelligence and its evolution. These includes (i) behavioral measures which may involve naturalistic observation or analyzing responses in laboratory experiments, (ii) artifactual measures which involve analysis of tools, art and so forth, (iii) anatomical/neurological measures which involve studies of the brain and cranium. Ideally, all three would converge upon a unified picture of how human intelligence evolved. However, this not always the case and indeed the assessment of human intelligence is still under several challenges.

3. Models of human intelligence

Basically there are four important models of human intelligence:

i. Psychometric model

ii. Cognitive model

iii. Cognitive and contextual model

iv. Biological model.

In this chapter, we consider the first three models which essentially deal with crystalized intelligence, fluid intelligence and combination of these two. We try to approximate or crudely approximate the above features of intelligence through deep learning, meta learning and deep meta learning approaches. We try to adopt in a very crude way the three stratum of Cattel-Horn-Carroll (CHC) theory of intelligence [5].

3.1 Psychometric model

Psychometric model is based on a composite abilities measured by mental tests. This model can be quantified.

One of the earliest of the psychometric model came from the British psychologist Charles E. Spearman (1863–1945), who published his first major article on intelligence in 1904: The Abilities of Man: Their Nature and Measurement.

Spearman did not know exactly what the general factor was, but he proposed in 1927 that it might be something like "mental energy."

The debate between Spearman and Thurstone has remained unresolved.

The American psychologist John B. Carroll, in 1993, proposed a "three-stratum" psychometric model of intelligence that expanded upon existing theories of intelligence. The third stratum consisted solely of the general factor, *g*, as identified by Spearman. It might seem self-evident that the factor at the top would be the general factor, but it is not, since there is no guarantee that there is any general factor at all. Though there is long pending debates on g (general factor), in this chapter, we discuss this particular issue, based on some conjecture, in section 4.

3.2 Cognitive models

Underlying most cognitive approaches to intelligence is the assumption that intelligence comprises mental representations (such as propositions or images) of information and processes that can operate on such representations.

Other cognitive psychologists had studied human intelligence by constructing computer models of human cognition.

3.3 Cognitive-contextual models

Cognitive-contextual theories deal with the way that cognitive processes operate in various settings. Two of the major theories of this type are that of the American psychologist Howard Gardner and that of Sternberg.

4. Putative test of intelligence

The term putative is commonly used to describe an entity or a concept that is based on what is generally accepted or inferred even without direct proof of it. It means something like an inference or a supposition. There are several examples on putative test of intelligence, like picture completion, picture arrangements, block design, object assembly, etc.

4.1 Culture-fair test

A 'culture-fair' or culture-related test makes minimal use of language and not ask for specific facts. On culture-fair tests, Euro-American and African-American children differ because culture can influence a child's familiarity with the entire testing situation.

Cattell argued that the observed variation among individuals in their scores on any intelligence can be regarded as depending on:

G: variation in the innate gene endowment.

dG: variations in environmentally-produced development of general ability.

C: variations in the closeness of the individual's cultural training and experiences to the cultural medium in which tests are expressed.

t: variations in familiarity with tests and test situations generally.

f: fluctuations in the underlying capacity.

fr: fluctuations in the effective expression or application of the ability through strength and direction of volition.

s: specific abilities.

e: chance errors of measurement.

In describing the G term in this expression, Cattell had reference to a culture-fair concept of intelligence:

This being the case, *a combination of dG and C* would constitute a manifest general ability, *crystallized intelligence,* which might, if there was any validity to the notion of culture-fair tests, be distinguished from G, *fluid intelligence.*

Later Cattell made these ides more explicit. He said general ability is of two kinds; (i) fluid ability which manifests perception in new situation, and (ii) crystalized ability which manifests itself in known situation.

He argued that the two abilities should show different development patterns of change.

4.2 Definitions of fluid and crystallized intelligence

Fluid Intelligence (G_f) involves concepts and can be obtained from experiences and opportunities that are afforded to the vast majority.

Thus, G_f involves learning and is a product of acculturation, *but it does not result primarily from differential opportunities in learning or from highly intensive acculturation, such as is promoted through educational programs, which, in one way or another, exclude substantial numbers of individuals.*

The mathematical model which would best represent the lawful combination of the above (and probably many other) factors might be highly complex, but in general form the theoretical terms can be represented as follows:

$$G_f = f(H, M, I, L1, T1, O1) \tag{1}$$

where G_f represents a performance involving fluid intelligence almost exclusively, f represents a function. H refers to a hereditary component. M to the maturation rate, I to injury, $L1$ to learning, $T1$ to the time over which these factors have operated, and $O1$ indicates the extent to which each of these factors has interacted optimally with each other and with environmental circumstances.

Crystallized intelligence (G_c) *is an outgrowth of* G_f. In the early years of development and under certain other conditions *the two may be so highly related* and *cooperative as to be virtually indistinguishable.* But over the course of development, when a properly broad view of this is taken, they may be seen to become separated by virtue of the fact that manifested intelligence is produced by a large number of factors which operated largely independently of those seen as accounting for basic intellectual potential. In general these can be classified as factors promoting intensification of acculturation.

$$G_c = f\left(G_f 1, C, B, P, R, L, 2, T2, O2\right) \tag{2}$$

where G_c represents a performance involving crystallized Intelligence to a high degree, C refers to opportunities and encouragements (chances), E to ergs and sentiments (motive traits), P to non-intellectual personality traits (temperament), R to a factor of longterm memory, $L2$ to the degree of intensive 1earning distinct from that which is provided for most people. $T2$ to the time over which these factor have operated, $O2$ to the extent to which the combination of factors and development stages was optimal for development of G_c, and G_f refers to the level of Fluid intelligence that operated over this period.

Thus a performance which is said to characterize crystallized intelligence is also seen to contain at least a trace of fluid intelligence, so that to some extent this G_c *measure can be said to be confounded with measure of* G_f.

Practically, it must be recognized that the learning component in G_f is not completely devoid of exclusive and intensive acculturation, so that it too, is to some extent confounded with G_c. But the essential hypothesis is of this study is that the functions of equations of G_f and G_c can be separated as distinct linear components in performances on a wide sampling of putative tests of intelligence (see **Figure 1**).

4.3 The Cattell-horn-Carroll (CHC) theory of cognitive abilities

The Cattell-Horn-Carroll (CHC) theory of cognitive abilities is the most comprehensive and empirically supported psychometric theory of the structure of cognitive abilities to date. Simplified version of the Cattell-Horn and Carroll model of the structure of abilities is shown in **Figure 2**.

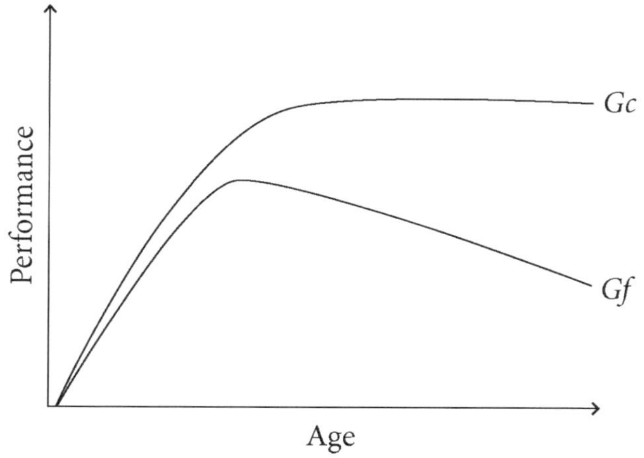

Figure 1.
Performance study between G_c and G_f.

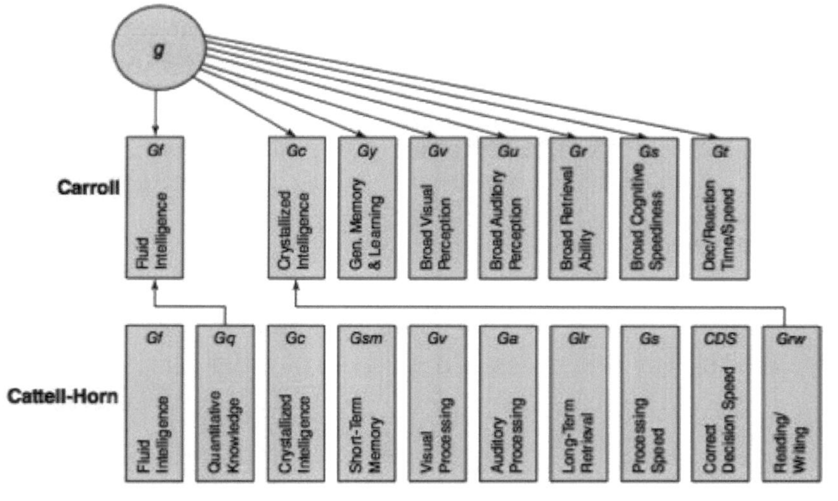

Figure 2.
Representation of Cattell-horn-Carroll three stratum theory.

5. Variant of putative test of intelligence: the factor structure of spearman

In section 3.1, we have already discussed Spearman's g-factor.

Spearman's theory postulated a general capacity, termed g — a kind of "mental energy/neural energy" ... from which all cognitive processes are derived. g-factor is a commonly accepted entity, but there is no evidence of how mental energy (neural energy) is generated. There are several pending debates on this particular issue. Setting aside the debates (section 3.1) we replace g-factor by a more intuitive term "Mood" which is also not measurable but which is more pragmatic to assume in the present context of a cognitive process. The mood is a favorable state of mind consists of the nervous system, to do something through a hierarchy of levels. The mood is placed at the top of the hierarchy and factors of varying degrees of generality further down. Thus, when a person is in a favorable state of mind to solve any problem, the person is in the right mood to solve it. That means, under a favorable state of mind (i.e. in the right mood) neural energy is charged at an absolute magnitude and initiate several levels of intelligence to solve a problem. If a person is in the off mood, then neural energy of the mind is not sufficiently charged to handle a problem.

5.1 Mood

The mood is a favorable state of mind of a person to do something with rationality.

5.2 Difference between mood and emotion

The mood can last for hours. It should not be confused with emotion which lasts, at most, anywhere from second to minutes. It is typically easier to identify emotional trigger but difficult to pinpoint the trigger for our mood. The mood does not have its unique facial expression, whereas emotions do.

5.3 Emotion intelligence

Emotional Intelligence (otherwise known as emotional quotient or EQ) is the abilities to understand, use and manage your own emotion in positive ways to relieve stress, communication effectively, empathize with others, overcome challenges and defense conflict. According to Goleman, emotion can be viewed as:

- Self-awareness; this is the ability to recognize and understand personal mood, emotion, drive and the effect of them on both self and others.
- Self-regulation.
- Internal motivation.
- Empathy (the ability to understand and share the feelings of another).
- Social skills.

In 1927, Spearman stated that g-factor might be something like "mental energy". Alternatively, it might be viewed as neural energy of brain. But the question is how the energy is generated in brain.

5.4 Where the energy comes from?

Recent neuroscientific evidence suggests brain function is a product of the organization of energetic activity in the brain.

Treating brains as neural information processors does not help understand brain function (consciousness) as a physical process because information, according to the commonly accepted definitions, is not a physical property of brains at the neural level; there is no information in a neuron.

5.5 Brain energy and oxygen metabolism

Dynamic metabolic changes occurring in neurons are critically important in directing brain plasticity and cognitive function.

With dynamic changes in oxygen metabolism occurring during neuronal activity, dynamic changes are likely to be reflected in level of oxygen concentration, potentially having secondary effects on protein function and gene expression.

5.6 Link between mood states and creativity

Creativity is a multifaceted construct, in which different moods influence distinct component of creative thoughts.

Mood shifts are crucial in scaling creativity. The activating moods induce more creative fluency and originality (i.e. novelty) than deactivating moods.

Based on the above discussion in Section 4, we state that the long-pending debates on g-factor of Spearman can be replaced by the new conjecture as follows:

- **Kumar's conjecture:** g-factor should be replaced by mood which, under favorable mental condition, can generate sufficient mental/neural energy inside the brain to activate different cognitive activities.

Thus, "g" of **Figure 2** is replaced by "mood" and generate a modified three stratum approach to Cattell-Horn-Carrol (CHC) theory of intelligence shown in **Figure 3**.

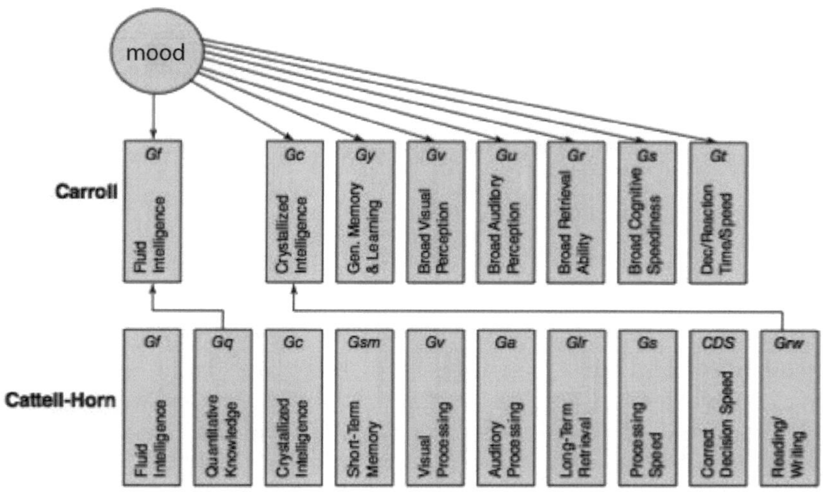

Figure 3.
Modified three stratum approach to C-H-C theory of intelligence.

6. Definitions of CHC abilities

These definitions are derived from an integration of the writings of Carroll (1993), Gustafsson and Undheim (1996), Horn (1991), McGrew (1997, 2005), and Schneider and McGrew (2012).

6.1 Fluid intelligence (G_f)

Figures 2, 3, **Tables 1** and **2** provide the definition of CHC abilities.

6.2 Crystallized intelligence (G_c)

It reflects the knowledge and experience of a person.

G_c includes both declarative (static) and procedural (dynamic) knowledge. **Table 2** shows the definition of narrow crystallized ability.

Definitions of broad crytallized and fluid abilities are available in **Figures 2** and **3**.

Narrow Stratum I Name (Code)	Definition
Fluid Intelligence (G_f) Induction (I)	Ability to discover underlying characteristic of a problem.
General Sequential Reasoning (RG)	Ability to discover rules to solve a novel problem.
Quantitative Reasoning (RQ)	Ability for inductively and deductively reasoning.

Note. *Definitions were derived from Carroll (1993) and Schneider and McGrew (2012).*

Table 1.
Narrow G_f stratum I ability definitions.

Narrow Stratum I Name (Code)	Definition
Crystalized Intelligence (G_c)	Depth and breadth of acquired knowledge.
General (verbal) Information (K0)	Domain of knowledge.
Language Development (LD)	Understanding of native language.
Lexical Knowledge (VL)	Content of vocabulary for oral communications.
Communication Ability (CM)	Speaking ability.
Grammatical Sensitivity (MY)	Knowledge of grammar of native language.
Oral Production and Fluency (OP)	Narrow oral communication skills.

Note. *Definitions were derived from Carroll (1993) and Schneider and McGrew (2012).*

Table 2.
Narrow G_c stratum I ability definitions.

7. Approximate model of crystalized intelligence: a non-elusive attempt

Crystalized intelligence (G_c) includes both declarative (static) and procedural (dynamic) knowledge (see Section 6.2). In the following section, we try to model G_c in an approximate sense through deep neural network model considering only declarative (static) knowledge. Convolutional neural network (CNN) is an implementation of deep neural network architecture. There are several variations of CNN architecture, e.g. Alexnet, Inception, Resnet, Demnet, etc. Input to the CNN is a static representation of knowledge represented by a matrix.

7.1 Why CNN?

Suppose, we have a 28 × 28 RGB image. So, the total number of inputs in a neural network will be 28 × 28 × 3 = 1872..

Let we have a 1000 × 1000 RGB image. In this case the total number of inputs in a neural network will be 3 million, which is pretty large.

Since, the number of inputs have increased, the number of weight parameters, will also increase. If there are 1000 nodes in the first layer, the number of elements in the weight matrix of the first layer will be, 3 billion.

We see that with the increase in the dimension of the image, there is a huge increase in the number of parameters, in a feedforward neural network. Thus, it is pretty difficult to train a neural network with such a large number of parameters.

7.2 Computer vision problem

Suppose we have 6 × 6 grayscale image.

3	0	1	2	7	4
1	5	8	9	3	1
2	7	2	5	1	3
0	1	3	1	7	8
4	2	1	6	2	8
2	4	5	2	3	9

We wish to detect vertical edges in it.
So, the filter or kernel we use is as follows:

1	0	−1
1	0	−1
1	0	−1

After convolution, the resultant matrix, we get as:

−5	−4	0	8
−10	−2	2	3
0	−2	−4	−7
−3	−2	−3	−16

The filter can be learnt using neural networks, which will determine the 9 values of the filter.

We treat each element of the filter as parameters and learn these parameters using back-propagation, similar to the ordinary neural network.

7.3 A short summary of convolutional operations

Summary of convolutions

$$n \times n \text{ image} \quad f \times f \text{ filter}$$
$$\text{padding } p \qquad \text{stride } s$$
$$\left\lfloor \frac{n+2p-f}{s} + 1 \right\rfloor \times \left\lfloor \frac{n+2p-f}{s} + 1 \right\rfloor$$

How to do convolutions on RGB Images?
Since an RGB image consists of 3 channels, we need to have 3 filters for each channel. So, for an image $6 \times 6 \times 3$, we need a filter of shape $3 \times 3 \times 3$.

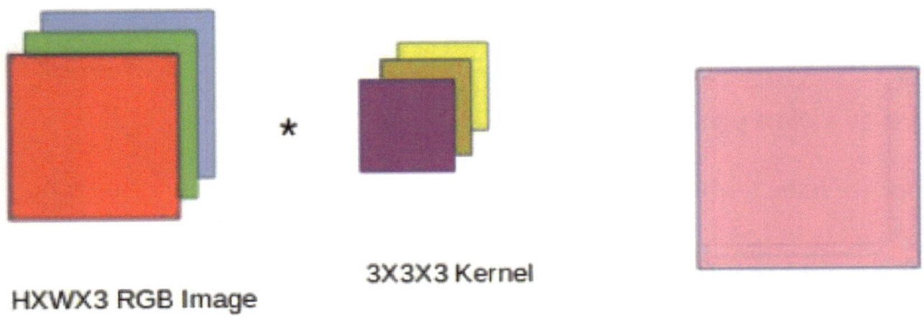

How is this convolution computed?
As in 2D convolution, the first filter is convoluted with the Red channel, the second filter with the Green channel, and the third filter with the Blue channel. The values at each convolutional step are added over the channels to give the final result, which will output a single channel, or a 2D matrix.

Suppose, the above $3 \times 3 \times 3$ filter used is for detecting vertical edges. Now, suppose that we also want to detect Horizontal edges. So, we need another $3 \times 3 \times 3$ filter for that purpose, which will again output a 2D matrix.

By stacking the output of these two filters, we get as folows:

$$[(H-f+1) \times (W-f+1) \times 2] \text{ output(considering no padding)}.$$

The number of channels in the output is equal to the number of filters we are using. And, the number of channels in each filter = number of filters in the input.

However, before stacking up the outputs, bias is added to the output and passed through the activation function, which is then used as input to the next layer.

Convolutional Layer.

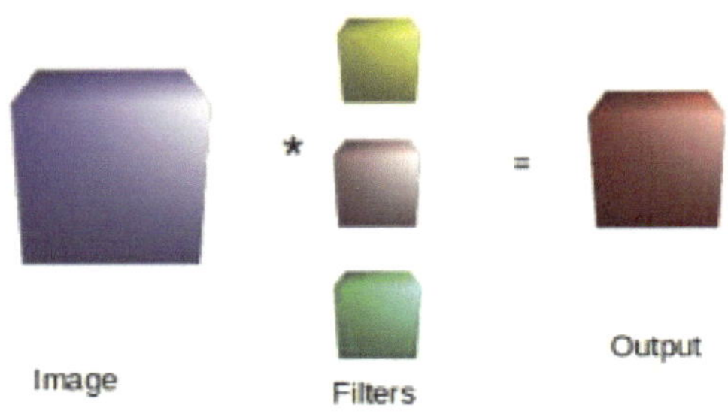

Now, there are various types of layers in a CNN:
1. Convolutional 2. Pooling 3. Fully Connected

Pooling Layers:
Let us consider a 2D matrix for Max-Pooling:

1	3	2	1
2	9	1	1
1	3	2	3
5	6	1	2

Max pooling takes the max of the elements in a $\mathbf{f} \times \mathbf{f}$ region.

Suppose, we take a 2×2 filter, with strides 2, the output will be a 2×2 2D matrix.

Now, the elements in the output will be max of the elements in the 2×2 region, the filter is passed over.

Going by this way, the output will be.

9	2
6	3

If we have a 3D input, the max-pooling output will have the same number of channels as in input. If the number of channels in the input is n_c, then the number of channels in the output of max-pooling will also be n_c.

Average Pooling

Instead of taking the max of the elements, we take the average in this technique.

3.75	1.25
3.75	2

One important point to note about Pooling layers is that, there are no trainable parameters in Pooling layers.

The two important features of CNNs are:

1. **Parameter Sharing**: A filter learnt can be used to detect a feature over all of the input image.

2. **Sparsity of Connection**?: In each layer, each output value is dependent only on a small number of inputs.

Unfortunately, Deep learning models are often problematic. Though Deep learning models are robust under declarative (static) knowledge, it is not sufficient under procedural knowledge which refers to the process of reasoning with previously learned procedures to transform learning. Further, several abilities being assessed by psychometric intelligence tests are crystalized abilities which are acquired through experience and which are not distinguishable from skills (multipurpose skills). On the other hand, AI tests showed a focus on capabilities that enable new skill acquisition; hence crystalized abilities are not acceptable for intelligent decision making [6].

8. Approximate model of fluid intelligence: a nonelusive attempt

In this section, we model, in an approximate sense, the above said concept of fluid intelligence (G_f) for on-spot problem solving of previously unseen problems through meta-learning (learning to learn) approach. Inductive and deductive reasoning are generally considered to be the hallmark narrow ability indicators of G_f. But in our study we do not consider such hallmark ability of G_f [7].

8.1 Meta-learning: learning to learn fast

Meta-learning, also known as "learning to learn", intends to design models that can learn new skills or adapt to new environments rapidly with a few training examples. There are three common approaches: 1) learn an efficient distance metric (metric-based); 2) use (recurrent) network with external or internal memory (model-based); 3) optimize the model parameters explicitly for fast learning (optimization-based).

We expect a good meta-learning model capable of well adapting or generalizing to new tasks and new environments that have never been encountered during training time. The adaptation process, essentially a mini learning session, happens during test but with a limited exposure to the new task configurations. Eventually, the adapted model can complete new tasks. This is why meta-learning is also known as learning to learn.

8.2 Define the meta-learning problem

A good meta-learning model should be trained over a variety of learning tasks and optimized for the best performance on a distribution of tasks, including potentially unseen tasks. Each task is associated with a dataset $\mathcal{D}$, containing both feature vectors and true labels. The optimal model parameters are:

$$\theta^* = \arg\min_\theta \mathbb{E}_{\mathcal{D}\sim p(\mathcal{D})}[\mathcal{L}_\theta(\mathcal{D})] \tag{3}$$

It looks very similar to a normal learning task, but *one dataset* is considered as *one data sample.*

Few-shot classification is an instantiation of meta-learning in the field of supervised learning. The dataset $\mathcal{D}$ is often split into two parts, a support set S for learning and a prediction set B for training or testing, $\mathcal{D} = \langle S, B\rangle$. Often we consider a K-shot N-class classification task: the support set contains K labeled examples for each of N-classes.

Figure 4 shows an example of 4 shot 2-class image classification.

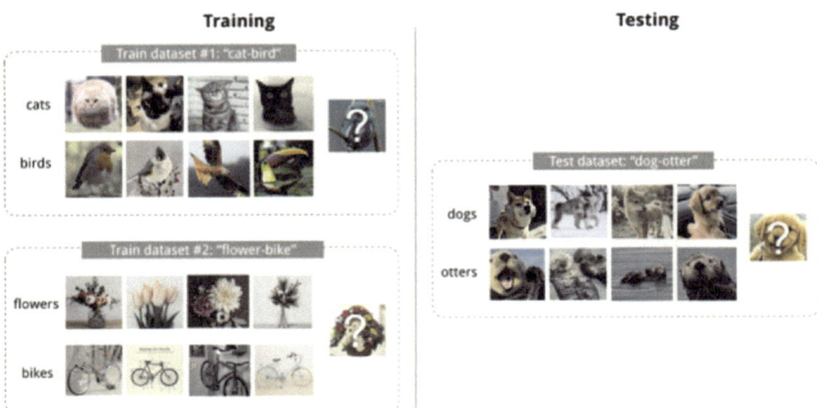

Figure 4.
An example of 4-shot 2-class image classification. (image thumbnails are from Pinterest).

From section 4.2, we understand that crystallized intelligence (G_c) is an outgrowth of fluid intelligence (G_f). Thus the performance of crystallized intelligence is influenced by a trace of fluid intelligence, though (G_c) and (G_f) are two separate distinct components in putative test of intelligence. Also from **Figure 2**, we understand that the component reasons (G_f) and acquired knowledge (G_c) are derived from the top level mental (neutral) energy g. Hence to make a very 'crude approximate' of three stratum theory of C–H–C (see **Figure 3**), we adopt deep meta-learning approach where we integrate the power of deep learning approach into meta-learning. The (G_f) and (G_c) are both derived from the top level mental (neutral) energy as shown in **Figure 2** and try to follow the hierarchy of three layers to derive the broad and narrow abilities to perform the specific task of given job. Here we consider the term 'crude approximation, because the top level of **Figure 2** or **Figure 3** can never be reached by the present state of art of artificial neural network. Specially "mood" at the top level of **Figure 3** is a biological phenomenon which generates sufficient mental energy (neural energy) inside the brain under favorable mental conditions. Hence, under such circumstances we assume sufficient neutral (mental) energy is generated for C–H–C theory to perform lower level of cognitive process like crystalized and fluid intelligence.

9. Concept space of deep meta-learning

Figure 5 shows the concept space of deep meta-learning. Eq. (4) represents the meta-learning process [8].

$$\min_{\theta_{\mathcal{G}}\theta_{\mathcal{M}}\theta_{\mathcal{D}}} \mathbb{E}_{\mathcal{T}\sim\mathcal{P}(\mathcal{T}),(\mathbf{x},\mathbf{y})\sim\mathbb{D}}\left[J\left(\mathcal{L}_{\mathcal{T}}(\theta_{\mathcal{M}}\theta_{\mathcal{G}}), \mathcal{L}_{(\mathbf{x},\mathbf{y})}(\theta_{\mathcal{D}}, \theta_{\mathcal{G}})\right)\right], \tag{4}$$

where $\theta_{\mathcal{G}}$, $\theta_{\mathcal{M}}$ and $\theta_{\mathcal{D}}$ are the parameters of deep meta-learning. We assume that the top level mental (neural) energy is available for C–H–C theory of intelligence and a crude approximation of C–H–C theory to mimic human intelligence can be achieved through deep-meta-learning approach. In deep-metal learning approach we crudely approximate to integrate crystalized intelligence (G_c) into fluid intelligence (G_f).

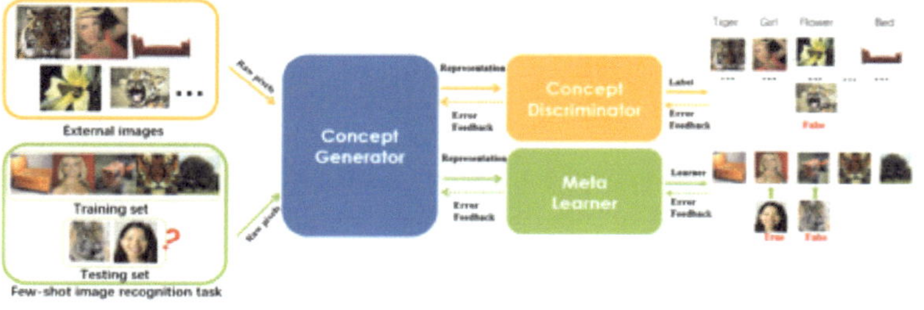

Figure 5.
Concept space of deep meta-learning.

10. Paradeigm shift from Von Neumann computing to neuromorphic computing

So far, we have approximately modeled the psychrometric model of human intelligence and implemented in Von-Neumann computer system. Now we seek a

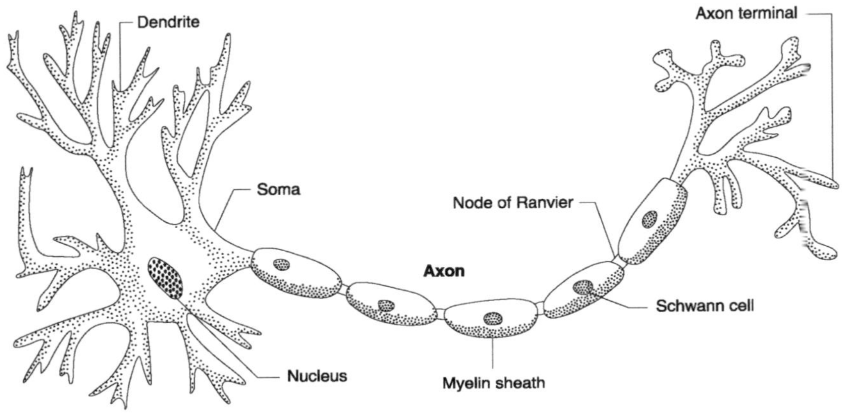

Figure 6.
Structure of simple neuron.

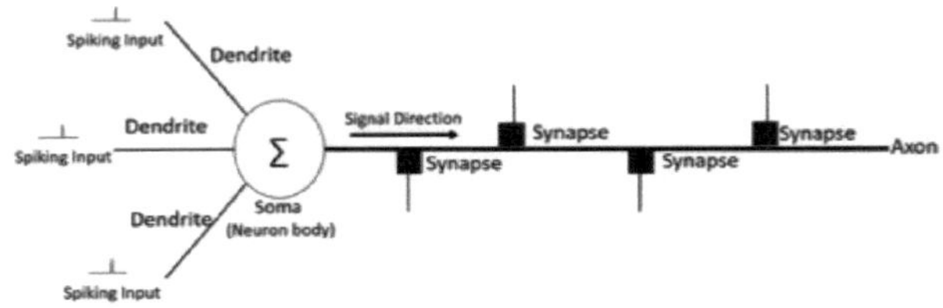

Figure 7.
Neuron design.

new type of computing device which is beyond Moore's law and Von-Neumann architecture. This new type of computer can proactively interpret and learn from data, solve unfamiliar problems using what it has learned and separated with the energy efficiency of the human brain [9].

Inspired by the working mechanism of the nervous system, the performance development of the computing system has led to a novel non-traditional computing architecture, namely, the neuromorphic computing system. The neuromorphic computing system was proposed by Carver Mead in the 1980s to mimic the mammalian neurology using the very-large-scaled-integrated (VLSI) circuit. In order to physically realize the biological plasticity of a synapse, neuromorphic is combined with computing architecture memristors as electronic synapses.

Although fundamental functions of the brain are still under investigation, two main elements: neuron and synapse are well studied at the cellular level. The structure of a simple neuron is shown in **Figure 6**.

There are four main parts of each neuron, whose functionalities are summarized as shown in **Figure** 7.

Several well-known neuron models are investigated, such as integrate and fire IX model, Xitzhugh-Sitzhudh-Naguno (XN) model, Hodgain-Huxley (HH) model, Leaky integrate an fire (LIS) model, etc.

11. Concluding remarks

In our non-elusive attempt to search for I (intelligence) in AI (Artificial Intelligence), in the first part of this chapter, we crudely approximate the Cattle-Horn-

DOI: http://dx.doi.org/10.5772/intechopen.96324

Carrol (C–H–C) theory of intelligence (see **Figure 3**) through Deep-meta learning approach where we integrate fluid intelligence (G_f) into crystallized intelligence (G_c). Thus problem-solving in unknown environment and robust task specific learning mechanism are combined. During this process of approximation of (C–H–C) theory of intelligence, we realize that with the present state of the art of Artificial Intelligence we can never reach the top-level g-factor/mood (see **Figures 2** and **3**). Hence the approximation process is crude. Though, g-factor as proposed by Spearman is not well defined, the mood which is an alternative conjecture to g-factor is basically a biological phenomenon which occurs inside the brain to generate sufficient mental (neural) energy under the favorable state of mind as stated above to perform lower level of cognitive activities. Thus, in the three stratum C–H–C theory of intelligence, we set aside all the debates on g-factor and inherently assume that such mental (neural) energy is already existing due to the above stated biological phenomenon, i.e. mood. Thus the lower level of cognitive activities can be performed. Hence we consider deep-meta learning approach to crudely approximate C–H–C theory of intelligence to mimic human intelligence in Artificial Intelligence (AI).

In the second part of this chapter, we consider a paradigm shift from Von-Neumann architecture to Neuromorphic computing. It is clear that an entirely new way of thinking about algorithm development is required for neuromorphic computing to break out of the Von-Neumann way of thinking. To develop new learning methods with the characteristics of biological brains, we need to learn from cutting edge research in neuroscience. As a part of this process, we need to build a theoretical understanding of "intelligence". Without the theoretical underpinnings, we cannot implement true intelligent neuromorphic systems. One of the key features of biological brains that likely enables speedy learning from limited examples or trials is the structural features that are present in biological brains as a result of evolution which should be customized through the learning process. A neuromorphic system may include a long-term off-line training or learning component that may create gross network structures or modules which may be refined and tuned by shorter-term on-line training or learning component. The goal of a neuromorphic computer should not be to emulate the brain. We should instead take inspiration from biology but not limit ourselves to particular models or algorithms.

From the above study we understand that the present state of art of artificial intelligence algorithms which are implemented through Von-Neumann computing cannot model the top level factor (g-factor/mood) of three stratum C-H-C theory of intelligence. Instead, with some assumptions about the top level factor (g-factor/mood) present AI approach can realized some lower level cognitive activities of fluid intelligence and crystallized intelligence. Thus the attempt to mimic human intelligence by conventional AI algorithms is not that much successful as much we except it to be through generalization of learning algorithm. On the other hand, alternative computing tool, i.e. neuromorphic computing device may attempt to adopt brain functioning for mimicing human intelligence provided the realization of plasticity of synaptic activity is achieved through electronic devices. Under the present scenario we should move towards native/natural intelligence (NI) which is organic/biological and which is essentially based on biological model of human brain. We should explore this new field and should no longer think of artificial intelligence as machines, robot and software code; rather we should think of biological artifacts. Thus in future we should welcome biological AI or BIO-AI.

Author details

Kumar S. Ray
Department of Computer Engineering and Applications, GLA University, Mathura, India

*Address all correspondence to: ksray@isical.ac.in

References

[1] A.M. Turing, Computing Machinery and Intelligence, MIND, vol LIX. No. 236. J, October 1950.

[2] Claude Shannon, A Chess-Playing Machine, Scientific American, vol 182, NO 2, February 1950.

[3] S. Legg, A Collection of Definitions of Intelligence, Proceedings of the 2007 Conference on Advances in Artificial General Intelligence.

[4] José Hernández-Orallo, Evaluation in Artificial Intelligence: From Task-Oriented to Ability Oriented Measurement, Artificial Intelligence Review, 48(3) 397–447, 2017.

[5] McGraw K.S., The Cattle-Horn-Carroll Theory of Cognitive Abilities: Past, Present and Future in D.P. Flanagan, J.L. Genshaft & P.L. Harrison (Eds.) Contemporary Intellectual Assessment Theories, tests and issue, (PP 136–182) New York, Guilford.

[6] Schmidhuber, J., Deep Learning in Neural Networks: An Overview, Neural Networks, 61: 85–117, January 2015.

[7] Chelsa Finn's BAIR blog on "Learning to Learn".

[8] M. Huisman, J.N. Van Rojn, A. Pleat, A Survey of Deep-Meta learning, Arxiv: 2010. 03522VI[CS. LG], 7 Oct 2020.

[9] Hongyu An, Kangjun Bai and Yang Yi, The Roadmap to Realize Memristive Three-Dimensional Neuromorphic Computing System, http://dx.doi.org/10.5772/intechopen.78986.